The WLP Scorecard:
Why Learning Matters

A Comprehensive User's Guide

Ray J. Rivera

ASTD
PRESS

Alexandria, VA

ASTD Press is an internationally renowned source of insightful and practical information on workplace learning and perform-ance topics, including training basics, evaluation and return-on-investment, instructional systems development, e-learning, leadership, and career development.

Ordering information: Books published by ASTD Press can be purchased by visiting our website at store.astd.org or by call-ing 800.628.2783 or 703.683.8100.

Library of Congress Control Number: 2007924169

ISBN-10: 1-56286-478-5
ISBN-13: 978-1-56286-478-1

ASTD Press Editorial Staff:

Director: Cat Russo
Manager, Acquisitions & Author Development: Mark Morrow
Editorial Manager: Jacqueline Edlund-Braun
Retail Trade Manager: Yelba Quinn

Developmental Editor: Lynn Lewis, Learning Solutions, LLC
Copyeditor: Maureen Soyars
Proofreader: Kris Patenaude
Indexer: April Davis
Interior Design and Production: Kathleen Schaner
Cover Design: Kristi Sone

For Peijie

我的心，我的灵魂，我的呼吸

Contents

Preface

In today's work world, organizations must reinvent themselves to survive. For example, military organizations no longer engage solely in defense and war craft, but provide humanitarian support and statecraft. Fire and law enforcement organizations have expanding reach and responsibilities as first respondents in all areas of civil need. Public schools need to produce graduates who are socialized into citizenry.

Not only do organizations need to change how they approach business, but nearly every business now competes in a global environment, and more sophisticated customers expect immediate access to goods and services. Innovation is not the vision of today's organizations; it is a requirement, and the means by which they are reinventing themselves is through learning.

Workplace learning and building a learning culture vies as the most critical aspect of reinventing business in any organization. So what exactly does it take to build a learning culture?

Change agents are people or groups who engage in the entire value chain to integrate disparate groups. Reinvention and growing a learning culture require a change strategy, sponsorship, and internal support at all levels to manage and implement the change. This change we are talking about is learning, and it permeates the entire process of creating and delivering value.

The Foundation in Building a Learning Organization

In a recent ASTD *T&D* magazine interview with *In Search of Excellence* author Tom Peters, Peters said, "Everything needs to change, so everybody then becomes a corporate change agent, and everybody becomes a trainer. . . . it means getting totally engaged in the client organization, and trying to change their culture, become a change agent, their trainer."

According to Peters, "[Training] is more relevant than ever. Where the hell is the border between training and learning? What is learning? Isn't learning the preoccupation of all human beings from birth to death? The problem with you guys, you trainers, is you won. Now what the hell do you do?" (Bingham and Galagan, 2006).

As Peters noted, to the victor go the spoils, and in the case of workplace learning, the spoils are significant. Like the idea of quality and total quality management three decades ago, the idea of a learning organization today means so many things to so many different people, and that's a big win for the workplace learning and performance (WLP) profession. The good news is that everyone talks about quality today. The bad news is there isn't really a standardized definition for quality. Some people implement quality poorly, whereas others implement it well. The WLP profession may well be in its infancy of defining and measuring learning organization performance, but there is hope that it will mature and become as widely known and valued as the focus on quality and the total quality management movement.

In this article, Peters alludes to the lack of clear definitions, and the fact that those who want change are hindered by the lack of a system for measuring learning. As a result, a big stumbling block to organizational learning hinges on the inability of management systems to measure and assure optimal performance.

Peters's words resonate with many learning and non-learning executives. As he says, "I'm 100 percent in favor of measurement, and I'm 100 percent terrified of it because most of the time we measure the wrong thing."

So how do we measure the right things?

Using the WLP Scorecard to Manage Learning Like a Business

Financial statements—performance measurement and management tools of the past—do not capture knowledge assets whose value and efficacy are increased through learning.

Intangible assets represent the unique capabilities and competencies of an organization, and learning is the means by which organizations increase and accumulate intangible assets. Most intangibles never make it to financial statements unless some transaction has occurred, making it a poor basis for measurement and probably the worst basis for managing.

Whereas financial statements measure tangible assets, the WLP Scorecard is a performance measurement tool for calculating intangible assets and benchmarking learning function expenditures and performance.

This is a book about management. It conveys the fundamental concepts required to manage the learning function, shares strategies for planning and collecting the data required for the WLP Scorecard reports, and demonstrates how to generate these reports and interpret the data to develop strategies and action plans. Taken together, these pieces enable measurement and evaluation of the learning function in terms of both tangible and intangible assets—providing the right mindset and the right tools required to run learning like a business.

Let's talk first about the right mindset. In preparing this book, I found very few sources that provided a comprehensive sense of the context in which today's learning executive must operate, and how the learning executive must think to run learning like a business function. In *Return on Learning*, Donald Vanthournout and his colleagues at Accenture eloquently described the three components of how to run learning like a business:

1. Plotting and measuring a course toward upside value creation, [and] determining the particular value objectives most closely linked to learning investments.
2. Putting in place the governance structures and decision-making mechanisms that enable the learning organization to understand the business well enough to direct the learning outcomes that affect business results.
3. Using the best cost management techniques to drive business results with the most efficient use of resources (Vanthournout et al., 2006).

Most initiatives consist of at least three phases: initiative, planning and executing. Part I of this book, chapters 1 through 5, focus on the initiating phase and present the theory of measurement and metrics that workplace learning professionals need to know when beginning the journey of measurement for the learning function. In particular this section expands fundamental principles and provides insight into how a learning executive must think about learning and organizational change to render learning into a value-producing, efficacious business function.

Part II includes chapters 6 and 7 and helps workplace learning professionals with the planning phase of implementing measurement. These chapters focus on strategies for identifying and gathering the data required to run the WLP Scorecard reports.

Part III of this book, chapters 8 through 12, detail the steps to execute the WLP Scorecard. Specifically, these chapters explain how to access, navigate, enter data, generate reports and analyze WLP Scorecard reports to make decisions and transform learning into a value-producing, results-driven business function.

Acknowledgments

Every author needs a group to help support the creative process and to bring a book to fruition. Thank you to

- Tony Davila, who taught me everything I know about performance measurement. Sarah Tasker, who provided me with one of the biggest "aha" moments of my life.
- Mark Morrow and Cat Russo, for being the kind of publishers that every writer should have, and Lynn Lewis, Jacki Edlund-Braun, and Maureen Soyars for likewise being the kind of editors that every writer should have.
- Erum Khan, Wang Wei, and Jennifer Homer: truly great partners.
- Ed Haertel and Susanna Loeb, for many years of support and patience.
- Tony Bingham, for being the kind of executive sponsor that makes things happen.
- My WLP Scorecard colleagues, Brenda Sugrue, Kyung-hyun Kim, Tony O'Driscoll, and Mike Czarnowsky. Very special thanks to Daniel Blair, for being a rock of strength, and Neville Pritchard, our Éminence Grise.
- Our special WLP Scorecard friends: Jeff LaBrache, Suzi Dunford, Miki Hespeth, Bruce Batton, Beth Mielwocki, Patricia Todd Byers, Wendy Witterschein, Kathy Shurte, Martyn Sloman, and Ron Dickson, the first-ever user of the WLP Scorecard.
- The WLP Scorecard Think Tank, acknowledging all their heavy lifting in conceiving and laying the foundation for the WLP Scorecard, especially Brenda Sugrue, whose efforts in particular merit this second and unique mention.
- Everyone in ASTD for putting up with all my eccentricities and non-sequiturs, especially Richa Batra, Dawn Baron, Greg Akroyd, Julie Nielsen, and Pat Galagan. Special thanks to Stephen Earnest, who provided timely assistance in communicating important performance management aspects of the WLP Scorecard.
- To our partners at Intrepid: Mike Tessem, David Atack, Darin Hartley, Jason Gorfine, Elizabeth Pearce, with a very special acknowledgement to Sharon Vipond, who has been with us from the very beginning.
- To the many very kind flight attendants and land personnel who supplied me with drinks, good cheer, and some words of inspiration while I was on their aircraft or in their stations, where much of this book was being composed and edited, especially Kim, Susan A., Laura M., Chip T., David Z., Frank M., and Sharon W.

- Ben Ho, who infected me with the concept that, in his words, "economics is psychology," and backed it up with even more punch.
- To Lisa Wong, a true practitioner of the medical art as it was conceived by its founders in antiquity; W. Mark Smith and his wonderful family, you are an inspiration to me in ways I cannot express; and Grace Chang—it's all good.
- Dana Wenjun Liu, Clayton Shunquan Shen, for many years of warm friendship and introducing me to an entirely new world.
- For the teachers who really made a difference in my life: Stephen Alessi, Stephen Barley, Jack Brower, Nancy Buchenauer, Nancy Hogan, Michael Littleton, Jim March, Pat Mendius, Leo Raditsa, Ola Svein Ressel, Nancy Rolph, Susan Schelonka, Brother Robert Smith, Myra Strober, David Townsend, and Walter Vispoel. Special thanks to some teachers who let me stumble around in areas where I was out of my league—and where I learned the most: Gene Awakuni, Tom Cover, John Etchemendy, Ira Friedman, John Hennessy, David Kreps, Luigi Pistaferri, Woody Powell, and Ed Vytlacil.
- To my beautiful bride, Peijie; my parents, Patsy and John, and my brother Tony; my parents-in-law, Mao Huiqing and Luo Lingdi; sister-in-law Mao Peiqian; and all the wonderful relatives in Shanghai and all over Zhejiang—there is no greater gift than a loving, warm, close family.

Part I

♦

Initiation Phase:
Understanding Why Learning Matters

Chapter 1

The WLP Scorecard: A New Tool for a New Kind of Executive

In This Chapter

- What is the WLP Scorecard?

- Who is the new learning executive?

- What are the four keys for new learning executives to focus on when measuring and managing the learning function?

Workplace learning professionals know the value of learning and talent development better than anyone in the organization. Like their non-learning executive counterparts, workplace learning professionals want evidence that investment in learning is appropriate, targeting the right people and competencies, and is driving productivity, innovation, differentiation, and readiness.

Demonstrating organizational value is the daily mantra of learning professionals working to increase the respect and clout afforded the profession by top management.

Many workplace learning professionals struggle to quantify the work they perform and to fend off proposed reductions or elimination of learning budgets during economic downturns. Although senior management values learning and talent development, they also need evidence that investing in learning is appropriate, targeting the right people and competencies, and driving productivity, innovation, and differentiation.

Few tools provide comprehensive measurement and reporting systems for the learning function. Many measurement and reporting systems track only a fraction of the learning activities that occur within organizations. In many cases, data collection and reporting are based on learning-oriented models rather than on solid business metrics.

What Is the WLP Scorecard?

So how do workplace learning professionals overcome these barriers to demonstrate value? All business functions rely on measurement as a means of finding gaps and targeting improvements. Measurement enables management to identify, develop, and implement strategies based on hard and soft targets to drive performance. For most learning functions, measurement currently focuses on

- levels 1-4 evaluation
- amount/quality of throughput (for example, number of learners, number of courses, percent completion, and others)
- learning function efficiency.

Although many of the measurements are relatively easy to gather because they focus on tangibles, they are often inadequate. In addition to the measurements listed above, learning functions should focus also on

- direct feedback from business unit leaders
- return-on-investment (ROI)
- alignment with organizational objectives
- scorecard measures.

Scorecard measures have emerged in the last 15 years in response to the challenges of managing business organizations that are increasingly becoming more complex. The number of measures that describe business function activity have exploded.

Scorecard methods reduce complexity by rendering sets of metrics into fundamental managerial categories. These methods often use inventive visualizations such as dashboards and ensure that each category receives due attention. Perhaps most important for managers, scorecard methods connect investments of resources with strategic objectives and illuminate the processes that need to be managed to transform resources into results.

Just as the traditional balanced scorecard is a management tool used to map an organization's strategic objectives into performance metrics, the WLP Scorecard is an online benchmarking, decision support, and performance measurement tool that connects learning investments to business results. The WLP Scorecard helps decision makers understand business drivers and how the organization currently stacks up based on a variety of metrics and indicators for work-based learning, human capital, and business outcomes.

The WLP Scorecard provides instant comparisons on a broad range of learning and non-learning variables and diagnoses the strengths and weaknesses of each organization. The WLP Scorecard generates Scorecard Reports that cover financial, operations, customer, and innovation indicators as well as Index Reports that provide diagnostics on the alignment, effectiveness, efficiency, and sustainability of the learning function.

The WLP Scorecard reports are beyond descriptive, they are predictive, diagnostic, and prescriptive—that is, they tell you much more than where you have been. WLP Scorecard reports give you a sense of where the learning function is going, what it is going to take to get to where you really want to go, and what needs to be done to get there.

Ultimately the WLP Scorecard provides workplace learning professionals, learning executives, and upper management with a common language to communicate with one another about the diversity of learning function activities, the means by which learning is measured.

Who Is the New Learning Executive?

Look at a short history to understand the new learning executive. At one time, the job of the training manager was fairly simple. Firmly planted in the HR department, the training manager reported to one of the senior members of HR. Managing the learning function often involved setting up and coordinating logistics, creating workshops, equipping stand-up trainers with adequate materials, ordering food and beverages, and putting together evaluation instruments to satisfy both the head of HR and senior management.

In the infancy of training, even the idea of a learning executive would have seemed strange. The training manager, primarily a tactician, often executed someone else's larger plan. Senior management demanded training as a solution for problems not easily solved by shuffling people or tasks. Training wasn't regarded so much as a profession as an avocation. It is little wonder in times of tight budgets that training was thought of as "nice to have" and therefore expendable.

Technology Explosion

Learning has come a long way since the days of traditional classrooms and blackboards. Within the last few decades, new technologies have enabled training to be administered across distances—thus changing training from a social activity to more of an individual activity. An ever-changing world economy demands constant updates to training resources to arm employees with the resources to develop required knowledge and skills. The technological choices available to learning executives today were unthinkable only 20 years ago.

New Business Environment

Changes in the global economy and information technology impact the learning function as well. For example, an instructional program on network protocols, once suitable for only a small group of English-speaking learners, now requires repackaging for worldwide access. In today's economy many organizations must open markets and outsource labor to other continents to remain competitive. The responsibility to keep a global labor force skilled falls squarely on the learning function.

In short, the new learning executive is faced with many of the same fundamental challenges as other business leaders: making sense out of complexities and making the best decisions from a number of choices.

Four Keys for New Learning Executives

So with all this complexity and change, what should workplace learning professionals do to stay in the game? To begin, they need to understand that to manage the learning function as a business function, they must reverse the decades-old tradition of decoupling measurement and management.

Summative evaluation—benchmarking the learning function after learning programs have been delivered—just doesn't cut it anymore. As illustrated in figure 1-1, management systems need to *feed back* measurement information flowing out of business processes and into decision-making situations. Only then can workplace learning professionals monitor and assess the flow of resources into value-creating business processes.

Four key concepts help workplace learning professionals focus on the right areas when measuring and managing the learning function:

- determining what needs to be managed
- selecting the right metrics
- creating compelling leadership and building partnerships
- communicating in business language.

Determine What Needs to Be Managed

Today, the learning portfolio in an organization consists of hundreds if not thousands of full-length courses. Learning executives find themselves solely accountable for more investments in the learning function and heavier demands to contribute to the bottom line. To achieve success,

Figure 1-1: WLP Scorecard Reports Overview

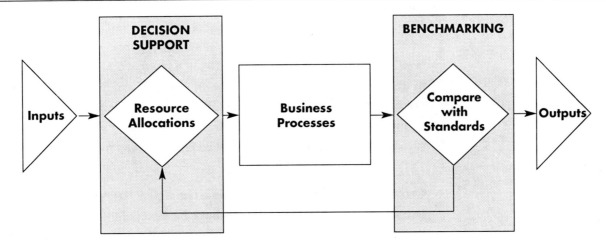

workplace learning professionals must assure that learning is reaching the right people, at the right time, and targeting the right competencies. In a word, learning has to be *right*.

Until now, many learning functions focused on managing learning *inputs* (people) and measuring *outputs* (courses, hours of learning, satisfied learners). With the number of learning function *processes* increasing exponentially in the past 20 years, which of these processes most deserve attention? Which processes contribute the most value to the organization? How do workplace learning professionals demonstrate that value to other business leaders? The success of the learning function in most of today's organizations now depends as much on knowing what dials and gauges to monitor and which levers to pull as it does producing hours of learning, workbooks, and posttraining tools.

With limited time to effectively manage all tasks needing attention, good management consists of giving the right amount of attention to the right tasks. Strong managers seek to strike a balance between what deserves attention and what requires attention, between details and fundamentals, between tactics and strategy.

Select the Right Metrics

A *metric* describes the distance of a phenomenon from a desired benchmark or standard. Metrics can describe either learning function inputs or outputs and can help to direct management action.

Metrics describe what is normal and abnormal and whether any one observation is part of a trend. For example, metrics that support decision making might include simple ratios of unit expenditures or difficult psychometric measures of how much people learn. Although metrics communicate, simplify, illuminate, and persuade, they ultimately represent opportunities for improvement.

Learning programs leading to performance improvement are not one-time events, but rather a series of events, each of which may be measured using separate sets of metrics. Several factors, including the amount of time between learning events and when the new information must be applied, may degrade the quality of how information gets translated into individual performance, and likewise how individual performance gets translated into organizational performance.

An *indicator* is usually a calculation or a ratio that describes the direction of a learning function input and gives some clue as to what might happen in the future if conditions remain the same. *Key indicators* are a set of indicators that concisely and comprehensively describe the direction of the most important inputs to the learning function. It is often challenging to translate information obtained from indicators into managerial action.

So how can metrics help to run training like a business? Successful learning programs accomplish these goals:

* Learners receive information and store it.
* Later, they must translate that information into individual performance behaviors.
* Individual performance behaviors conspire to achieve organizational objectives. Such an improvement is usually measured very tangibly, often in terms of dollar value.

In *Presenting Learning*, authors Tony Bingham and Tony Jeary discuss the skills and techniques that workplace learning professionals need to communicate to CEOs and other top decision makers about the value of learning as part of overall company strategy (Bingham and Jeary, 2007). This resource includes examples of and tips for developing strong leadership skills as well as stories about the power of learning in transforming organizations.

Metrics should derive from desirable behavior and favorable outcomes. The data that contributes to each metric is as important as the metric itself. Invalid and unreliable data and data collection methods result in untrustworthy metrics. Above all, metrics should be parsimonious. Workplace learning professionals need to identify the least number of metrics required to effectively manage processes, communicate with senior management, and execute learning strategy. Keep in mind that the same set of metrics may not be appropriate for all three of these areas. Some metrics are used to signal an emergency, whereas others are meant to be monitored more regularly.

Create Compelling Leadership and Build Partnerships

In a recent ASTD study, chief learning officers (CLOs) cited leadership as the most important characteristic for success (Sugrue and Lynch, 2006). Although almost all successful people attribute at least part of their success to leadership ability, this study found that many of the top learning executives attribute their greatest successes to the ability to build alliances across organizations and to be seen as a partner with other business owners. This may seem obvious, but many workplace learning professionals still rely almost entirely on their technical proficiency or mastery of learning science to gain credibility.

The majority of current CLOs come from outside the learning function (for example, production, finance, operations) and became conversant in learning science later in their careers. More recent trends indicate just the opposite with an increasing number of learning leaders who are rising through the ranks of the learning function and learning the lessons of leadership early in their careers.

Communicate in Business Language

As learning becomes more integral to business strategy, learning executives need to become more conversant in the language of business—that is, describing organizational learning in terms of value, the marketplace, learners, and learning function.

Value

Value means many things depending on the context. Successful CLOs describe value in vivid ways to produce both numbers and compelling stories. Discussions usually focus on the bottom line: How does learning impact the bottom line—both in business units and at the enterprise-level? The bottom line may refer to profit, net income, a definitive result, or a dollar figure.

Return-on-investment, another common framework for discussing value, describes how much profit or cost savings is realized as a result of an investment or expenditure. In the WLP profession, ROI reflects the dollar value of learning program outputs compared with the cost. This ratio of inputs to outputs, always expressed as a percentage, calculates the amount of learning program impact at an organizational level—that is, how well the organization performs under a given set of circumstances.

Successful learning executives communicate in business language and skillfully address common concerns regarding the real outcomes of learning programs beyond standard professional certification and efforts to integrate new employees into productive and committed members of the organization. They justify investments in learning, quantify the impact of expenditures, describe how investments link to organizational performance, and emphasize the competitive advantage that now exists due to differentiation in productivity and innovation.

In building a case for the strategic value of the learning function, you must identify if the organization is investing optimally in learning. Learning executives need to explain whether the current effects of learning could be achieved with a smaller budget, or conversely would greater investment yield increased benefits.

The Marketplace

Learning professionals collaborate with colleagues to expand the field, but these same professionals must also guard confidential information and competitive intelligence. So how can workplace learning specialists obtain information to benchmark learning expenditures, such as amount of expenditure per employee, within the context of the competition and not just an entire industry?

Strong workplace learning professionals are able to describe how key indicators and benchmarks of the learning function in their organization match up against those of direct competitors, the overall industry sector, and across a broad range of organizations. For example, they often discuss innovative learning strides implemented both successfully and unsuccessfully by the competition when communicating with senior management. They need to understand industry changes so that the learning function can continually adapt to remain effective and support the rest of the organization amid market changes. Because CEOs rely on the learning function as a competitive advantage, workplace learning professionals must become trusted advisors with the ability to effectively communicate the value of the learning function, especially in relation to the competition.

The Learners

Learning executives constantly look at metrics and numbers—and rightfully so. Numbers, however, tell only part of the story, and understanding the full story requires talking to the people behind the numbers.

Speaking directly with learners provides invaluable intelligence about the wealth of an organization's human capital and where it clusters. Taking time to do walk-around management and cultivating relationships with leaders of other business units in the organization provide a sense of how the learning function is perceived by others—including the learners.

Workplace learning professionals need to identify what employees see as the benefit of learning. Do they perceive learning as a worthwhile task to help accomplish personal or professional goals and make them more marketable? Or do they see training as time away from *real work?*

For any industry, remaining competitive requires the learning function to help retain and nurture the leadership and talent that already exists in the organization. By tightly partnering with HR and senior management, the learning function plays a vital role in planning and equipping employees and future leaders with crucial skills.

The Learning Function

As a learning executive, if you don't boast about the value of the learning function and the talented staff within it, who will?

Take a page out of the playbook of other senior managers who showcase the talent that surrounds them! Many organizations like to boast about their partners. As the saying goes, you can learn a lot about somebody by the company they keep.

Successful learning executives imitate the way their organizations show off portfolio partners. During a recent multimillion dollar learning center tour, every hallway, wall, and room of the facility displayed powerful messages about organizational values and commitment to learning. The ultimate message: show off the learning function talent and partners!

Walking the talk and ensuring that the learning function staff participate in their own personal and professional development are also mission critical. Do the workplace learning professionals in the organization develop their own skills as learning professionals and possibly future leaders or is it learning for everybody else?

If the learning function is to be seen as a strategic learning partner, then this area needs to have the right people, in the right place, targeting the right competencies, and receiving the right amount of investments and attention from senior management.

In summary, every learning executive needs to impact the seven *right things*: the right people, in the right jobs, in the right places, at the right time, with the right competencies, using the right programs, and nurtured in the right environment.

Chapter 2

Five Fundamentals for Managing Learning Like a Business

---※---

In This Chapter

- Treating learning like a capital investment
- Engaging learning resources from outside the learning function
- Evaluating marginal impacts
- Making learning transparent and reducing complexity
- Determining critical success factors

---※---

So how should workplace learning professionals approach managing learning like a business? To be effective, they should provide reports that satisfy senior management, establish credibility, earn the respect of management and peers, and demonstrate the value of the learning function in contributing to the organization's success. These professionals will possess strong business acumen and are not reactive to daily demands and emergencies; rather, they focus on organizational goals and driving results.

What exactly does business acumen mean in this context? In training, how often do learners "not rise to the level of expectations, but rather fall to the level of training?" Regardless of the training goal—executing a championship football season, exceeding sales goals, leading an organization, developing armed combat skills, training law enforcement officials—a learner's success depends on mastering a set of fundamentals and repeatedly practicing those fundamentals to be able to execute them successfully in a real performance situation. Likewise, business acumen requires professionals to master a set of fundamentals and rehearse authentic situations to execute those fundamentals on a moment's notice.

This chapter discusses the fundamental competencies required to effectively manage learning like a business, including

- ❋ treating learning like a capital investment
- ❋ engaging resources outside of the learning function
- ❋ evaluating marginal impacts
- ❋ making learning transparent
- ❋ determining critical success factors.

Fundamental 1: Treat Learning Like a Capital Investment

Workplace learning professionals must communicate in the language of financial terms and investments, especially when making a case for budgets and stating the value of the learning function. The WLP professional's business language, however, is often naïve and sometimes turns off the exact people he or she wants to persuade!

Senior management evaluates opportunities quantitatively. They carefully analyze financial inputs, expected outcomes, and results for a variety of scenarios. Although senior management talks about the value of employees, they need better tools to describe that value. That's where workplace learning professionals with strong business acumen can play a vital role. By communicating the establishing measurements, they can best convey the value of the learning function in terms that management deems essential.

Any important initiative undertaken by an organization is treated like a capital investment—that is, resources invested will have a predictable flow of benefits and will ultimately be regarded as productive long-term assets. Capital assets drive, create, and extract tangible value after their initial funding.

The fact is that learning programs create valuable assets that have some of the same underlying dynamics as traditional capital assets, and non-learning executives need help in identifying ways that investments in learning can be treated as capital investments. Start by demonstrating to management that investment in the learning function is not an open-ended commitment. Then evaluate learning investments using the same techniques that financial managers use to evaluate investment opportunities. This means tying hard investments to hard outcomes and showing the links.

Fundamental 2: Engage Learning Resources From Outside the Learning Function

Although a learning function's budget fluctuates from year to year, the WLP profession generally sees increased investment in learning in most

Treat Learning Like a Capital Investment

The following questions can help you to begin thinking strategically about and treating learning like a capital investment:

- ❋ **Estimating the benefits of learning over time:** Are the benefits greater as time goes by or immediately after the learning event? Do the benefits increase or decrease gradually? How long are the benefits expected to last? What forces dilute the benefits before they are fully realized?
- ❋ **Assessing the risks:** What is the contingency plan to obtain required resources? What functional areas within the organization have resources with the required skills to help with resource issues? Is this a one-time investment, or are additional investments likely if the program succeeds? If the program does not succeed, is further investment justified or is it better to stop the initiative?
- ❋ **Discussing the full value of benefits:** How can a particular learning program be leveraged for other parts of the organization rather than reinventing the wheel? What alternative strategies can be used if this program is no longer feasible? What potential revenue streams could be realized from a successful learning product, for example, customer education programs or consultancy?

industries every year. Organizations, however, are not solely responsible for the learning process. As organizations increase the training investment per employee each year, they expect employees to stretch each learning dollar and use learning resources beyond those directly provided by the organization.

In lieu of unlimited funding, workplace learning professionals need to build partnerships with other business units in the organization to access and leverage resources for learning programs. By pooling and sharing resources with other business units, the learning function and its internal partners benefit by reinforcing each others' efforts, thereby forging a strong partnership. Learning programs extend beyond division and business unit boundaries to improve performance across the organizations. In the same manner, the learning function needs to partner with business units and identify resources for cross-organizational learning programs. By sharing resources, the learning function continues to deliver high-quality, targeted learning programs at a potentially lower cost on a per-participant basis, and the business units gain knowledgeable resources who can readily coach and support the transfer of learning back on the job.

Centralizing the learning function provides many benefits to individual learners, business units, and the organization as a whole. For example, learners can readily access the learning programs they need. Training redundancies are uncovered based on what the learning function needs to provide and what individual business units are already providing. Removal of these redundancies frees up business unit resources to support the objectives of the learning program before, during, and after the training to maximize application and retention.

So how does this help to demonstrate the value of the learning function? Truly strategic learning functions complement the efforts of other business units in the organization and help them to drive the required behavior to achieve their performance goals. Strong learning executives recognize these dynamics and benefits and seek opportunities to enable success in business units by creating strong partnerships within the organization.

Fundamental 3: Evaluate Marginal Impacts

The saying "employees respect what management inspects" conveys the idea that the measures and concerns of senior management drive the measures and focus of everyone else in the organization. Management in any organization tries to avoid uncertainty because it often involves more risk and unexpected costs. As a result, some workplace learning professionals prefer to take small steps when the amount of risk in pursuing an initiative is high or uncertain.

Marginal analysis, an economic tool, enables better decision making by comparing the marginal costs with the marginal benefits when producing one additional unit. Some examples of marginal costs include

- investing $100,000 *more* in computer security
- hiring 10 *new* employees
- providing three *more* hours of training per employee
- developing 100 hours of *additional* content.

As senior management asks more questions about the impact of increasing learning function investments on other areas of business performance, marginal analysis enables workplace learning professionals to articulate which investments are likely to yield the greatest business impacts, both positively and negatively.

Fundamental 4: Make Learning Transparent and Reduce Complexity

Management is a paradox. Nearly everyone has been managed at some point in his or her career and has probably said to himself or herself, "I could do what my boss does." Yet those achieving management positions in their careers quickly find that no matter how much preparation they received beforehand, either through education or apprenticeship, they still lack many skills needed to be an effective manager. The higher they climb in the management hierarchy, the more difficult management becomes. Few workplace learning professionals received training on how to effectively communicate with senior management using the language of business.

Successful managers simplify the facts and discuss key points quickly. Unfortunately, many learning professionals, used to explaining the complexities of evaluation and competency mapping or the difficulties of measuring learning, often overwhelm the intended audience and end up losing them. Many senior managers do not have time for details of how workplace learning professionals arrived at their findings; they just need to know what is important in plain English.

The precise speech of the WLP profession often makes it difficult to convey ideas quickly and simply. Workplace learning professionals must trade highly precise but possibly incomprehensible speech for highly concrete yet easily understandable speech.

The good news is that as trainers and workplace learning professionals, we are experts at communicating and imparting knowledge. We have experience simplifying key concepts and communicating them concretely. These WLP professional competencies just need to be applied in the boardroom as well. Through this process, successful learning executives often find that they have much in common with other business unit managers who they initially thought were cut of an entirely different cloth.

Fundamental 5: Determine Critical Success Factors

In his book, *Good to Great*, Jim Collins explains how companies leaping to the status of elite performers identified a unique and definitive ratio (containing an economic denominator) within their organizations that illustrated where value is really created in the economic engine (Collins, 2001). For most of Collins's great organizations, this ratio was rarely an "off-the shelf" or ROI-type measure. In nearly every case the ratio was simple, yet not always intuitive. For Walgreens, the ratio that drove their business turned out to be amount of *profit per customer per visit*. From this ratio, Walgreens determined that the key driver of success was the convenience the customer experienced during each store visit. Collins noted that many organizations struggle for years before determining the unique ratio driving value for their organization. After identifying the magic ratio and driver, these organizations discovered a fountain of prosperity: They found one critical success factor, which if managed properly, served as the principle for strategic decisions and maximum profits.

Collins suggests that for some organizations, one critical success factor in the form of a ratio defines the value proposition for the entire organization. Several critical success factors relating to mission, culture, ethics, commitment to excellence, or positioning of products and services drive the profitability of other organizations. The value of identifying these efficacious critical success factors is not only to drive profitability but also to serve as the final arbiter for management making crucial decisions.

The Wrong Brothers: Defining the Right Critical Success Factors

A story that illustrates the great power of authentic critical success factors as well as the futility and wastefulness of false critical success factors comes from a famous engineering professor, who happened to be an expert in the history of aviation and a great admirer of the Wright brothers. He often told the story of how the Wright brothers were obsessed with flight and had a great passion to create a machine that would allow them to have the same experience as seabirds swooping down on the beaches of North Carolina.

Yet their greatest passion was not to fly but to understand the wondrous phenomenon of flight. They toiled and experimented endlessly until they found the principle by which they believed anything could fly. When they found that mechanism, they were both amazed at its simplicity. They felt lucky that of all the people who would study flight, they were the ones who found what really could make an object fly. From that simple principle, they were able to design an entire machine that could suspend itself and maneuver through the air in flight.

The professor then told us about the Wright brothers' competitors—the Wrong brothers. The Wrong brothers built outhouses for a living and loathed the task of transporting the newly built outhouses throughout the swamps to their final destinations. The Wrong brothers found out that the Wright brothers were experimenting with making machines that could fly and came upon the great idea that if they could build a machine that could fly, then they would have a much easier time transporting outhouses to customers up and down the mid-Atlantic coast. So, while the Wright brothers were seeking the simplest mechanism by which any common object could fly, the Wrong brothers were busy designing a flying machine around the outhouses that they hoped to transport. The rest is history. The Wright brothers introduced the age of flight, and the Wrong Brothers disappeared in obscurity. Both in aviation and sanitation.

What is the point of the professor's story? An authentic critical success factor is extremely powerful and is worth the great effort to discover it. A false critical success factor will seem sensible at first but will always lead to failure. Discover and explore the principles that make the organization fly. Spare the talk of how to move an outhouse from one place to another.

Now that we've discussed the importance of selecting the right critical success factors, the next chapter focuses on key measures that every learning professional should know to be able to clearly articulate how the learning function demonstrates value.

Chapter 3

How to Demonstrate Value: Key Measures Every Learning Professional Should Know

---

In This Chapter

- Defining productivity
- Exploring organizational capacity and growth
- Seizing opportunities
- Reducing scrap and rework
- Analyzing customer satisfaction
- Identifying employee satisfaction and retention
- Minimizing inefficiencies

Organizations that have already streamlined and tweaked their business processes to drive profit need to find more innovative ways to grow—and developing and retaining top talent is a key priority. In many organizations, upper management now views the learning function as a strategic driver and integral to the organization's profitability and growth. Upper management expects great results for the dollars invested, and learning initiatives are no exception.

Finding opportunities to support or enhance the organizational strategy isn't easy, and implementing them isn't a simple task either. Large projects depend on the success of the smallest details, and even the most seasoned workplace learning professionals find that demonstrating the value of the learning function with hard evidence is a daunting task.

Many workplace learning professionals go overboard by developing costly and arcane studies to demonstrate value. Some try to oversell the value of the learning function and end up attracting suspicion rather than inspiring confidence. Organizations that develop idiosyncratic or firm-specific measures of value, while quite impressive and rigorous, often find the results to be limited in use and incomparable with more standard ways of measuring value.

When analyzing organizational strategy, workplace learning professionals need to identify ways to help the CEO and management achieve their goals—specifically, how learning can leverage strengths and shore up weaknesses in the organization. This section provides a brief primer of ways the most successful workplace learning professionals demonstrate value effectively and convincingly. Although demonstrating value is unarguably one of the most difficult problems faced by the profession, workplace learning professionals have several ways to solve this problem. Even though this is not a comprehensive list, any workplace learning professional with a working knowledge of these measurements is way ahead of the game.

Productivity

Productivity means different things within different organizations. Successful learning programs, even those without explicit economic or financial goals, enable an organization to produce an increase in items that can immediately be exchanged for cash or that can be booked as a sellable asset in the future. Thus, productivity often refers to a greater output of goods, services, or anything that can be placed into the organization's inventory.

Organizational Capacity and Growth

An IBM study cited hundreds of interviews with CEOs worldwide about their vision for the future of their organizations (IBM, 2004). The results? These CEOs direct their efforts toward growth to sustain profitability rather than cost cutting. In practical terms, this suggests that most organizations are betting their future competitive advantage on the talents they nurture rather than the talent they acquire. Organizations that wish to grow organically must engineer the organization's key value-producing areas for expansion.

What can workplace learning professionals do to support this growth? For organizations to successfully grow they must have scalable business processes—that is, as demand for a product grows, the supporting business structure also grows to meet the demand. Growing businesses need to decrease marginal cost while increasing efficiency.

Organizations operating at full capacity possess very limited ability to scale. Scalability requires organizations to create standardized and easily duplicated processes that draw from reusable resources. When demonstrating value, learning professionals look for efficiency in terms of standardization and replication.

To derive a good estimate of organizational capacity, identify increases in inputs to outputs and compare those to the expected learning costs required to support the increased capacity.

Seizing Opportunities

Success for many organizations requires the ability to identify and pounce on opportunities, some of which exist for only a brief period of time. Learning programs can create necessary slack (excess capacity) and equip organizations with the competencies needed to seize future opportunities.

Highly influential organizations cause changes in their industries that lead to new opportunities—opportunities that leaner, hungrier, and more nimble companies can seize. Organizational *nimbleness*, as many learning executives like to call it, depends on the ability to adapt, retool, and refocus. Many ASTD BEST Award winners excel at using the learning function to create nimble organizations that quickly enter into markets and enjoy first mover advantages.

Reduced Scrap and Rework

No organization is 100 percent efficient in converting raw inputs into inventory-ready outputs. Every organization produces some amount of defective product or scrap. Many elite-performing learning functions successfully use workplace learning to reduce scrap to a level below industry benchmarks. These outcomes generate several economic benefits including reduced disposal costs, streamlined production processes, and fewer accidents.

Customer Satisfaction

According to the ASTD's 2006 *State of the Industry Report,* 97 percent of ASTD BEST Award winning organizations use customer satisfaction to measure learning function effectiveness (Rivera and Paradise, 2006). In this report, product quality and customer satisfaction top the list of fundamental measures indicating how well the learning function supports value creation and high organizational performance. Organizations striving for

Who Do the ASTD BEST Awards Recognize?

The ASTD BEST Awards recognize organizations that demonstrate enterprise success as a result of employee learning and development. Award winners show that they are **BEST** at **B**uilding talent, **E**nterprisewide, **S**upported by the organization's leaders, and fostering a **T**horough learning culture. The BEST organizations provide metrics and evidence of strong links between learning activities and business results that are strategically important to the company. BEST Award winners are able to show learning's relevance to organizational goals.

"best of breed" customer satisfaction reap several benefits including creating higher barriers to entry for competitors, protecting market share, justifying price premiums, and building customer loyalty. Despite the fact that the learning function can positively influence customer satisfaction metrics, many organizations still see the customer service function as an expense and not as a means to generating increased value through high customer satisfaction.

Employee Satisfaction and Retention

Employee satisfaction is a hallmark of the perennial ASTD BEST Award winning organizations as well as the ASTD Benchmarking Forum members. Most organizations, particularly public companies, are primarily interested in performance and profit. Because employees are part of this equation, organizations need to develop and challenge employees and try placing them in the right positions to aid retention.

Employee satisfaction promotes strong morale, greater eagerness to perform well, increased propensity to capitalize on improvement opportunities, higher employee and team cohesion, and reductions in lost productivity due accidents, sickness, and undocumented absences. Although the learning function plays a significant role in facilitating employee satisfaction and retention, ultimately employees need to ensure that the training received is applied and reflected in their job performance.

Minimize Inefficiencies

Time-crunched workdays force employees to effectively use time management techniques and to work smarter. Tasks need to be done right the first time. Employees struggling to perform at expected levels waste not only their own time but also that of co-workers and managers who must overcompensate for poor performance. Workplace learning professionals diagnose causes of underperformance and prescribe learning solutions to shore up gaps in knowledge or skills required to effectively perform job requirements. Reducing the time it takes for an employee to become proficient minimizes organizational costs, increases efficiency, and is one more way learning functions demonstrate value.

Percentage of Efforts Focused on Value-Producing Goals

Many organizations, especially in scientific, medical, legal, consulting, and research and development professions, require managers and employees to log activities. For example, in consulting organizations where the percentage of billable time makes or breaks profitability by project phase, employees track the time spent on administrative tasks, research, design, development, testing, evaluation, and documentation.

This data, especially when compared with historical data for other projects, serves as a powerful management tool. Astute managers use the distribution of time spent on tasks to accurately estimate costs, cycle time, and resource requirements. They can also discover what specific allocation of time to tasks maximizes value creation. Management sets the goals and metrics for time spent in each of these areas, but the learning function enables workers and managers to achieve those goals. To the extent that workplace learning professionals can help workers and managers focus on efficiently spending time on tasks that return the most value, learning is itself a valuable good.

Lower Operational and Franchise Risks

Every manager, regardless of the industry, must focus on some level of risk management and risk avoidance. The right learning and performance programs equip managers with the skills to effectively assess, prioritize, plan for, manage, and reduce possible organizational risks including operational and franchise risks.

  * *Operational risks* refer to major disruptions in production due to employee negligence or carelessness. One cause of operational risk is inadequate employee response during irregular production operations. In some industries, operational risk can result in additional compensation or extra effort to satisfy an inconvenienced customer, delays in the launch of mission-critical products, or the prevention of key deliverables from reaching the customer. For example, learning programs that equip customer service agents with techniques to retain high levels of customer satisfaction during irregular operations reduce the risk of order cancellations and, ultimately, customer loss.
  * *Franchise risks* refer to catastrophic disruptions of operations caused by employee recklessness, sabotage, misconduct, or malevolence. Losses due to franchise risk are usually sufficient for the businesses to lose favorable position in the market. In this case, organizations often terminate some or all of the operations; hence, the business loses its franchise.

In recent years, many high-profile organizations were devastated and forced to liquidate as the result of the behavior of a few employees. Programs that successfully reduce this risk require deep partnerships among the learning function and senior management of each business unit, such as accounting, finance, marketing, manufacturing, and others.

Managers of these departments understand better than anyone that an effective learning program focused on minimizing operational and franchise risks serves as an inexpensive and valuable insurance policy.

Reduction in Poor Management Decisions

Decision analysis evaluates and quantifies business opportunities and the consequences of pursuing different options. Although mastering this field's intricate techniques is not a requirement, decision analysis proceeds from two important principles that every workplace learning professional should know:

1. Every decision contains uncertainty, and with uncertainty comes a price tag. Knowing more about an opportunity often reduces uncertainty; however, obtaining additional information also has its costs. Effective learning programs equip managers with the capabilities to obtain information inexpensively. Several ASTD BEST Award-winning organizations create learning opportunities around decision making. This focus increases the quality of managerial decision making and simultaneously reduces the risk and cost of obtaining information.
2. Every decision carries direct and indirect costs for the decision taken, the next best course of action, and alternatives not taken. For example, taking a course of action ties up resources that might be deployed elsewhere in the organization to realize payoffs in different ways.

Eliminating Skills Gaps

Skills gaps top the list of concerns for senior management in any organization—and rightly so! Skills gap issues cause jobs to remain unfilled after reasonable recruiting and screening efforts and plague areas of organizations struggling to get past a certain point of growth or performance.

Many government leaders believe the national skills gap crisis is caused in large part by intense global competition, inadequate public education, a shrinking labor force, and expected retirement trends associated with the baby boomers. Learning functions focused on retooling employee knowledge by identifying and closing skills gaps positively impact the growth and competitiveness of organizations.

Reducing Replacement Costs Through Succession Planning

Let's face it. Notwithstanding the efforts of a number of gifted minds in the WLP profession, it isn't easy to come up with a number that describes the dollar value of an employee's productivity and knowledge or their economic value contributed to the organization. It would be easy to determine the consequences of human assets if they were to just walk out the door and never come back. Many organizations successfully give an accurate, albeit conservative, estimate of the direct expenses of hiring and replacing a departed employee, but that is only the beginning. Lost productivity—sometimes very evident in terms of lost sales, client migrations, or reduced output—often dwarfs the costs of training replacement employees and the development time required to achieve the same level of proficiency as their predecessors.

By proactively focusing on succession planning, an organization can quantify the required investment for developing talent to build the bench strength of key positions. Succession planning also serves as an insurance policy against incurring the unlimited costs associated with lost productivity plus replacement costs, compounded over time if the position remains unfilled.

Increasing Ties to Organizational Strategy

The changing role of workplace learning professionals requires developing a greater set of skills. Learning's increasingly important role in business strategy and organizational effectiveness involves far more than an understanding of sales and marketing.

Even the most budget-conscious senior executives want employees to be happy and inspired by their work. They want to create an environment in which everyone is working at capability and developing new skills needed for the future. They count on the learning function to help create a dynamic culture that influences the quality and suitability of people they hire, as well as the organization's ability to adapt to changes in the marketplace.

In facilitating organizational culture and change, many learning functions leverage instructional technology and more readily capture and retain tacit knowledge, often called institutional memory.

A Final Word about Value

Workplace learning professionals struggle to communicate the value of the learning function because they don't understand the value themselves and have difficulty putting a dollar value on the contribution. This chapter presents some of the methods and tools used to describe, calculate, and demonstrate value; however, no single measure of value is suitable in all cases.

Unfortunately, because so few learning professionals know how to define value, they have not focused on communicating it to colleagues, peers, and senior management. Communicating the value of the learning function isn't just a priority; it's a requirement for survival. Communicating value requires simplification to make it compelling and readily understandable. The next chapter defines learning assets and presents strategies for demonstrating learning function value.

Chapter 4

How the WLP Scorecard Measures and Manages Organizational Performance

---
✳

In This Chapter

- Learning products do not deplete with use
- Understanding learning's small marginal costs
- Creating unfair advantages
- Temporary monopolies
- Resistance to commoditization
- Costs of learning

✳

Ever since Kaplan and Norton introduced the Balanced Scorecard in the mid-1990s, the learning dimension holds greater weight in many organizations. In fact, the Balanced Scorecard requires organizations to allocate as much weight to certain intangible assets (that don't appear in financial statements) as the hard assets in the financial and operations dimensions.

As a result, many organizations consider learning assets less as per capita expenses and more as pillars that support sustainable success. For the first time in business history, upper management recognizes the positive economic and financial benefits of learning assets.

This chapter presents some of the reasons why learning assets have taken center stage among economists and academic accountants, and are on the tips of the tongues of so many CEOs. In particular, this section discusses the power of learning assets and how they can be treated as business resources; this section will also help you to facilitate conversations on how the learning function creates value both strategically and economically.

Learning Products Are Not Depleted as They Are Used

Much of the wealth created over the last century was developed by acquiring assets (inputs), and then using most of them up through a process of creating valuable outputs. For many decades, wealth has been accumulated by using natural resources and certain manufactured goods to produce products and services, thereby creating capital. In the process of converting inputs to outputs, natural resources become depleted, and the manufactured goods used in production wear out their useful lives. In nearly every case, those assets must be replaced. An appliance manufacturer uses metal and rubber to shape components, which are then assembled using electrical power, and then delivered to market using trucks. A certain amount of metal, rubber, electrical power, and life of a truck are used up.

Accountants use precise measures for calculating the amount, rate, and costs of resource depletion, namely, depreciation and amortization. Although depreciation and amortization derive from standard formulas, professionals use a great deal of judgment and prudence applying these measures to an organization's assets. The book value of an organization is greatly impacted by the correct judgment of the rate at which assets deplete.

This practice differs, however, for the WLP profession. Although most learning programs contain content that requires occasional replacement to keep it up to date, learning function products do not wear out from use. For example, a learning program used to train 100 new employees yesterday does not lose any of its potency, and it is just as capable of producing the same positive effects when delivered to 250 newly hired employees six months later, assuming the content is still relevant.

Learning's Small or Negligible Marginal Costs

In many manufacturing and service industries, expanding production capacity or increasing the scope of service comes at a considerable price. For example, a manufacturing organization may find that the price of producing 5 percent more of its signature product results in a variable cost increase of more than 5 percent. Although this increase would generate more top-line revenue, the more costly variable expense devours the excess income and contribution margin. Workplace learning professionals, in contrast, develop learning assets once and deploy everywhere without incurring increases in variable costs.

According to the 2006 *ASTD State of the Industry Report,* elite-performing learning organizations show increases in costs to produce one hour of learning (Rivera and Paradise, 2006). The average cost to deliver one hour of learning content, however, steadily decreases. By leveraging reusable content, the costs to deliver additional content to learners decreases dramatically. According to this report, in some organizations these costs are negligible, and as learning becomes further integrated into workflow, costs to deliver additional learning decrease further.

So what is the key takeaway point? After the initial investment in production and delivery, the costs to support learning decrease and knowledge assets become more valuable.

Nonrivalry

Nonrival assets are able to support multiple, simultaneous uses within an organization. However, many organizations are heavily invested in hard assets that cannot be used simultaneously in multiple situations. For example, a Boeing 747 flying from Washington, D.C., to San Francisco cannot simultaneously be used to transport other passengers traveling from New York to London. It is unavailable for any rival use until it lands in San Francisco, at which time it is becomes usable for transport only from San Francisco to its next destination. Now, imagine if this flight to San Francisco is only half-full, but in Chicago there are as many people wanting to fly to Shanghai as a 747 can hold. The aircraft could not stop in midair and transfer those passengers to a smaller Boeing 757 for the remaining duration of their flight, while the 747 hurries off to take those passengers waiting in Chicago to Shanghai.

In contrast, one learning program can be applied to many distributed groups, both in real-time and asynchronously. If one person or one group participates in (and then benefits from) learning, it does not prohibit other learners or other groups from simultaneously enjoying the same benefits. There is more to the nonrivalry of learning assets than the simultaneous access that learning programs allow. The benefits of a successful learning program, such as improved performance, do not come at the cost of something else, but rather support other success objectives.

Put simply, nobody gets a free lunch in producing effective learning programs that improve performance or increase competitive knowledge; but then again, nobody is eating somebody else's lunch, nor is anyone stuck eating lunch alone.

Scalability

Effective use of learning technology plays a big role in making learning products scalable. According to the 2006 *ASTD State of the Industry Report,* many ASTD BEST Award-winning organizations as well as ASTD Benchmarking Forum organizations experienced large efficiency gains in the learning function based on realizing learning technology investments. As the reach of the learning function increased along with the number of learners participating in learning opportunities, these organizations delivered learning at a lower cost per hour of learning content. Lower per unit costs coupled with an increasing scope provide clear evidence of the importance of scalability in these learning functions.

Unfair Advantages

Some of the companies listed by John Nesheim as having unfair advantages include members of the ASTD's Benchmarking Forum and those regularly seen on the list of ASTD BEST Award-winning organizations.

Scalability

Scalability means that something can be expanded without incurring excessive additional costs or burden. For example, organizations with a scalable product line expand and deploy the product in several other markets without making fundamental changes to the product line or the mechanisms that support production and delivery. Scalable organizations can produce more without having to be redesigned.

Scalable learning functions deliver reusable content in different locations, at different times, to an increasing scope of learners. Scalable learning creates replicable results even as the number of learners and delivery channels expand; performance resulting from this scalability can be appropriated across regions and nations.

Learning Creates Unfair Advantages

Both entrepreneurs and venture capitalists seek what John Nesheim, author of *The Power of Unfair Advantage: How to Create It, Build it, and Use It to Maximum Effect* (2005), calls an *unfair advantage.* An unfair advantage is defined as an organization occupying a place that nobody else can occupy. Expansion of these places creates greater interest and attraction—often forming the basis of business empires.

According to Nesheim, organizations create an unfair advantage by combining several ingredients that result in products characterized as unique, hard to duplicate, highly differentiated, highly adaptable, scarce, and desirable. Most of the ingredients that produce an unfair advantage include the skills and areas of knowledge of employees. Fortunately, learning functions focused on building truly strategic learning programs can expand and cultivate these skills and areas of knowledge. The most effective learning programs precisely target the special features and characteristics that drive an organization's uniqueness within an industry.

Temporary Monopolies

An unfair advantage refers to an organization's ability to remain differentiated over a long period of time. Most organizations, however, cannot maintain an unfair advantage through just one product or service. Every organization experiences extreme pressures to innovate and differentiate. Organizations must continually produce products in the short term in areas in which they have an unfair advantage to keep their edge. Such products create temporary monopolies and consequently create very high barriers to competition.

So what does learning have to do with temporary monopolies? The key to extracting the most value from a temporary monopoly involves quickly expanding the organization and equipping the key personnel with new knowledge and skills before the competition even knows what hit them. For example, salespeople must be equipped with a convincing presentation and attractive purchasing incentives for the customer. Marketing personnel need to clearly articulate the benefits of the new products and must reach their channels immediately. Line workers require instruction in production techniques to create products within business specifications. An effective learning function oils the hinges and enables rigid organizations to become fluid enough to expand into a new space before the competition.

Resistance to Commoditization

New product or service launches require specialized learning programs to equip employees with the required knowledge and skills to meet the challenges posed by the new item. The unique nature of products, along with learning programs tailored to specific learner profiles, creates an effective learning program with results that are not easily replicated by competitors. Learning reinforces the uniqueness of products or services. Even if the knowledge of how to produce a special product were acquired by a competitor the day after it appeared on the market, it would be unlikely that the competitor would be able to reap the same benefits without the support of the unique learning function tied to it.

The key message? Unique organizations, unique products, and unique learning functions greatly impact the success of one another. When all three are aligned, superior results occur.

Full Costs of Learning Shared

The majority of assets acquired by a company are paid in full by the organization. Although organizations can negotiate discounts, in most cases organizations cannot transfer the majority of costs of acquiring goods and capital.

Learning is different.

Every employee within an organization brings a unique set of skills and aptitudes to the workplace. These skills, developed over many years, offer fertile ground for future growth and development. The costs to equip employees with basic skills such as literacy, numeracy, consumer awareness, and social consciousness, as well as more advanced skills that are pertinent to the job, have already been paid for either through formal education, personal development in higher education, or by a previous employer's training programs. The learning function adds proprietary and organization-specific knowledge and skills required for employees to perform their jobs exceptionally.

This chapter, dedicated to defining the meaning of learning assets and identifying strategies for demonstrating learning function value, establishes a baseline of measurements for building a business case. Learning professionals are often stymied and must figure out some way to deliver high-level reporting, results, and proof of alignment with organizational goals. Identifying meaningful measurements is half of the battle. The next chapter focuses on how balanced scorecard–style tools force workplace learning professionals to determine measurements that senior management values and to align learning function efforts in support of organizational goals.

Chapter 5

Why Learning Is Hard to Measure and How the WLP Scorecard Can Help

Workplace learning professionals want evidence that investment in learning is appropriate, targeting the right people and competencies, and driving productivity, innovation, differentiation, and readiness.

How is this accomplished?

To begin, it is essential to focus on the metrics that really matter. Meaningful measurements differ for every organization but all have one thing in common: They are defined by the CEO or other senior manager in charge of learning or performance issues.

Too many workplace learning professionals focus on data quantifying the number of courses taken or hours of training per employee. But upper management wants to see the impact of learning in terms of addressing the needs of the organization. When deciding what to measure, focus on data that is directly relevant and meaningful to executives.

What Are Balanced Scorecards?

The Balanced Scorecard, developed by Robert Kaplan and David Norton in the 1990s, has emerged as the most prominent strategic management and performance measurement system used by organizations today (Kaplan and Norton, 1992). The Balanced Scorecard derives its name, and achieves its thrust, by balancing traditional performance measures with more forward-looking indicators in four key dimensions:

- **Financial**—To succeed financially, how should we appear to our shareholders?
- **Integration/Operational Excellence**—To satisfy our shareholders and customers, at what business processes must we excel?
- **Learning and Growth**—To achieve our vision, how will we sustain our ability to change and improve?
- **Customers**—To achieve our vision, how should we appear to our customers?

Figure 5-1 is an example of a balanced-scorecard-type planning chart for a regional airline. The strategic vision of the airline is to continue building on its unique position as "the only short-haul, low-fare, high-frequency, point-to-point carrier in America." The theme of this scorecard is "operating efficiency," and the card is read from left to right.

Notice that the strategic objective—greater operating efficiency—is in the left-hand column, whereas the actual initiatives are in the right-hand column. Between them are objectives, measures, and targets. In this example, training is on the bottom row, but the arrows indicate that the entire value chain depends upon aligning the ground crews, which will help improve turnaround times, which in turn will lead to more on-time flights, the ability to serve more customers, and ultimately drive more revenue and profits.

The balanced scorecard facilitates the alignment of individuals and corporate strategic objectives, accountability, cultures driven by performance, and support of shareholder value creation. There are also versions of scorecards related to marketing, sales, training, accounting, and so on.

Benefits of Using the WLP Scorecard

The WLP Scorecard provides the perspective and tools to transition from only measuring descriptive data for formal learning; it focuses on measuring performance-driving organizational outcomes. The WLP Scorecard investigates direct and indirect relationships and makes it possible to create prescriptions for maximizing the value of learning.

By understanding the learning function as multidimensional, workplace learning professionals will be able to manage learning with the same kinds

Figure 5-1: Example of a Balanced Scorecard for a Regional Airline

Mission: Dedication to the highest quality of Customer Service delivered with a sense of warmth, friendliness, individual pride, and company spirit.

Vision: Continue building on our unique position—the only short-haul, low-fare, high-frequency, point-to-point carrier in America.

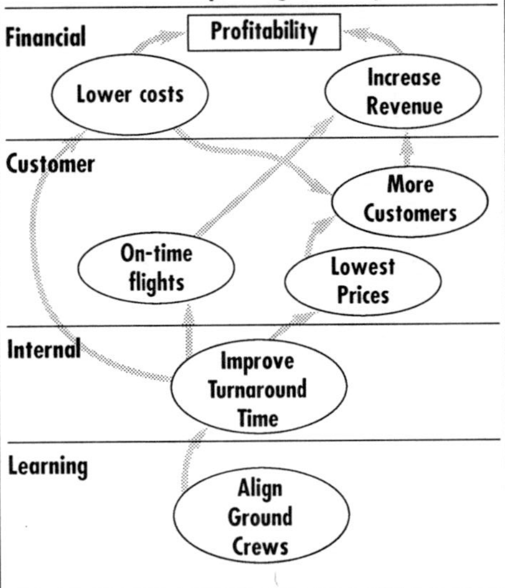

Theme: Operating Efficiency	Objectives	Measures	Targets	Initiatives
Financial	• Profitability • Fewer planes • Increased revenue	• Market value • Seat revenue • Plane lease cost	• 24% per year • 20% per year • 5% per year	• Optimize routes • Standardize planes
Customer	• Flight is on time • Lowest prices • More customers	• FAA on time arrival rating • Customer ranking • Number of customers	• First in industry • 96% Satisfaction • % Change	• Quality management • Customer loyalty program
Internal	• Fast ground turnaround	• On ground time • On-time departure	• < 25 minutes • 93%	• Cycle time optimization program
Learning	• Ground crew alignment	• % Ground crew stock-holders • % Ground crew trained	• year 1: 70% • year 4: 90% • year 6: 100%	• Stock ownership plan • Ground crew training

Financial: Lower costs, Profitability, Increase Revenue

Customer: On-time flights, More Customers, Lowest Prices

Internal: Improve Turnaround Time

Learning: Align Ground Crews

Source: Reprinted with permission from the Balanced Scorecard Institute, 2006.

of tools used to manage other business functions. There are six key benefits that workplace learning professionals gain by using the WLP Scorecard:

- identifying areas of performance
- leveraging report ratings
- facilitating effective planning
- allowing for comparison with similar organizations
- performing sensitivity analyses
- communicating the value of learning.

Identifying Areas of Performance

Traditional learning benchmarks, such as expenditure per employee, learning hours per employee, and expenditure as a percent of payroll, are simply baseline measures. They offer a useful retrospective yet give few clues as to which areas of the learning function deserve attention and resources for the future. Today's learning functions need much more information to operate. Keep in mind that more information is useful only when it can be visualized and understood without burdensome effort.

Just as the dashboard of a car indicates key information about the performance of the vehicle, the WLP Scorecard offers a comprehensive, dashboard-like approach full of just the right workplace learning information to determine which specific areas of the learning function exert the greatest effect and require immediate attention and which only need occasional monitoring.

The WLP Scorecard doesn't just report on the learning function accomplishments in the past year. By incorporating indicators of informal (also called work-based learning), human capital, and business outcomes, the WLP Scorecard helps to predict which areas of the learning function will generate the most value for the organization.

Leveraging Report Ratings

Over the years, ASTD has studied hundreds of organizations and found that top-performing organizations share common characteristics with respect to the learning function. *(See sidebar.)*

These ASTD report findings are corroborated by a 2004 Accenture study of high-performing learning organizations, which cited many similar characteristics among their banner organizations:

- alignment of learning strategy with business need
- competency development focused on families of critical jobs
- leadership development marked as high priority
- blended delivery approach, relying heavily on the use of technology
- learning integrated into other processes and the daily life of the employee

Top-Performing Learning Function Characteristics:

Analysis of past ASTD BEST Award winners reveals the top characteristics of a championship learning function:

- higher than average investment in the learning function when compared with all organizations as well as industry peers
- deliberate alignment of learning with business needs and strategy
- maximized efficiency in production and delivery, often facilitated through innovative use of instructional technology
- demonstrated effectiveness proven by multiple, yet simple, business measures
- systematic, thorough, and definitive measurement of effectiveness and efficiency
- a broad range of learning opportunities available throughout the enterprise, both formal and work based
- innovative non-learning solutions combined with learning for performance improvement
- high levels of involvement and support from C-Level management (Sugrue and Rivera, 2005).

◈ a well-conceived measurement system in place, with a focus on effectiveness, efficiency, and organizational impact

◈ learning extended across the value chain, including customer education (Accenture, 2004).

Facilitating Effective Planning

Aside from aligning strategy and initiatives, the WLP Scorecard introduces measurements that go beyond the strictly financial. Using this tool reinforces a planning process that mobilizes for measurement by first identifying the vision and desired results then identifying strategies and measures of performance based on outcomes. Planning is a fundamental part of the process. It provides workplace learning professionals with the opportunity to discuss measurements and the means for acquiring them.

Comparing with Similar Organizations

Measurements don't exist only to prove that progress is being made; they also exist to give workplace learning professionals and senior management some basis for comparing the learning function performance in one organization against some established norm.

The WLP Scorecard, useful to organizations of any size and budget, facilitates comparisons among learning functions by size, industry sector, region, and organization type. Using this tool guarantees a deeper understanding of how the learning function stacks up against those of peers and helps to diagnose strategies needed to gain an advantage.

Performing Sensitivity Analyses

Sensitivity analysis, a fundamental activity in the accounting and finance professions, allows managers to determine what effect small changes in inputs or processes will have on outputs. The WLP Scorecard brings this powerful management tool to the learning function by providing "what-if" scenarios:

◈ How will changes in key learning processes affect the efficiency and effectiveness of the learning function?

◈ What are the biggest risks to sustaining the learning function?

◈ What measures should be taken to immediately strengthen the sustainability of the learning function?

◈ What improvements will have the greatest impact on the learning function for the least amount of money?

Communicating the Value of Learning

Unless the learning function has a stellar record to draw upon with impressive measurements of past contributions, discuss value in terms of the future. An organization's challenges lie ahead. History shows lessons learned, so focus the analysis and communication of the value of the learning function on current organizational goals and how to achieve desired outcomes.

The WLP Scorecard is more than a souped-up benchmarking database; it helps to manage day-to-day operations by providing a model for monitoring and reporting on internal learning operations.

Many homegrown "value of learning" models based on evaluation frameworks are familiar only to learning professionals. The WLP Scorecard, however, is a business-driven approach to learning management that precisely and vividly articulates the value of learning.

Advantages for Business Professionals

For workplace learning professionals to produce the forward-thinking value that senior management expects, they must deeply understand the organization based on research of publicly available material, conversations with co-workers and colleagues, purposeful interviews, and daily experiences. Time is precious and brevity is important. Workplace learning professionals know the importance of strategic learning but don't have the time to sort out all the theories about learning and performance. Quick decisions must be made with limited time to reflect on the past.

The WLP Scorecard stops metric madness and identifies those indicators that most affect the performance of the learning function. These indicators enable workplace learning professionals to select the right metrics to monitor as well as focus the right amount of attention on managing strategic learning in the organization. With a solution in place to measure and manage performance, the next step involves identifying and collecting the required data to populate the WLP Scorecard.

Part II

◆

Planning Phase:
Strategies for Identifying and Gathering Data

Chapter 6

Setting Up Your Organization to Track and Obtain Data

In This Chapter

- Examining principles to set up the learning function for success
- Determining approach to measurement and measurement strategy
- Establishing the right focus and measurements
- Determining the right number of measures

No matter what factors drive the need for measurement, the ultimate goals of developing measures are communication and decision making. Indicators and metrics are numerical ways to explain the relationships of data. Indicators provide information about the *direction* of an activity or set of activities within an organization, and in some cases the environment within which the organization exists. A metric describes the *distance* from an organization's activities to a desired benchmark or standard.

Many workplace learning professionals steer clear of metrics and measurements fearing they will be held accountable to achieve target performance goals. But to run learning like a business, professionals must be held accountable to the bottom line and need the tools to assess situations to be able to make decisions based on the wealth of data collected.

Workplace learning professionals must justify the existence of the learning function and convincingly discuss accomplishment of goals. Measuring and tracking the learning function activity is not a matter of punctilious monitoring of individuals. The cornerstones of tracking and obtaining data

Principle One
Probing Questions

Use these questions to help sharpen your knowledge of your organization's goals and learning outcomes so that you are able to respond succinctly in any discussion about learning in the organization. Be prepared to elaborate if prompted by upper management.

* What is the value that the learning function provides in the organization?
* What is the most compelling reason for management to continue funding the learning function at current levels?
* What learning function investments are required in the future and what type of benefit or return will the organization realize as a result?
* What is the biggest risk to the organization if the investment in the learning function is reduced?
* How much is learning a part of your organization's culture?
* How do you know when learning occurs?
* How do you convince stakeholders outside the learning function that learning has occurred?
* If funding for the learning function were reduced significantly, what strategies could be implemented for the organization to continue to learn?

are *resourcefulness* and *relationships,* not just the tactics of implementing sophisticated information systems.

Nothing enables the learning function to affect change in an organization more than consistent sponsorship and support from top management. Without that support, the workplace learning professional's job might consist of constant uphill battles to justify budgets and existence of the learning function. Articulating learning's impact on the organization in terms that senior management understands and appreciates begins with identifying what measures matter most and planning to gather the data.

Most initiatives consist of at least three phases: initiating, planning, and executing. The previous chapters focus on the initiating phase and present the theory of measurement and metrics that workplace learning professionals need to know when initiating measurement of the learning function.

This section focuses on planning what data is needed for measurement and strategies for obtaining such data. In particular, chapters 6 and 7 emphasize the best practices and core principles used by the most successful learning executives to build credibility, relationships, and business acumen to ensure the success of the learning function.

The Six Principles to Set Up the Learning Function for Success

Based on core practices of some of the world's top learning functions, the following six principles outline strategies for promoting the learning function and running learning like a business:

* simplifying the concept of learning
* creating partnerships with upper management and functional area leaders
* delving into the organization's financial statements
* auditing all learning management systems (LMSs)
* reviewing survey results for the last three years
* balancing hard and soft data.

Principle One: Simplify the Concept of Learning

Most people would agree that learning is valuable. Workplace learning professionals need not plead too hard to make the case for new hire or basic skills training. However, when senior executives start asking "Why?" "How much?" and "What's the payoff?" today's professionals struggle to state a convincing case without hard data and evidence. Clearly, measurements do matter.

Part of the reason that senior executives recoil at anything sounding like it came from an educator—for example, competency mapping—is the perception that learning appears complex and obscure. This trap snares many workplace learning professionals.

Today's learning function leaders must produce results that executives value but also must clearly and succinctly communicate the value of those results. The problem isn't always caused by a lack of evidence but rather the incorrect selection of what to measure. If the CEO doesn't value the selected learning function metrics, then the learning function is focused on the wrong measurements.

Four criteria can help simplify the concept of learning in the organization: Learning is a change in behavior, either individually or as a group, that can be

1. attributed to something an employee or the learning function enabled
2. measured
3. executed successfully the majority of the time
4. applied to a practical performance situation.

By understanding the organizational goals and desired outcomes and by clarifying the measurements that do matter to senior management, workplace learning professionals will set up the learning function to collect the right data and simplify the concept of learning in the language of business.

Principle Two: Create Partnerships with Management and Business Unit Leaders

The most savvy workplace learning professionals recognize that senior management and business unit leaders serve as the most fertile source of both anecdotal and quantitative data about the effectiveness of learning within their respective areas. These functional area leaders also often exert the greatest influence on the success of learning programs occurring in their domains. These leaders either make or break learning programs based on their willingness and motivation to champion and drive support. They create the incentives for employee participation and evaluate subordinate managers on the success of fostering the learning back on the job.

Similarly, management and business unit leaders (the learning function's internal customers) strongly influence senior management's perceptions and advocacy for learning.

Based on that insight, what should workplace learning professionals do to cultivate relationships with these champions?

Successful learning function leaders actively network and build credibility and trust with leaders in the organization. Forging strong relationships

Principle Two
Probing Questions

Use these questions to assess your current understanding of the organization, goals, and business performance:

* Who are the key business leaders in the organization?
* How often do you meet with them?
* Are you consulted or asked to take part in their strategy meetings?
* What do you think they say about the learning function to other business leaders and to the senior managers to whom they report directly?
* What do you think they say about the learning function to their subordinates and to the business lines under their jurisdiction?
* How do they measure the performance of their business units?
* On what criteria are they evaluated?
* How does learning help them meet their strategic objectives?
* If business leaders had a wish list of things they could get from the learning function, what would it contain?
* Do senior leaders and business leaders publicly attribute their successes to anything the learning function is doing?
* How often do senior leaders teach programs and courses developed or administered through the learning function?

41

Principle Three
Probing Questions

Use these questions to assess your financial business savvy about your organization:

* How is the learning function budget determined and who signs off on it?
* Who pays for the development and the use of your products?
* Under what line items do the cash flows associated with the learning function appear on income statements?
* If you knew how much your competitors were spending on their learning function, would you be able to justify your expenditures? Be more competitive? Obtain more resources? Suggest improvements to enterprise strategy?
* Is the learning function prudently managed? Would the CEO, COO, and CFO agree with you?
* What are the annual revenue and net income of the organization this year? Were these increases compared to last year's allocations?
* Are organizational earnings improving year to year? Could the learning function help to improve these earnings?
* How much revenue is the organization generating from new products and services?
* Did the learning function contribute to these figures?
* If management decreased the learning function budget next year, what economic arguments could you make to persuade the decision makers not to decrease the learning function budget?
* If your learning function had to pay for itself, what business case could you make?
* What were the unplanned expenditures that occurred in each of the last five years?
* What factors caused these surprise expenditures?

requires scheduling regular meetings, engaging department leaders to understand their operations and pain points, and strategizing solutions to problems caused by gaps in knowledge or skills. Workplace learning professionals need to serve as internal consultants by collecting and synthesizing information to understand business needs. They then must devise the most effective way to help departments and the organization accomplish performance goals. The anticipatory nature of this process enables these learning professionals to educate business unit leaders about training's ability to solve certain problems and to clearly convey that not all performance problems are solved with training.

In building these partnerships with internal customers, workplace learning professionals need to avoid jargon understood only by those in the WLP profession, actively listen rather than talk, discuss custom learning solutions to improve performance, and communicate in the language of business.

Involving these leaders in the learning function by leveraging their knowledge, for example, as subject matter experts for key initiatives impacting their functional areas, forges a stronger relationship and helps these business leaders to experience first hand the value of the learning function. As is often the case, by working closely with the learning function, these managers can become the staunchest allies to help sell the value of training to all levels in the organization.

Principle Three: Delve into the Organization's Financial Statements

There's no way around it. Workplace learning professionals must master business and finance principles if they want senior management to view them as strategic partners with something useful to contribute. Money metrics form the language of business, and communicating in terms of money is as fundamental as understanding adult learning, pedagogy, instructional design methodology, or measurement and evaluation theory.

Entire courses are dedicated to financial statement analysis. Some of the most influential analysts on Wall Street drive the behavior of equity markets by their analyses and interpretations of financial statements. Mutual fund managers, investment bankers, and institutional investors decide where to place hundreds of millions of dollars based on their understanding of the financial statements for potential investments. If the people managing the largest accumulations of capital in the world consider reading financial statements as a fundamental part of knowing where to spend money, why would that be any different for workplace learning professionals who manage the largest and most fertile store of human capital in any organization?

A surprising number of learning executives never read their organization's financial statements outside of internal budget documents or expenditures within the learning function. Some consider the mere sight of ledger lines as intimidating, whereas others fail to see understanding financial statements as a required skill in the WLP profession.

Learning executives lacking knowledge of the organization's financial statements increase the risk of learning function failure. An inability to read and understand financial statements seriously constrains effective communication with non-learning executives and senior management.

Financial statements reveal important information about strategy and the projected direction of an organization. They reveal how resources ought to be managed to effectively execute strategy. And they contain dozens of concrete measurements to help predict the future and discover where value is created within the organization.

Principle Four: Audit All Learning Management Systems (LMSs)

Facilitated by the explosion in technology and networking, many organizations centralized their learning functions in the last 10 years. Centralization brought with it the development of corporate universities, occupation of dedicated training facilities, and use of highly customized instructional technology.

For some organizations, the corporate university exists without bricks and mortar and leverages a virtual location on the intranet, whereas for others, the corporate university can boast of physical locations on a campus near the corporate headquarters. No matter whether the learning function operates primarily in physical facilities or a virtual environment, all corporate universities possess the means to develop, store, administer, and deploy the portfolio of learning content.

Successfully centralizing the learning function is no small feat! Whether large or small, these learning functions must catalogue volumes of courses and learning programs and carefully weigh decisions to acquire learning solutions that will continue to meet employee knowledge and skill needs.

According to ASTD research, the most successful learning executives put a great deal of effort in selecting the platform to launch learning programs and the information systems to simultaneously design and develop instruction, and manage administration and evaluation activities for all learning initiatives (O'Driscoll, Sugrue, & Vona 2005).

In this study, as organizations successfully centralized the learning functions, many learning executives identified great inefficiencies due to redundant

Principle Four
Probing Questions

Use these questions to assess your current knowledge of the learning function and key metrics in the organization:

* How many platforms does the organization develop, deploy, and administer to support the learning function?
* How many LMSs are currently deployed? What is each LMS's share of usage? Are any managed by external partners, and if so, to what degree?
* What notable additions or changes occurred with the LMSs in the last year?
* If a senior executive asked for a brief report about the throughput of the LMSs, what measures and points should be highlighted?
* How much of the learning portfolio is delivered electronically or in a blended environment?
* What are the signature items in the learning portfolio? Who accesses them, how often, and what strategic objectives do they support?

learning materials and learning activities conducted without approval or supervision from the learning function.

Upper management highly regards several tangible metrics that gauge learning function effectiveness—most of them available through any LMS:

* number of courses offered and completed
* hours of learning consumed
* cost per learning hour consumed
* number of new hours of content developed
* amount of content reuse
* increases in knowledge repositories
* the number of certifications granted.

Learning executives need to be able to recite these statistics and communicate them as easily as the CFO recites earnings multiples, income figures, and expenditure categories.

As a best practice, perform a thorough audit of all LMSs in the organization and determine which learning metrics already exist in those systems. Consider setting up a mechanism to extract and monitor these figures weekly, perhaps even daily. Evaluate the strengths and the weaknesses of all LMSs and create an electronic fact sheet of key metrics that could be emailed to non-learning executives on a periodic basis.

Principle Five: Review Survey Results for the Last Three Years

For organizations to grow and reap expected profits, customers must first be happy with the products, service, and support they receive. Because customers drive incoming revenue, organizations pay close attention to customer feedback. Positive customer comments help management to know that they are doing some things right, but how much more revenue would be realized if customers were happier? Valuable feedback coming from dissatisfied customers enables the organization to identify problems and to quickly develop a plan to remedy the issues. The same is true for internal customer feedback—that is, employees who rely on the learning function to equip them with the required skills to perform on the job.

To measure overall satisfaction, organizations can send surveys to employees and customers. Annual surveys measuring overall employee satisfaction often focus on employee engagement as well as confidence in senior management and the organizational vision. Departments and divisions can also distribute surveys more frequently to gauge the vital signs or general atmosphere of the department or division.

Level 1 evaluations administered at the completion of a course provide a plethora of learner reactions regarding the learning environment, course content, type of instruction, presentation skills (if relevant), and the success of the course in accomplishing the stated objectives. These evaluations often solicit input regarding what other types of training learners feel they need to be successful in their jobs.

Occasionally IT or other departments might distribute surveys to learn more about employee needs or satisfaction related to, for example, email server performance or virtual networking capabilities.

Internal surveys are most likely administered and collected by the HR department. Consider starting with HR to research what surveys have been conducted in the last year or so and identify where the findings from those surveys now reside.

Most organizations have dedicated staff to determine client or customer satisfaction, customer demographics, segmentations, preferences, quality of supplier relationships, brand recognition, price sensitivity, and perceptions of the organization. This staff, perhaps housed in market research or the public relations departments, often uses rigorous collection methods and gather and analyze large amounts of data. Their reports, while sometimes only shared with key internal personnel, carry a great deal of weight in strategic decision making and can shed valuable light on customer satisfaction and customer experience with new products and services. Research by Rivera and Paradise (2006) indicates a strong association between employee satisfaction and the quality of an organization's learning function. Workplace learning professionals and executives who focus primarily on smile sheets and course evaluations can miss a substantial segment of data that can illuminate aspects of the learning function far beyond whether or not a particular course was worth the learner's time.

Learning executives need to establish strategic relationships with HR, marketing, and public relations research personnel to gain access to and evaluate employee and customer satisfaction survey results. By virtue of their larger and more representative samples, these survey results explicitly illustrate the strength and fitness of a learning function as well as the association with performance metrics that relate to business outcomes.

Reviewing several years of employee engagement results and customer satisfaction research gives workplace learning professionals a keen and intuitive sense of how much the learning function permeates organizational culture. The results also show the learning function's ability to positively influence the quality of products and services that an organization offers. Likewise, the learning executive who understands the sentiments of

Principle Five
Probing Questions

Use these questions to assess your current knowledge and to explore ways of seeking out the answers:

* How many organization-wide surveys did the organization conduct last year and what were the key findings?
* What are the current levels of employee satisfaction, employee engagement, customer satisfaction, and customer engagement, and how have they changed in the last three to five years?
* If there have been dramatic increases or decreases, how were they explained?
* What are the biggest contributors to employee satisfaction and employee engagement in the organization?
* What are the major markets and market segments for the organization's products or services, and how has each of these changed in the last three to five years?
* What are the organization's competitive advantages and risks, and how has the learning function helped in increasing the former while reducing the latter?
* How does the market perceive the quality of the top five revenue-producing products or services?
* What are the major reasons that employees have voluntarily left the organization in the last year?
* What are the major reasons that high-potential employees chose to work in the organization and not for the competition?

employees and customers is in a better position to build relationships outside the learning function and to increase the reach of learning into aspects of the business that are fundamental to creating business value.

Principle Six: Balance Hard and Soft Data

The most successful learning executives excel at presenting a balance of definitive hard metrics and compelling anecdotes and are often more rigorous about quantitative metrics than is required of them by non-learning executive sponsors. Unfortunately, some learning executives overstate the case for learning by presenting abstract metrics that fail to illustrate key points in business terms or by failing to communicate learning activity measures in crisp, concrete, analytical terms.

Consider punctuating the hard metrics with vivid anecdotes describing successes or learning function dashboards with graphical representations of metrics. For example, demonstrating a graphic of a needle's progress in the right direction and relating an anecdote that plausibly explains the movement demonstrates value and creates a memorable message. This process often prompts workplace learning professionals and management to think about which right metrics to use.

How to Approach Measurement and Measurement Strategy

A few words of caution.

A former professor of statistics, fond of beginning some classes by reviewing current research appearing in various journals, often pointed out where researchers, who ought to know better, misused measurement.

The professor's words also apply to the practice of measurement in workplace learning and business performance. Countless managers confine themselves to a few pet measurement techniques. Other learning professionals, stubborn about measurement, think that they have some conception of what a good number looks like. For organizations that design and implement poor measurement systems, the hope is that they just waste money and time for one accounting period and quickly realize the fallacy in the selected measurements.

Getting SMART to Establish the Right Focus and Measurements

Get SMART, really SCHMART.

Anyone who has ever developed a system of measurement, whether related to individual performance goals or business-unit financial goals, will likely

**Principle Six
Probing Questions**

* What type of annual and semi-annual reporting is required by the CLO's supervisor?
* What metrics do executives regularly monitor in the organization? Where is the effect of learning seen on this dashboard or report?
* How does the CEO evaluate the effectiveness of organizational learning?
* What does it take to persuade senior management to continue allocating resources and attention to the learning function?

be familiar with the SMART acronym. The SMART acronym describes five features that measurement systems should strive to attain to be worth-while to the business.

The experience of ASTD research culled over many years, however, suggests that SMART represents the bare minimum requirements of both individual and enterprise metrics. To establish a truly comprehensive system, consider SCHMART:

> Sensible
> Concise
> Handy
> Manageable
> Articulable
> Reliable
> Transferable

Sensible

Does it pass the laugh test, the furrowed-brow test, or the "my frequent flyer program is easier to understand than this" test?

Concise

Do the metrics describe phenomenon as succinctly as possible, without describing confounding events or a bunch of irrelevant events that are happening around the thing being measured? Similarly, do the metrics speak for themselves, or do they require multiple rounds of elaboration?

Handy

Do the measures serve you like your most trusted business tools such as your PDA?

Manageable

Does the activity of measurement ultimately free up attention and resources, or does it drain resources and become a task with a life of its own?

Articulable

Can you make it understandable to an intelligent professional who nevertheless does not have an extensive educational background or specialized training? Or do the metrics require layer upon layer of opaque mathematical, statistical, or methodological treatment?

Reliable

Do the measures strike where they are aimed each time?

Transferable

Can the measurement system be linked to performance measurement systems outside the learning function?

SMART MEASURES

The five features that commonly compose a **SMART** measure are

* **S**imple (or **S**pecific)—must be easily understood and unambiguous
* **M**easureable—requires no special methodological training
* **A**ctionable (or **A**chievable or **A**vailable)—has readily available data
* **R**elevant (or **R**ealistic)—ties to a clear tactical or strategic objective rather than a vague sense of "the way things ought to be"
* **T**imely—is time sensitive.

The Purposes of Measurement

Measurement seeks to

* communicate strategy, expectations, and the value proposition
* enable organizations to make the best decisions with the highest quality information and the least amount of risk
* promote good practices of managing—and not managing
* determine where resources are needed, deserved, and how to best allocate them accordingly
* establish whether a set of behaviors constitutes a trend
* describe what is normal behavior, what are the characteristics of exceptions, and what is an acceptable amount of variance
* feed back timely information from processes to manage inputs and from outputs to manage processes.

Determining the Right Number of Measures

Workplace learning professionals and business leaders using measurement systems struggle with knowing how many dials, gauges, and consoles to monitor. When things are going smoothly and all that is required is to stay the course, then monitoring a few measures suffices. When the weather, terrain, or conditions change, or when a significant amount of change occurs, then monitoring several measures simultaneously is imperative. Too few measures fail to capture all the information needed to manage; too many measures obscure, confuse, create, and encourage micromanagement.

Measurement is both art and science; the art consists in knowing where to look, and the science in knowing what tools to use to focus on what's important. Some stock traders monitor an astonishing number of highly technical measures, whereas others only a few fundamental measures. Yet there are numerous examples of both types being highly successful. Some workplace learning professionals remain informed by reading dozens of academic journals, trade publications, newspapers, blogs, and weekly magazines. Others only glance at a few Internet sites. Yet both groups remain sufficiently informed to participate in high-level discussions.

As a best practice to get started, select the number of measures that are not burdensome but yet provide relevant data. Too few measures make the unimportant important; too many measures make it difficult to discern what's important. Consider balancing individual-level, process-level, and organization-level measures to enhance management.

One tool, the WLP Scorecard, enables learning functions to begin measuring metrics that matter and discover the core measures that drive what the organization does best. The next chapter focuses on the nine broad areas of data used in the WLP Scorecard to describe and define the learning function.

Chapter 7

How to Gather the Right Data

※

In This Chapter

◉ Preparing for the WLP Scorecard journey

◉ Developing techniques for good estimates

◉ Exploring nine WLP Scorecard categories

※

This chapter, part of the section dedicated to planning, covers the basic categories of data needed to populate the WLP Scorecard. Some of the data will be readily available from documents and reports. Other data will require some detective work and judgments based on your knowledge and expertise. The suggestions for obtaining data, as well as the guidance for estimating figures where hard data is not available, all prepare workplace learning professionals to successfully complete the WLP Scorecard.

Embarking on the WLP Scorecard Journey

Prepare to embark on a journey of discovery. This journey will emphasize the connections between learning and business, and provide a renewed vision of how learning permeates an organization. The WLP Scorecard paves the path on this journey as a powerful tool for measurement, performance management, and decision support within an organization.

After a few glances at the WLP Scorecard, some may feel intimidated by the amount of data requested. Organizations with well-established LMSs, highly centralized learning functions, and stable leadership are much more likely to have this information at their fingertips. Based on previous WLP Scorecard user experiences, some organizations take as little as a few hours to enter a useful amount of data, while other organizations take substantially more time, sometimes over 100 hours. Regardless of the time required to gather and enter the data, every WLP Scorecard organization using the tool found immediate value—making the effort to enter the data worthwhile.

Learning any new tool requires ramp-up time for users to become proficient. Although the WLP Scorecard is relatively easy to use, practice builds mastery of entering data and generating reports.

Techniques for Developing Good Estimates

The quality of data is imperative. Period. As the saying goes, "garbage in, garbage out." Avoid the tendency to gather large quantities of data at the expense of quality, validity, reliability, accurate measurement, and comparability of data to that of other organizations. There are no hard and fast rules to determining whether a particular data point is an adequate representation of what it aims to measure. In some cases, where hard data does not exist, workplace learning professionals need to exercise judgment in developing the best estimates. There are two techniques to assess confidence in the data and estimates before entering them into the WLP Scorecard: the senior manager/member of the press test and the income tax form test.

The Senior Manager/Member of Press Test

To determine if data is fit to be entered in the WLP Scorecard, consider if the figure is accurate and precise enough to present to senior management or a member of the press for publication. If so, then use the figure for data entry. For any data entered into the WLP Scorecard that is later found to be incorrect, update the information in the WLP Scorecard as soon as the correct information becomes available.

The Income Tax Form Test

When preparing and submitting income taxes, most preparers have a good idea of the adjusted gross income, the expected amount owed, and whether or not a refund is likely before jotting any information on the tax form. When gathering data for the WLP Scorecard, consider using the income tax form test for any data requiring best "guesstimates"—that is, if you are confident enough with a figure to enter it on a tax form and not worry about being audited, then it is fit to use. If lack of confidence persists, then do more detective work to find or develop better estimates.

Exploring Nine Categories of the WLP Scorecard

The WLP Scorecard includes nine broad areas of data that describe and define various dimensions of learning functions. The nine dimensions correspond broadly to the foundational competency of "Business/Management," and the areas of expertise described in ASTD's Competency Model that especially influence the roles of "business partner" and "learning strategist" (Bernthal et al., 2004). These nine dimensions are

1. financial
2. qualitative/impressionistic
3. learning function
4. learning function organization
5. satisfaction
6. formal learning
7. human capital
8. work-based learning
9. workforce.

Financial Data

Financial data exists in organizational financial statements, which typically include the balance sheet, income statement, and statement of cash flows. Publicly held organizations, as well as many governmental and nonprofit organizations, are required by law to make their financial statements available to anyone who requests them. Most organizations publish annual reports that include these financial statements.

Privately held companies, as well as some governmental organizations, are not required by law to make these documents available to the public and may be very reluctant to share them except on a need-to-know basis. In these organizations, the financial officers will need to share the financial data for the WLP Scorecard, since workplace learning professionals may not be allowed to see these entire financial statements.

Possessing a background or experience in analyzing financial statements makes identifying the information needed for the WLP Scorecard a simple matter. If the thought of analyzing this data sparks a spiral of dread, ask the financial officer in the organization to supply the figures required for the WLP Scorecard. Keep in mind that as the learning function transforms into more of a business function, workplace learning professionals need to build their business acumen to include understanding and interpreting financial statements.

Although revenue, income, and profits appear on income statements, they are often calculated and represented according to the customs and

WLP Scorecard Resources!

Appendix A displays a grid of all WLP Scorecards by report and also outlines which fields are required to generate the desired level of reporting.

To aid in the data-gathering process, Appendix B provides a worksheet of all WLP Scorecard input fields and the format of data required (for example, $ or %).

WLP Scorecard Financial Data

Some of the financial data fields in the WLP Scorecard include

* revenue
* income/profit
* revenue from new products and services.

conventions of an organization or a particular industry. Revenue from new products and services usually appears on income statements but these may be difficult to locate. It should be listed as a separate item but may appear as an aggregate with other revenue figures. If this is the case, work with a financial officer in the organization to determine the appropriate number.

Qualitative/Impressionistic Data

Some of the qualitative/impressionistic data fields in the WLP Scorecard include

* Individual and Organization Goal Linkage
* Individual Performance Goals
* Employee Alignment with Culture/Values
* Integration with Business Planning
* Maturity of Work-Based Learning Infrastructure.

Qualitative/Impressionistic Data

Qualitative and impressionistic data requires the most judgment on the part of the gatherer. All qualitative/impressionistic data is rendered on a scale from zero to 10, where zero represents complete absence and 10 represents complete achievement. Because these figures do not require a great deal of calculation, resist the temptation to enter off-the-cuff guesstimates. Beware of entering haphazard figures in these data fields. Qualitative data is just as valid as quantitative data and often provides richer and more actionable information. As such, this type of data analysis requires more care and reflection.

In formulating judgments about qualitative/impressionistic data, first consult relevant surveys, reports, or other sources of data in the organization. This information, coupled with data gathered from stakeholder interviews, enables workplace learning professionals to formulate a reasonable range of data to enter in the WLP Scorecard. For example, asking several stakeholders, "What is your impression of the organization's documentation of key learning processes on a scale from zero to 10" often results in similarity of answers. If one of the stakeholders has the most intimate knowledge related to a topic during this interviewing process, consider a weighting system in which his or her judgment is given the most weight.

In this process, judgments need to be backed up by internal data, interviews, past behavior, and above all common sense. Avoid overstating data to drive favorable outcomes. Be honest when entering data for values that truly rate as poor, mediocre, or excellent. When needed, use the "tests" presented at the beginning of this chapter: if the figure entered in the WLP Scorecard could be confidently broadcast to the entire industry with your name and organization attached to it, then it should be suitable for the WLP Scorecard.

Learning Function Data

Some of the learning function data fields in the WLP Scorecard include

* Total Direct Learning Investment
* Unplanned Learning Expenditure
* External Services Expenditure
* Learning Staff Costs (Excluding Benefits and Taxes)
* Expenditure on Technology Infrastructure.

Learning Function Data

Most learning function data resides in one area although it could be diffused depending on the organizational structure. Figures related to direct investments may not be available until the organization performs a trial balance or closes the books at the end of the fiscal year. Standard learning function measures (such as tuition reimbursement, external services, and investments according to formal, work-based, or non-learning solutions) may not be tracked and may need to be imputed. When data required for the WLP Scorecard is unavailable, apply the tests presented at the beginning of this chapter and update later when more precise figures are available.

Learning Function Organization Data

Most workplace learning professionals gather information about the size and staffing of the learning function with relative ease. In cases in which the learning function is part of the HR department, more work may be required to extract the learning function data because it may be rolled up in the HR data.

Satisfaction Data

Use employee satisfaction surveys—most likely available from HR, customer service, or market research—as a key input to identifying satisfaction. Ideally, use at least three years' data to identify if the feedback is a new occurrence or part of a bigger trend. This healthy reality check prevents casting current levels of satisfaction either too positively or negatively.

Examining external customer satisfaction surveys provides indicators of both customer and internal employee satisfaction. Customer satisfaction often appears in the mirror as employee satisfaction; however, do not inappropriately infer one from the other during the same accounting period. In some organizations, customer satisfaction lags employee satisfaction, and vice versa.

The second source of data to gauge satisfaction is interviews with business unit leaders and senior managers. Interviewees provide candid responses when workplace learning professionals pose point-blank questions. For example, asking senior managers to describe their satisfaction with the learning function on the scale from zero to 10 (zero being complete dissatisfaction and 10 being high satisfaction) provides invaluable insight. If senior managers gave recent public recognition of the learning function, more weight might need to be given to their feedback.

Formal Learning Data

Formal learning comprises structured learning activities that are conducted separately from the workplace. The most common example is a classroom event but could also include online lessons or a coaching event conducted separately from work.

Formal learning has been the bulwark in the WLP profession for many decades and will likely form the core of many learning functions for decades to come. Formal learning provides workplace learning professionals with

Learning Function Organization Data

Some of the Learning Function Organization data in the WLP Scorecard includes

* Learning Staff Size
* Learning Staff Reporting
* Learning Staff Turnover
* Standardization
* Automation.

Satisfaction Data

Some of the satisfaction data fields in the WLP Scorecard include

* Employee Satisfaction
* Employee Satisfaction with Learning Opportunities
* Customer Satisfaction
* C-Level Satisfaction
* Business Unit Leader Satisfaction.

Satisfaction Data Tip!

If many measures exist for customer satisfaction, consider simplifying this process by choosing one external customer satisfaction measure that best represents external customer satisfaction at its most general level.

Formal Learning Data

Some of formal learning fields in the WLP Scorecard include

* total formal learning hours available
* number of new hours available
* number of formal hours by content area (for example, sales, marketing, and so on).

hard data regarding costs, usage, and efficiency. Most organizations collect a great deal of data about formal learning and include these analyses in regular reporting on learning function effectiveness and efficiency.

Human Capital Data

Like any other form of capital, human capital represents an accumulation of assets used to create value and realize organizational strategy. Human capital is intangible and is characterized by

- a front-end measure that describes a ready capability to be employed by organizational strategy
- a back-end measure that describes immediate results of its use.

Reduction in the time it takes an employee to achieve competence (time to competence, for short), for example, describes the ease of engaging human capital assets into high-value work and is often a good estimate of human capital accumulation. Successful development of a new product or service provides an example of a good back-end measure.

Reduction in time to competence is a figure that, although not often captured in profit plans, is on the tip of somebody's tongue. The trick is finding the right people in the organization. When trying to identify this information within any organization, consider interviewing several business unit leaders and even line managers. They often give accurate estimates regarding the skill changes and the time to competence for employees within their purview.

When gathering this data, exercise some judgment in weighting the estimates received. For example, some business units may already be highly optimized, where any improvements in time to competence are incremental. For other business units, experiencing any reduction in time to competence would be a welcome improvement.

Also use common sense when weighting the responses from multiple line personnel. Try to spend the majority of time and effort finding those people in the organization who can give you the most accurate estimates. In truth, only the most sophisticated financial reporting systems are likely to have reduction in time to competence figure available automatically.

The development of new products and services, though managed by several areas of the business, proceeds more directly from human capital accumulations than other capital accumulations. Most organizations keep detailed and comprehensive records of their new products. Workplace learning professionals shouldn't have to dig far below the surface of the organization to locate data relating to new products and services. Good sources of data include annual reports, materials presented to the board of

Human Capital Data

Some of the human capital data fields in the WLP Scorecard include

- New Products and Services
- Human Capital Readiness
- Reduction in Time to Competence/Performance
- Organizational Readiness.

directors, and leaders within marketing departments. Most workplace learning professionals will not have to calculate this figure so time is best spent seeking out the resources who readily know this information.

Work-Based Learning

Work-based learning refers to activities embedded in, or coincident to, an employee's normal work activity. Common examples include use of knowledge repositories, job aids, knowledge sharing, and coaching while doing work tasks.

Work-based learning is likely to be the most challenging dimension to gather for the WLP Scorecard. Workplace learning professionals often need to "back in" to this data when it is not readily available.

Fortunately, obtaining this data will not be just a shot in the dark either. LMSs usually track learner activity and usage, but many LMSs are unable to capture all the activity related to work-based learning. In this case, workplace learning professionals need to rely on personal experience and the experience of the most knowledgeable learning function colleagues to determine level of usage, the kinds of people that are using knowledge repositories, and how workers spend their downtime while on the job.

Many workplace learning professionals can leverage their instructional design skills to ask questions and determine how experts and novices use job aids, online resources, both online and offline knowledge repositories, and how they spend any downtime. For example, an expert customer service representative might spend his or her downtime engaging in self-directed learning: improving product knowledge or job-related skills. In contrast, during downtime, novices might be bidding on an eBay auction or chatting about non-work-related items with co-workers. Consider observing novice and expert workers to arrive at estimates of how non-structured learning time is spent.

Workforce

HR departments maintain rigorous personnel information including figures on hires, departures, salary, and many other aspects of individuals and groups of workers. Depending on whether or not the learning function is housed within the HR department, workplace learning professionals will need to work through the appropriate chain of management in the organization to obtain this data.

This chapter wraps up part II of this book, which is dedicated to defining the type of data that workplace learning professionals will need to gather and strategies for obtaining it. The next chapter details how to get started using the WLP Scorecard including how to enter data and generate reports.

Work-Based Learning Data

Some of the work-based learning data fields in the WLP Scorecard include

* Number of Hours Used of Knowledge Repositories
* Number of New Hours of Expert Knowledge Entered into Repositories
* Time on Challenging Work Assignments
* Time on Other Discretionary Learning.

Workforce Data

Some of the workforce data fields in the WLP Scorecard include

* Workforce Size
* Payroll
* Turnover
* Job Competency Documentation.

Part III

◆

Executing Phase:
Using the WLP Scorecard to Transform Learning into a Value-Producing, Results-Driven Business Function

Chapter 8

Getting Started with the WLP Scorecard

✳

In This Chapter

- Identifying WLP Scorecard Report levels
- WLP Scorecard system requirements and optimization
- WLP Scorecard functionality and home page overview
- Navigating and entering data
- Staging WLP Scorecard planning and usage

✳

Workplace learning professionals have amazing opportunities to communicate the measurements that non-learning executives demand—those that communicate the true value of the learning function and benchmark the current learning function performance of their organization as compared with other organizations. The WLP Scorecard is the tool to capitalize on these opportunities.

The WLP Scorecard system enables workplace learning professionals to

- monitor the efficiency and effectiveness of organizational learning and performance operations
- provide report-based information that can be integrated with business-critical success factors
- facilitate comparison of the cost-effectiveness of learning and performance activities, and not just levels of expenditure
- explore the causal chains and relationships to help predict the effects of changes in single or multiple indicators on overall efficiency and effectiveness of the learning function
- manage learning with the same kinds of tools that non-learning managers use to manage other business functions.

This chapter begins Part III of this book; it provides an overview of the WLP Scorecard reports, discusses how to navigate and enter data into the WLP Scorecard, and identifies some staging strategies for a phased approach to implementing the WLP Scorecard in any organization.

Identifying WLP Scorecard Report Levels

Four reports, as described in table 8-1, enable workplace learning professionals and organizations to transform the learning function from an expense function into a powerful business function that is able to communicate the direct and indirect relationships between learning and business value.

Each report is available in the WLP Scorecard, depending on the level of service purchased. Appendix A provides a quick-reference table that details the required or optional data needed to generate each of the WLP Scorecard reports.

Table 8-1: WLP Scorecard Reports Overview

Report Name	Description
Free Key Indicators Report	This report displays many of the same key learning indicators found in ASTD's annual State of the Industry Report. Taken together, these indicators are useful for benchmarking the effectiveness and efficiency of learning investments, the production and delivery of learning content, and usage.
	Benchmarking allows workplace learning professionals to compare their learning investments to best practices and industry leaders, and to obtain guidance regarding an acceptable range for various learning investment areas.
Scorecard Reports	Scorecard Reports contain rankings of standard sets of learning and performance indicators and metrics within a balanced scorecard framework. Learning indicators and metrics are classified according to the performance dimensions of financial, operations, customer, and innovation.
	Users may compare their organizations' learning and performance indicators to those of other organizations. Customized Scorecard Reports allow users to select the indicators and metrics of greatest interest, and compare with organizations across different industries. This enables workplace learning professionals to make comparison with organizations of similar size and in different geographic regions.
	This tool helps to feed back information about the performance of the learning function to the point where resource allocation decisions are made. Such an approach provides proper decision support and illuminates the power that learning has in many organizations.
WLP Index Reports	WLP Index Reports, the highest level of reporting, allow users to measure and manage the learning function strategically and over a longer-term view than with Scorecard Reports. WLP Index Reports map a standard set of learning function measures to four WLP Indexes—alignment, efficiency, effectiveness, and sustainability. These reports allow users to visualize the areas of the learning function that contribute most to its strength and fitness.
	A comprehensive WLP Index Report displays index scores for four WLP Indexes, a comprehensive index score, and separate diagnostic reports for each of the WLP Indexes (that is, alignment, efficiency, effectiveness, and sustainability.
Benchmarking Forum	As part of their membership, ASTD Benchmarking Forum members have access to all three levels of reporting, and are able to make organization-by-organization comparisons to other Forum members.

Depending on the subscription level selected, the WLP Scorecard screens display different features and functionality. Figure 8-1 depicts these WLP Scorecard report functionality differences. For example,

◈ Workplace learning professionals using the Free Key Indicators report, referred to as Level 1 users, have access to all input fields required to generate this report and only this report.

◈ Level 2 subscribers have access to all Level 1 input fields, and all additional input fields required to generate the Scorecard Reports.

All data entered into the WLP Scorecard remains strictly confidential. Users will only see the data entered for their organization. The summary statistics, used to compare an organization against others based on size, industry, and other segments, are an aggregate of all organizations that have entered data into the WLP Scorecard website.

ASTD Benchmarking Forum subscribers are able to access organization-specific data for all member organizations. Subscribers are bound by the member confidentiality agreement prohibiting sharing of individual organization member data outside the Benchmarking Forum.

WLP Scorecard System Requirements and Optimization

The WLP Scorecard reports run best on personal computers with the Microsoft Windows operating System, Microsoft Internet Explorer 6 or later,

WLP Scorecard System Requirements

The WLP Scorecard is a web-based application that should run on any platform/browser combination (that is, iframes, SSL, session cookies, and JavaScript including Firefox, Netscape, Safari, etc.) and support for the tool is available for Microsoft Windows and Microsoft Internet Explorer 6 or later.

Figure 8-1: WLP Scorecard Reports Overview of Functionality Differences

Feature	Free (Level 1)	Scorecard Reports (Level 2)	Index Reports (Level 3)	ASTD Benchmarking Forum
Input Data (Key Inputs)	X	X	X	X
Input Data (Scorecard Inputs)		X	X	X
Input Data (All Inputs)			X	X
Save and Reuse Data	X	X	X	X
Basic Scorecard Reports	X	X	X	X
Comprehensive Scorecard Reports		X	X	X
Customized Scorecard Reports		X	X	X
Index Scores	X	X	X	X
Diagnostic Index Reports			X	X
Sensitivity Analysis			X	X
Custom Reports by Organization				X

61

and a high-speed Internet connection. It is is best viewed at a resolution of 800 x 600 or higher. The following steps verify and edit the Internet Explorer settings and optimize the performance of this web-based tool.

To Enable the Web Browser to Accept Session Cookies:

To use the WLP Scorecard, the browser must be configured to accept session cookies.

1. Open **Internet Explorer.**
2. Click **Tools, Internet Options...** on the menu bar.

3. The Internet Options... dialog box appears.

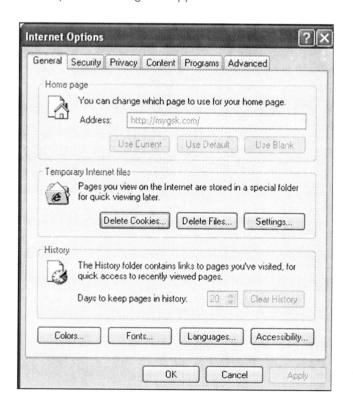

4. Click the **Privacy** tab.

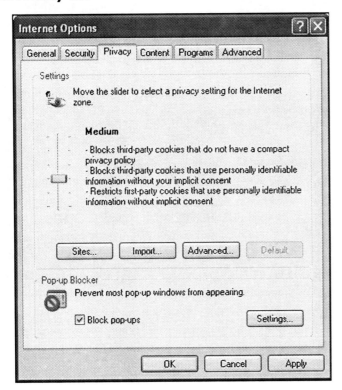

5. Drag the slide bar to **Medium.**
6. Click **OK.**

 To Enable JavaScript:

JavaScript must be enabled in the browser to use all features in the WLP Scorecard to their best advantage.

1. Open **Internet Explorer.**
2. Click **Tools, Internet Options...** on the menu bar.

3. The **Internet Options...** dialog box appears.

4. Click the **Security** tab.

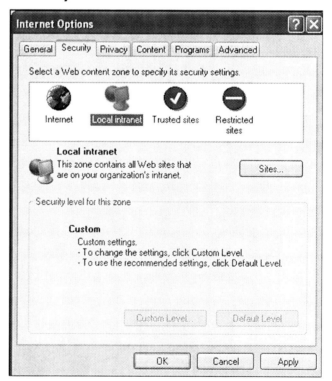

5. Click the **Custom Level...** button.
6. Scroll down to **Scripting.**
7. Check **Active Scripting** and **Scripting of Java Applets,** if needed.
8. Click **OK.**

Exploring the WLP Scorecard Functionality and Home Page

ASTD provides subscribers with a unique Organization ID and password to log in to the WLP Scorecard website. After registering as a WLP Scorecard member, the primary contact (designated during the registration process) and will receive one Organization ID to access the tool.

 To Subscribe to the WLP Scorecard (New Users):
1. Open **Internet Explorer.**
2. Type **http://wlpscorecard.astd.org** in the address bar. The WLP Scorecard home page appears.
3. Click the **Register** link on the blue navigation bar to subscribe to the WLP Scorecard.
4. Follow the instructions to register for an ASTD login, if needed.
5. After logging in, you will be redirected to the WLP Scorecard home page (http://wlpscorecard.astd.org).
6. Complete all registration fields, including the desired subscription (desired product) level (i.e., Level 1, Level 2, or Level 3).
7. Click **Complete Registration.**
8. You will receive an ASTD login and password to access the WLP Scorecard tool at any time and as many times as you want.

 To Access the WLP Scorecard for Current Users:
1. Navigate to WLP Scorecard (http://wlpscorecard.astd.org).
2. Click Login on the blue navigation bar. A single sign-on page appears.
3. After logging in, you will be redirected to the WLP Scorecard home page (see figure 8-2; http://wlpscorecard.astd.org).

Figure 8-2: WLP Scorecard Home Page

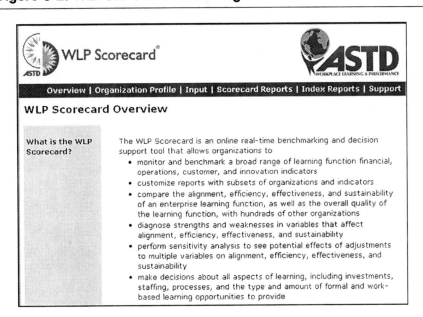

Navigating within the WLP Scorecard

The navigation bar appearing at the top of every WLP Scorecard page (see figure 8-3) provides quick access to each page and report in the tool. Click the label on the navigation bar to display the desired page.

Table 8-2 provides an overview and describes key functionality available by selecting a label from the Navigation Bar.

Figure 8-3: The WLP Scorecard Navigation Bar

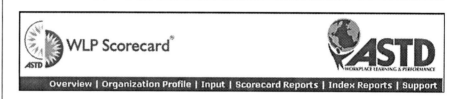

Navigating the WLP Scorecard Input Screen

The WLP Scorecard enables quick and easy access to key features including entering data and generating reports. Figure 8-4 illustrates each element appearing on the Input screen. Descriptions for each of these elements appear in table 8-3.

To Navigate to the Input Screen:
1. Open the WLP Scorecard.
2. Click the **Input** label on the Navigation Bar. The Input screen appears.

Figure 8-4: WLP Scorecard Input Screen

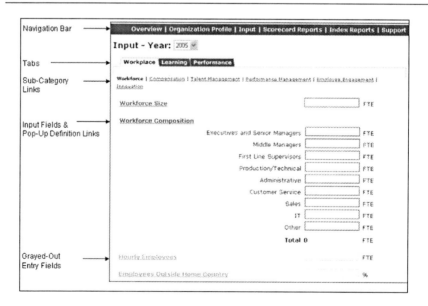

Table 8-2: WLP Scorecard Navigation Bar Overview

Navigation Bar Label	Description
Overview	Displays the WLP Scorecard home page as well as links for new user registration to subscribe to the tool, and a link to log in to the tool.
Organization Profile	First-time users need to complete the Organization Profile page completely before entering any data into the WLP Scorecard. After entering this information, this screen does not need to be revisited unless changes need to be made to the profile information.
Input	This page facilitates the entry of all data for reports depending on the subscription level selected. The **Input-Year:** drop-down menu at the top of the screen enables data entry and viewing of reports for a selected year.
Scorecard Reports	This page provides access to four Scorecard Reports—financial, operations, customer, and innovation—represented by the tabs along the top of this screen. Click the Customize tab to customize a report. Benchmarking Forum members will see an additional tab labeled BMF for additional customization options.
Index Reports	This page displays an aggregated WLP Index report as well as four diagnostic reports on efficiency, effectiveness, alignment, and sustainability. Click the tabs at the top of the screen to access each report. Benchmarking Forum members will see an additional tab labeled BMF to access member company scores.
Support	The Support page includes hyperlinks to display and print the WLP Scorecard Guide for Users and WLP Scorecard Worksheets. The Contact Us hyperlink provides a form to email questions to the WLP Scorecard team.

Table 8-3: WLP Scorecard Input Screen Elements

Input Screen Element	Description
Input Year	Data inputs and reports represent data from one year. Select the year to enter data or to view reports using the Input Years: drop-down menu.
Tabs	Three tabs organize data inputs by grouping (that is, **Workplace, Learning,** and **Performance**) to facilitate quick data entry.
Sub-Category Links	These hyperlinks display more granular categories to enter data used to generate the WLP Scorecard reports.
Input Fields	The color-coded fields appearing on each Input screen indicate which data is required to generate reports vs. nice-to-know information that provides details when generating reports. <ul><li>Red text and data input boxes indicate required fields.</li><li>Blue text and data input boxes indicate nice to know information—however reports can still be generated without this data.</li></ul>
Input Definition Links	Click the Input Definition link to display a pop-up window to view the definition of the data to input as well as tips and examples.
Grayed-Out Entry Fields	The fields available for data entry on the Input screens vary depending on the reporting subscription level selected for the organization. For example, grayed-out entry fields are not available. To upgrade subscriptions, contact the WLP Scorecard team at wlpscorecard@astd.org.

Note! Enter all monetary figures in U.S. dollars. Do not enter the words *thousands* or *millions* in the score-card. For example, if the annual learning function budget is $5,700,000, enter 5700000. Do not enter 5.7 million. Organizations using currencies other than USD must convert all monetary figures from the home currency to USD using the exchange rate effective on the date of entering figures into the WLP Scorecard.

Note! Closing the WLP Scorecard automatically saves all data entry items or changes.

Entering Data in the WLP Scorecard

To enter data into a WLP Scorecard input field, navigate using the tabs and subcategories available on the navigation bar at the top of the screen. The WLP Scorecard automatically saves all data entered into a field as soon as another input field is selected.

To Complete the Input Screens:
1. Open the WLP Scorecard.
2. Click the **Input** label on the Navigation Bar. The Input screen appears.
3. Select the **Input-Year:** drop-down menu, if necessary, to select the appropriate year.
4. Click the desired **Sub-Category Link.**
5. Enter the data in the input fields.
6. After entering all required data in the Input fields for a report, click the appropriate reports tab (that is, Scorecard Reports, Index Reports, and so on) on the Navigation Bar to view the report.

Staging WLP Scorecard Planning and Usage

Some WLP Scorecard users, excited about the measurement and bench-marking possibilities, want to immediately jump in and start leveraging all WLP Scorecard reports. Others decide to start to gather all required information for the Free Key Indicators Report and set milestones to begin implementing each WLP Scorecard report over a period of time—usually

Figure 8-5: WLP Scorecard Input Screen

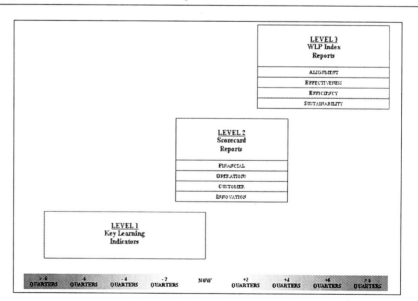

months or years. No matter what the goal, the fact is it takes time to execute proper planning to obtain the data and then to determine the important measures to demonstrate the learning function

Figure 8-5 represents a phased approach to implement the successive levels of scorecard reports over time. For example, workplace learning professionals may want to begin using the Free Key Indicators Report that requires 13 pieces of data.

After taking several quarters to implement the Level 1 report, gathering all data required for the Level 2 report should take place over two to three subsequent quarters. This phased approach enables workplace learning professionals to begin using the Level 1 reports in a relatively short period of time while planning for gathering the data required for the next level of reports. The process of asking questions and gathering the data for additional WLP Scorecard reports is an invaluable process in and of itself. The discovery and analysis process arms users with insightful information for making decisions as well as focuses efforts on efficiency, performance, and alignment of the learning function with organization performance goals.

Chapter 9

Free Key Indicators Reports: Finding Out Where You Have Been

---❊---

In This Chapter

- Entering Free Key Indicator Report data
- Defining input indicators
- Generating the report
- Interpreting the report data

---❊---

For workplace learning professionals who want to use the WLP Scorecard but don't know where to begin, a great place to start is with the first level of service—the Free Key Indicators Report.

This report includes most of the key learning indicators found in ASTD's annual *State of the Industry Report*. These indicators form the core of practically all successful performance measurement and management systems. As a group, they represent a set of fundamental measures used for benchmarking the effectiveness and efficiency of overall learning investments, the production and delivery of learning content, the amount and quality of learning program usage, and the operational stability of the learning function.

Workplace learning professionals use benchmarking to compare their organization's learning investments to industry norms, determine how well they stack up with industry leaders, and to find an acceptable range for their particular areas of learning investment, such as technology or outsourcing partners.

Benchmarking is usually performed upon completion of periodic learning investments, or at the conclusion of a major learning initiative. Nearly every organization determining its learning budget refers to benchmarking data—sometimes spanning several years—to discern trends and determine acceptable ranges for the various areas of learning investments.

Entering Data to Create the Free Key Indicators Report

To help get started with the WLP Scorecard reports, table 9-1 summarizes the 13 pieces of data required to generate the Free Key Indicators Report.

The first three columns of the table indicate the "path" that users need to navigate to each of these required fields when entering data in the WLP Scorecard Input screen. Follow the steps to begin entering the data to generate this report.

Tip! Appendix B provides a worksheet that workplace learning professionals can copy and use when gathering the data required for any of the WLP Scorecard reports.

To Complete the Input Screens:
1. Open the WLP Scorecard.
2. Click the **Input** label on the Navigation Bar. The Input screen appears.
3. Click the **Input-Year:** drop down menu, if needed, to select the appropriate year.
4. Click the desired tab **Sub-Category Link.**

Table 9-1: Free Key Indicators Report Required Data

Tab	Sub-Category Link	Input Indicator	Input Indicators Importance
Workplace	Workforce	Workforce Size	R
	Compensation	Payroll	R
	Investment	Total Direct Learning Investment	R
		Total Indirect Learning Investment	R
		Percentage of Direct Cost for Learning By Type of Solution	R
		External Services Expenditure	R
		Tuition Reimbursement Expenditure	R
Learning	Learning Function Staff/Talent	Learning Staff Size	R
	Output (Formal Learning)	Total Formal Hours Available	R
		Formal Hours by Content Area	R
		Formal Hours by Delivery Method	R
Performance	Business Outcomes	Revenue	R
		Income/Profit	R

R = indicates required field

5. Enter the data in the required input fields (indicated with red text and boxes).
6. Closing the WLP Scorecard automatically saves all data entry items or changes.

Defining Input Indicators for the Free Key Indicators Report

Most of the input indicators required to generate the Free Key Indicators Report will be familiar to many WLP Scorecard users or those users who have spent any part of their careers in HR management.

These input indicators represent critical areas that workplace learning professionals and HR managers have traditionally monitored. In particular, these indicators help to determine the costs associated with acquiring and maintaining human capital and the benefits that accrue from maximum employee performance. Together they form the basis of most discussions related to the effectiveness of the learning function, even if the precise figures are not explicitly mentioned.

Every workplace learning professional should be as familiar with these input indicators as the CFO is with the organization's earnings, working capital, and cost of goods sold.

Workforce Size
Path: **Workplace** tab**Workforce** link

Enter the average number of total employees for a year (a full 12 months). Resist the temptation to enter the largest or smallest number of employees over the year, the number of employees from a month that may seem representative, or an end-of-year or end-of-fiscal-year figure. Learning functions within banking institutions may alternatively enter an end-of-year figure.

The Human Resource Information System (HRIS) most likely contains this information. Organizations experiencing major reductions in force, reorganizations, or mergers within the last year should contact the WLP Scorecard Team for assistance in determining this figure.

Tip! In this section, the "paths" listed below each input indicator denote the navigation needed to locate each of these input indicators on the WLP Scorecard Input screen.

Workforce Size Includes:	Workforce Size Excludes:
• employees of consolidated domestic and international subsidiaries • part-time and seasonal employees • employees classified as FTEs (full time equivalents) • corporate officers	• contracted workers and consultants • board members • employees of unconsolidated subsidiaries

Payroll
Path: **Workplace** tab**Compensation** link

Enter total salary and wages only. Do not include benefits plans and taxes. In most organizations, this figure is available from the HR or finance departments.

Total Direct Learning Investment
Path: **Learning** tab**Investment** link

Total direct costs for learning include formal learning, work-based learning, and the learning function's contribution to non-learning performance improvement solutions. For many organizations, gathering this figure will be easier to obtain than individual breakdowns according to formal, work-based, and non-learning solutions. However, workplace learning professionals may enter an aggregate figure for this category for ease of use and if the budget is divided into sections that readily map to formal, work-based, and non-learning solutions. Consider the explanations for each category:

- **Formal learning** comprises structured learning activities conducted separately from the workplace. Some examples are classroom events, online lessons, or a coaching event conducted separately from work.
- **Work-based learning** refers to activities embedded in, or coincident to, an employee's normal work activity. Some examples are job aids, use of knowledge repositories, knowledge sharing, and coaching while performing work tasks.
- **Non-learning solutions** refers to the time that learning staff members are involved in performance improvement activities such as organizational development, process analysis, talent management, and performance management.

Direct Costs Include:	Direct Costs Do Not Include:
• learning and performance staff salaries including gross wages without benefits or employer-paid taxes • travel costs for learning and performance staff • administrative costs • non-salary development costs • non-salary delivery costs (such as classroom facilities, online learning technology infrastructure) • Outsourced activities • Tuition reimbursements	• learner's travel expenses • costs of conference attendance, fees, and travel • cost of lost work time while engaged in learning formal activities • costs of internal subject matter expert time for content analysis, coaching, and knowledge sharing

Total Indirect Learning Investment
Path: **Learning** tab**Investment** link

In the WLP profession, total indirect learning investment costs include expenses related to formal and work-based only. Indirect costs for learning include

- learner travel expenses
- conference attendance, fees, travel, lodging, meals, and ground transportation
- lost work time while engaged in learning formal activities
- internal subject matter expert time for content analysis, coaching, and knowledge sharing
- reasonable opportunity costs if recognized in organizational or industry common practice.

Percentage of Direct Cost for Learning by Type of Solution
Path: **Learning** tab**Investment** link

Enter a breakdown of the percentage of direct learning *expenditures* devoted to formal learning, work-based learning, and activities related to non-learning performance improvement solutions.

External Services Expenditure
Path: **Learning** tab**Investment** link

For external services expenditures—sometimes called outsourcing, outtasking, vendor profiles, or learning partners, depending on the organization—enter the percentage of total *direct* learning expenditure for external services.

Direct Expenditures Include:	Direct Expenditures Do Not Include:
• consulting services • content development and licenses • workshops and training programs delivered by external providers	• payments made in the form of employee tuition reimbursements for educational programs at educational institutions

Tuition Reimbursement Expenditure
Path: **Learning** tab**Investment** link

Enter the percentage of total direct learning expenditure for employee tuition reimbursement for educational programs at educational institutions.

Learning Staff Size
Path: **Learning** tab**Learning Function Staff/Talent** link

Enter the number of learning function staff *expressed as full-time equivalents* (FTEs). Although it might be tempting to enter only a simple head count of the learning function, do not use this figure as the indicator input unless that figure equals the total FTEs.

As part of an overall employee development plan, many organizations are now identifying high-potential personnel and putting them on an accelerated career development track, similar to medical students completing their clinical training by rotating through major medical specialty areas. Such tracking of key personnel often includes rotation through important business functions, including the learning function. If your learning function staff includes personnel who serve in a rotational capacity, include their FTE totals *only* if their FTEs are specifically allocated to the learning function.

Total Formal Hours Available
Path: **Learning** tab**Output (Formal Learning)** link

Perform a one-time count of the total number of hours of formal learning content available and enter the figure into the WLP Scorecard as number of hours. This value should include live classes, workshops, seminars, online course catalog content, video, and print. Although many learning functions determine this figure with relative ease, it may be more difficult to calculate for highly decentralized learning functions.

Formal Hours by Content Area
Path: **Learning** tab**Output (Formal Learning)** link

For organizations submitting data for previous years' *ASTD State of the Industry Report*, the following should be readily available. In this section, determine and enter the percentage of formal learning content by these common content areas:

- executive development
- managerial and supervisory
- sales (not including product knowledge)
- customer service
- mandatory and compliance (for example, safety, security)
- processes, procedures, business practices, and quality
- information technology and systems (for example, enterprise and desktop software)
- interpersonal skills (for example, communication, team work)
- new employee orientation

- basic skills
- profession-specific or industry-specific (for example, engineering, accounting, legal, medical)
- product knowledge
- other.

Formal Hours by Delivery Method

Path: **Learning** tab**Output (Formal Learning)** link

Formal hours by delivery method figures are closely monitored by elite-performing learning functions. This input indicator focuses on the distribution of technology versus non-technology delivery methods. Enter the percentage of formal learning hours available through each of these delivery methods:

- live instructor-led real classroom
- live instructor-led virtual (online) classroom
- live instructor-led remote, but not online (for example, satellite, video conference, teleconference)
- self-paced online (networked)
- self-paced stand-alone (non-networked) computer-based (that is, CD-ROM)
- mobile technology (for example, PDA, MP3, cell phone)
- technology other than computer and mobile (for example, videotape, audio CD)
- self-paced non-technology delivered (that is, print)
- other.

Formal Hours Used

Path: **Learning** tab\\ **Usage (Formal Learning)** link

Calculate the total formal learning hours for content accessed or completed by learners. To perform this calculation, multiply the number of hours available by the number of employees who accessed or completed the learning content. For example, if 100 new employees participated in an eight-hour workshop on consultative selling techniques, the total hours used equals 800.

Revenue

Path: **Performance** tab\\ **Business Outcomes** link

Most workplace learning professionals locate this information from the finance department or the organization's annual report. When determining the total revenue generated by the business, include all recognized customer, operating, investment, rent, and accrued, unbilled revenue. For governmental organizations, enter the budget figure in place of revenue.

Income/Profit

Path: **Performance** tab\ **Business Outcomes** link

Enter the net profit or net income *before taxes*. Consult with the finance department or refer to the organization's annual report to locate this information. Since many organizations maintain several financial measures describing profit in varying levels of detail and complexity, enter the simplest and most precise number possible.

Some organizations have difficulty locating this value. Subtract the sum of expenses and losses from the sum of revenues and gains. For organizations that have more sophisticated accounting systems set up, include any effects related to discontinued operations, extraordinary items, total income taxes, and minority interest.

For all organizations that issue stock, do not include payments of stock dividends as an expense. Banks should include securities gains and losses. Governmental organizations should enter 0.

Generating the Free Key Indicators Report

After entering the data required for the Free Key Indicators Report, click the Scorecard Reports label on the blue navigation bar at the top of the screen to view the report data.

To Generate and View the Free Key Indicators Report:

1. Open the WLP Scorecard.
2. Click the **Scorecard Reports** label on the Navigation Bar. The Free Key Indicators Report appears.
3. Click the **Financial, Operations, Customer,** or **Innovation** tabs at the top of the screen to navigate to the desired indicators.

Exploring the Free Key Indicators Report Data

For over a decade, the *ASTD State of the Industry Report* has included industry-wide data so that learning managers can benchmark key indicators of learning efficiency and effectiveness against both industry averages and elite-performing learning functions.

In the Free Key Indicators Report, users will be able to view individual values for most of the Key Indicators that appear in ASTD's *State of the Industry Reports* annually, and compare them to industry averages (see figure 9-1). The industry averages are calculated from data of all organizations in the WLP Scorecard database. Additionally, a Free Key Indicators Report

Figure 9-1: The Free Key Indicators Report

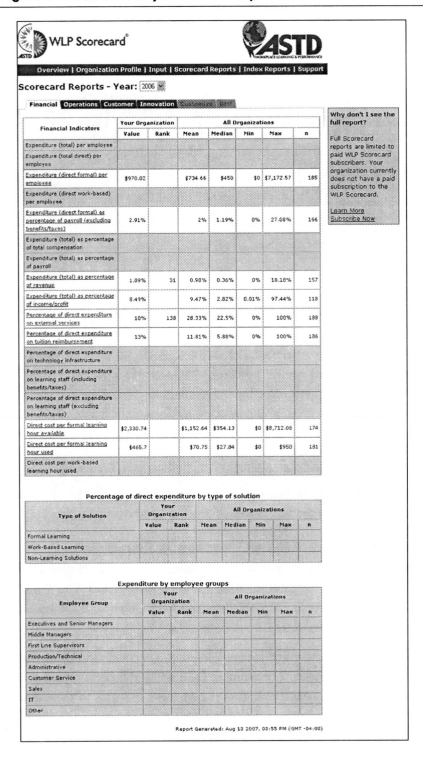

The following data appears within the figure:

Scorecard Reports – Year: 2006

Tabs: Overview | Organization Profile | Input | Scorecard Reports | Index Reports | Support

Tabs: **Financial** | Operations | Customer | Innovation | Customize

Financial Indicators	Your Organization		All Organizations				
	Value	Rank	Mean	Median	Min	Max	n
Expenditure (total) per employee							
Expenditure (total direct) per employee							
Expenditure (direct formal) per employee	$970.02		$734.66	$450	$0	$7,172.57	185
Expenditure (direct work-based) per employee							
Expenditure (direct formal) as percentage of payroll (excluding benefits/taxes)	2.91%		2%	1.19%	0%	27.08%	166
Expenditure (total) as percentage of total compensation							
Expenditure (total) as percentage of payroll							
Expenditure (total) as percentage of revenue	1.09%	31	0.98%	0.36%	0%	18.18%	157
Expenditure (total) as percentage of income/profit	8.49%		9.47%	2.82%	0.01%	97.44%	118
Percentage of direct expenditure on external services	10%	138	28.33%	22.5%	0%	100%	138
Percentage of direct expenditure on tuition reimbursement	13%		11.81%	5.88%	0%	100%	136
Percentage of direct expenditure on technology infrastructure							
Percentage of direct expenditure on learning staff (including benefits/taxes)							
Percentage of direct expenditure on learning staff (excluding benefits/taxes)							
Direct cost per formal learning hour available	$2,330.74		$1,152.64	$354.13	$0	$8,712.08	174
Direct cost per formal learning hour used	$465.7		$70.75	$27.84	$0	$950	181
Direct cost per work-based learning hour used							

Why don't I see the full report?

Full Scorecard reports are limited to paid WLP Scorecard subscribers. Your organization currently does not have a paid subscription to the WLP Scorecard.

Learn More
Subscribe Now

Percentage of direct expenditure by type of solution

Type of Solution	Your Organization		All Organizations				
	Value	Rank	Mean	Median	Min	Max	n
Formal Learning							
Work-Based Learning							
Non-Learning Solutions							

Expenditure by employee groups

Employee Group	Your Organization		All Organizations				
	Value	Rank	Mean	Median	Min	Max	n
Executives and Senior Managers							
Middle Managers							
First Line Supervisors							
Production/Technical							
Administrative							
Customer Service							
Sales							
IT							
Other							

Report Generated: Aug 13 2007, 03:55 PM (GMT -04:00)

contains simple descriptive statistical values that help WLP Scorecard users better determine how an individual organization compares to the rest of the organizations in the database.

Figure 9-2: The Free Key Indicators Report

Overview | Organization Profile | Input | Scorecard Reports | Index Reports | Support

Scorecard Reports - Year: 2006

Financial | Operations | Customer | Innovation | Customize | BMP

Operations Indicators	Your Organization		All Organizations				
	Value	Rank	Mean	Median	Min	Max	n
Integration of learning requirements and business planning process							
Ratio of employees to learning staff	472.35	27	276.88	141.83	7.19	3,333.33	185
Centralization of learning staff							
Centralization of learning budget							
Education level of learning staff							
Turnover of learning staff							
Tenure of learning staff							
Hours of formal content available per learning staff member	196.58	77	534.93	123.93	1.28	4,942.75	183
Hours of formal content usage per learning staff member	983.87	136	5,756.1	2,851.44	1.06	45,220	185

Tip! Keep in mind that because the WLP Scorecard is a real-time tool, the values displayed in the reports may change each day as organizations enter and update information.

Statistics allow workplace learning professionals to quantitatively describe and draw inferences about people, things, or events. In other words, statistics allow data to be organized and summarized. This makes it possible to draw generalizations and inferences. Statistics enable these professionals to document current levels of performance, measure the impact of their learning programs, and offer well-grounded feedback for change. This report provides descriptive statistics (that is, mean and median values) for all organizations entering data for the input indicators. These measures of central tendency, or averages, each serve a unique purpose. Table 9-2 explains these measures and all columns of data appearing in the Free Key Indicators report shown in figure 9-2, as well as tips for interpreting the data.

Understanding Drivers of Variation in Report Data

After generating reports and reviewing the data, some discrepancies may jump off the page when comparing the data in the **Your Organization** columns to the values in the **All Organizations** columns. If accurate data entry occurred, then indeed the numbers don't lie!

Variation in investment and internal practices may make it challenging for an organization to select a benchmark for any WLP Scorecard indicator or to make meaningful comparisons of the data. So how does this variation in the **Your Organization** and **All Organizations** columns impact the selection of benchmarks?

Gaining a keen understanding of the variation between industry benchmarks and an individual organization's figures helps workplace learning professionals argue that current learning function practices rank at least within the range of what others organizations do. The WLP Scorecard report findings and benchmarking comparisons also enable justification of

Table 9-2: Free Key Indicators Report Data Descriptions

Your Organization Column	Description
Value	A calculated number describing the quantity of an indicator or metric. **Example:** Based on the "ratio of employees to learning staff" value in figure 9-2, there are 472.35 employees in the organization for each full-time equivalent learning function staff member.
Rank	The location of a particular value in the set of all values for a particular indicator or metric. **Example:** In this example, the "ratio of employees to learning staff" has a rank order of 27 out of a total of 185, making it one of the higher values in the distribution.

All Organizations Column	Description
Mean	The mean score is considered the most robust, or least affected by the presence of extreme values (outliers), of all types of central tendency measures, because each number in the data set has an impact on its (mean) value. The mean is represented by the following formula: **Mean = Sum of all numbers / by the # of values that make up that sum** The mean is a good measure of central tendency for roughly symmetric distributions but can be misleading in skewed, or nonsymmetic, distributions because it can be influenced a great deal by extreme values. Therefore, other statistics, such as the median, may be more informative and appropriate for distributions that are quite often skewed. **Example:** In figure 9.2, the mean value for the "ratio of employees to learning staff" is approximately 276. This benchmark indicates that for all organizations that responded for this indicator in the WLP Scorecard, they have approximately 276 employees in the organization for each full-time equivalent learning function staff member.
Median	The median is the middle of a distribution arranged by magnitude: half of the scores are above the median, and half are below. The median is less sensitive to extreme scores than the mean, which makes it a better measure than the mean for highly skewed distributions. For example, the median income of a demographic group is usually more informative than the mean income. **Example:** In figure 9.2, 50 percent of all organization learning functions entering data in the WLP Scorecard for the "ratio of employees to learning function staff" entered ratio values above 141 and 50 percent of the responding organizations entered values below the median.
Min	The minimum value of all valid entries for that indicator or metric. **Example:** figure 9.2 shows that the min. value is 7.19.
Max	Indicates the maximum value of all valid entries entered by all organizations who responded. **Example:** In figure 9.2, the maximum value entered for the "ratio of employees to learning staff" is 3,333—meaning that one organization using the WLP Scorecard has approximately 3,333 employees for each full-time equivalent learning function staff member.
n	The number of organizations that entered data for the input indicator. **Example:** Figure 9.2 indicates that as of the time this report was viewed, 185 organizations entered data for the "ratio of employees to learning staff" indicator. The number of organizations appearing under the "all organizations" section of the WLP Scorecard report may change daily—hence possibly changing the mean, median, min, and max values displayed in the report.

Real World Variation

* Some ASTD BEST Award winning organizations spend as little as $50 per employee per year, while others spend $6,000 or more per employee per year.

* Several examples exist where highly respected organizations provide employees with an average of only a few hours of formal learning per year, while other learning functions provide an average that is well over 200 hours per year.

* ASTD research found world-class learning functions spending as little as $15 dollars on average to provide an hour of learning content, where other organizations spend an average of more than $4,000 to provide an hour of learning content (Rivera and Paradise, 2006).

* As a general rule, organizations with larger populations of learners spend more to produce or provide learning content. For years it seemed plausible that larger organizations produced higher quality material. As the sophistication of the WLP profession increases, however, this research shows that larger organizations scale their learning portfolios more efficiently, and smaller organizations manage learning costs more adeptly to provide similar benefits found in much larger organizations.

* High-growth learning functions almost always spend more than similarly sized organizations not experiencing strong growth. This is especially true for organizations headquartered abroad in emerging markets.

* The maturity of an organization's instructional technology largely determines the degree to which the learning function has to bear the costs of acquisition, administration, maintenance, and depreciation of infrastructure.

learning function practices even if they appear to deviate from the norm. If what is appropriate for the organization at this time differs from the norm, chances are the learning function value is still within the range of industry peers indicators.

Understanding and Interpreting the Free Key Indicators Report Results

Understanding and interpreting the Free Key Indicators Report begins not with a list of numbers but instead with the knowledge that the numbers represent living phenomena within the organization. Each indicator or metric exists within a context, and in some cases defines the context in which it exists. Likewise, each indicator or metric contains assumptions that in some cases are as meaningful as the number itself. Each of the figures contained in the report should be thought of as the first word in a conversation, not the last; the figures should spur further questioning, not silence it. The key to unlocking the wisdom contained in each of the figures is to test them against other known facts and benchmarks, both within and outside of the organization, and most important against your learning function knowledge and the stakeholders knowledge! Doing so may require several rounds of inquiry to discover what is truly moving the needle.

Steps for Digging In and Interpreting Report Data

1. Understand the assumptions about the financial and organizational impact of the indicator or metric before analyzing it.

2. Try to tie the indicator or metric as concretely to actual resources flowing from the learning function to the rest of the organization. Treat the numbers as direction finders.

3. Avoid the urge to seek one definitive metric that supposedly tells it all. Such a metric does not exist for any organization. Understand the figures in the Free Key Indicators Report as events that contribute to the story of how learning is driving value in the organization

4. After viewing the value for the organization, take some time to understand the entire distribution of values. Begin by evaluating the minimum and maximum. Very likely your figure will not approach either of them. Nevertheless, take a moment to reflect on the range of values. In what kind of organization and learning function would such extreme values make sense? Don't assume that extreme values necessarily reflect excellence or mismanagement. Pay attention to your initial impression of how your organization's value compares to the minimum and maximum.

5. Finally, compare the mean and the median. The mean and median both describe the "average" value, but they do so in very different ways. The mean represents the sum of all the values divided by the

number of values. Although the mean is the most common way of describing the average, it is important to know that the mean is very sensitive to extreme values. In particular, if there is a high concentration of values toward the high end of a distribution, the mean will be misleadingly high, and misleadingly low for a concentration of values toward the low end of a distribution.

In such cases, the median value is often preferable. The median is essentially the midpoint in the set of values and is therefore less sensitive to extremes at either end. Average home prices and average household income are often presented as median values because of the concentration of values toward one end of the distribution.

Now, here is where knowing these properties becomes very powerful. If the median is greater than the mean, then the distribution in values is said to be skewed to the right. That means that the majority of the values in that distribution are tending toward the lower end. Similarly, if the median is less than the mean, then the distribution's values are said to be skewed to the left, as the majority of the values in that distribution are tending toward the higher end.

Evaluating these differences between the mean and median provides a better sense of what an average value really is, and how your organization compares overall. In cases where there is a substantial discrepancy between the median and the mean, the more accurate figure for the "average" will likely be closer to the median. In most cases, if the value for your organization lies between the mean and the median, it will be safe to say that your organization is within the norm. If your organization falls outside the norm, probe a little further with questions such as:

- Does your industry sector tend to be higher for that particular value?
- Does the value tend to increase depending on organization size?
- Is the organization experiencing high growth?
- Have there been recent substantial changes to the learning organization?
- Is your industry cyclical?
- When considering your organization's rank order, does it confirm or challenge the conclusion you might want to draw?

When reviewing numbers and your thoughts about them, evaluate whether you still have a clear sense of what assumptions go into the numbers and the phenomena they represent.

The Free Key Indicators Report includes the indicators in the list below. Use the next section to review the descriptions of each indicator to assess the current state of the learning function and to identify benchmarks and strategies to achieve future plans.

Expenditure per Employee

Learning expenditure per employee, a standard measure of the efficiency of the learning function, provides the most fundamental and widely used benchmark by organizations in all industry sectors. Learning expenditure per employee is frequently taken as a proxy for the overall value-add of the learning function to the organization. An efficient learning function that provides adequate learning has secondary effects of controlling personnel costs (remediation, turnover, minimal scrap). Similarly, learning expenditure per employee often serves as an indirect measure of the confidence in the learning function to drive value that exceeds the dollar amount of learning function overhead.

Despite the venerability of this measure, avoid looking for an optimal score, which would be a misuse of this measurement. An optimal score ignores the fact that there is often a lag between investment in learning and reaping the benefits of effective learning. Instead, use the expenditure per employee indicator as a simple benchmark that reveals information about how closely an organization's most fundamental learning investments match those of organizations similar in size.

In the example in figure 9-3, the direct formal expenditure per employee is greater than both the median and the mean but still quite a bit less than the maximum. The user might be satisfied that a moderately greater than average direct formal expenditure per employee will be in line with organizational objectives to provide high-quality classroom learning experiences. However, this figure might indicate that direct formal learning might be slightly overfunded in relation to other technology-based learning, for example, or perhaps there may be room for trimming direct formal costs.

A large deviation from the average expenditure can reveal as much information as a small one. For example, some organizations may spend much more than the norm, while others spend much less. Yet those investments may be exactly what the organizations should be doing. A lower-than-average expenditure does not necessarily mean a sub-par performing learning function, nor does it mean that the organization's learning function is necessarily more efficient than that of its peers.

Similarly, a higher-than-average expenditure does not mean better, nor does it mean inefficient. A small organization shouldn't necessarily try to approach the high limit roulette table just because the large organization its

Figure 9-3: Learning Expenditure Per Employee

Financial Indicators	Your Organization		All Organizations				
	Value	Rank	Mean	Median	Min	Max	n
Expenditure (direct formal) per employee	$970.02	49	$734.66	$450	$55.43	$7,172.57	185

management admires is tossing chips around like lawn darts. The key is not how much is spent, rather the results and outcomes achieved based on that investment.

Expenditure as a Percentage of Payroll

Many organizations view the measure of expenditure as a percentage of payroll with less and less relevance as organization payroll becomes more fluid. And although this measure reveals less than it did 20 years ago, it still helps organizations understand the range of what they could be spending for employee learning and development. This number should be used to benchmark and not as a prescription for what a company must spend.

Alternately, expenditure as a share of payroll is sometimes regarded as a measure of rightsizing: if the figure is increasing without accompanying revenue growth, it can indicate inefficiencies or duplication of job tasks among job categories.

In figure 9-4, the organization's figure is higher than both the median and the mean, but still quite a bit less than the maximum. In general, the larger the organization the more likely the expenditure as a share of payroll figure will fall near the mean and median. If possible, the user should try to compare recent years' payroll data with recent years' expenditure data to determine whether this figure is affected by either's rate of growth.

Report Location: Financial Tab

Figure 9-4: Learning Expenditure as Percentage of Payroll

Financial Indicators	Your Organization		All Organizations				
	Value	Rank	Mean	Median	Min	Max	n
Expenditure (direct formal) as percentage of payroll (excluding benefits/taxes)	2.91%	28	2%	1.19%	0.15%	27.08%	166

Expenditure as a Percentage of Revenue

Expenditure as a share of revenue can be used as a gross measure describing the ability of learning investment to drive top-line growth. However, since the effects of learning are complex and indirect, it is not feasible—in the case of the data in figure 9.5—to say that only 1.09 percent of learning investment is returned as revenue. Rather, this figure should be treated more as an index and should always be compared with expenditure as a percentage of income/profit.

Report Location: Financial Tab

Figure 9-5: Learning Expenditure as a Percentage of Revenue

Financial Indicators	Your Organization		All Organizations				
	Value	Rank	Mean	Median	Min	Max	n
Expenditure (total) as percentage of revenue	1.09%	31	0.98%	0.36%	0.02%	18.18%	157

Expenditure as a Percentage of Income/Profit

In a broad sense, learning expenditures and income/profit mirror one another: As one increases, so does the other. However, the correlation is far from perfect, and therefore this measure alone should not be used to attribute the impact of learning on profit. Rather, expenditure as a share of income/profit is a reflection of the ability of the organization's learning investment to drive both top- and bottom-line growth. This figure will typically be about five to 10 times larger than expenditure as a percentage of revenue because it accounts for more (though certainly not all) of the effects of learning on performance improvement, such as cost reduction, operational excellence, and market capture. By comparing expenditure as a percentage of profit/income with expenditure as a percentage of revenue, the user will gain a deeper sense of the degree to which learning facilitates sustainable growth and contributes to overall reinvestment. (See figure 9-6.)

Figure 9-6: Learning Expenditure as a Percentage of Income/Profit

Financial Indicators	Your Organization		All Organizations				
	Value	Rank	Mean	Median	Min	Max	n
Expenditure (total) as percentage of income/profit	8.49%	34	9.47%	2.82%	0.01%	97.44%	118

Percentage of Direct Expenditure on External Services

Percentage of direct expenditure on external services refers to the extent to which the organization can meet its desired competency profile and skills inventory internally. This measure reveals the extent to which management can leverage the learning function cost beneficially through the use of partners. For large organizations, percentage of direct expenditure on external services can describe the strength of its internal market for learning programs. This figure varies widely by industry, level of globalization, maturity of organization, and need for quick adaptation.

In figure 9-7, the proximity of the median and mean suggests that what most organizations spend on external services is in the range of 22.5 - 28.33 percent, suggesting further that an external spend of one-quarter may be reasonable. In this example, a figure of 10 percent may suggest opportunities for cost savings or leveraging of current competencies, or alternatively that this organization's learning function is not easily modularized beyond a certain point and that cost savings should perhaps not be sought using external partners.

Figure 9-7: Percentage of Direct Expenditure on External Services

Financial Indicators	Your Organization		All Organizations				
	Value	Rank	Mean	Median	Min	Max	n
Percentage of direct expenditure on external services	10%	137	28.33%	22.5%	0%	100%	188

Percentage of Direct Expenditure on Tuition Reimbursement

This indicator refers to the extent to which the learning function requires outside partnership to meet anticipated long-term competency/skills and credentialing needs (that is, for promotion of tracked personnel). It may be an internal signal of the ability of the learning organization to cost effectively invest in talent in the long-term through partnerships. Similarly, this figure depicts the portion of learning needs that are not currently being met by internal competencies.

This indicator can vary substantially by industry, maturity of organization, and size of organization. Smaller organizations will likely have a higher percentage than larger organizations due to increased purchasing power and economies of scale. Organizations anticipating increasing management headcount may tend toward a higher figure. In figure 9-8, the value of 13 percent is slightly greater than average, yet might be typical of a smaller, high-growth company, or a public sector organization that includes generous tuition reimbursement benefits as a retention incentive.

Report Location: Financial Tab

Figure 9-8: Percentage of Direct Expenditure on Tuition Reimbursement

Financial Indicators	Your Organization		All Organizations				
	Value	Rank	Mean	Median	Min	Max	n
Percentage of direct expenditure on tuition reimbursement	13%	49	11.81%	5.88%	0%	100%	186

Direct Cost per Formal Learning Hour Available/Used

The cost per learning hour available and used indicators, sometimes referred to as "learning hours provided" and "learning hours received," are fundamental measures of learning activity and learning function productivity.

Let's use a library analogy to elucidate the precise difference between learning hours *used* and learning hours *available*. Learning hours available is like the number of books in a library available for checkout, whereas learning hours used is like the number of times the books are checked out by all users. Therefore, cost per learning hour available refers to the cost of producing one hour of learning content, and the cost per learning hour used measures how much it costs to supply one hour of learning to one employee. Taken together, these measures are used in capacity planning and in determining how many learners must use a learning program for it to be cost efficient.

Cost per learning hour available and used are among the most fundamental metrics in the WLP field, and they will likely remain standards of measure for learning function efficiency for decades to come. All learning professionals need be familiar with this figure for their organizations and be able to communicate not just the surface information but also the story behind the

Report Location: Financial Tab

numbers. Be prepared to be asked questions about how this figure has been trending for the past few years as well.

According to the 2006 *ASTD State of the Industry Report,* the cost for one learner to use an hour of content is decreasing in many organizations, especially elite-performing organizations, despite the cost per learning hour available being on the rise. In many organizations, efficiency gains have penetrated learning delivery, but these gains are failing to reach learning production.

The most ready explanation is that the efficiency gains facilitated by instructional technology have yet to reach (or may not be able to reach) the production of new content. Although in some organizations, the cost per learning hour available has been falling for the last few years, many organizations expect production costs for learning to rise in the next few years. Many organizations are finding that the reduced up-front development costs are offset by increasing costs related to content reuse, such as increased administrative overhead. Yet in some organizations, greatly increased reuse has required substantial upgrades of learning technology. Also, despite being scalable, some larger-scale learning programs have required live instruction to supplement many e-learning programs, which adds to reuse costs.

In the sample in figure 9-9, both cost per learning hour available and used are well above average. In high-growth organizations, such an observation would not be surprising, as revenue growth would easily compensate for the increased learning costs to support the growth. Mature organizations or organizations with established LMSs and centralized learning functions, however, should be achieving economies of scale in their learning program production. They should find their costs of steadying, nearer the average figures displayed in the Free Key Indicator Report.

**Report Location:
Operations Tab**

Ratio of Employees to Learning Staff

When evaluating the ratio of employees to learning staff, it is important to note that a particular trend may affect the interpretation of this indicator. Decreases in FTE totals are often misinterpreted and lead to incorrect conclusions that the learning function is serving fewer employees.

Figure 9-9: Cost per Learning Hour Available/Used

Financial Indicators	Your Organization		All Organizations				
	Value	Rank	Mean	Median	Min	Max	n
Direct cost per formal learning hour available	$2,330.74	31	$1,152.64	$354.13	$3.06	$8,712.08	174
Direct cost per formal learning hour used	$465.7	9	$70.75	$27.84	$0.27	$950	181

A correct interpretation is that fewer FTEs served the learners—not necessarily that fewer individual employees served learners. This subtle difference is not just semantic.

One of the most common explanations of this trend relates to the fact that fewer FTEs were tied exclusively to the learning function. Many organizations actively leverage job rotation as a means of individual career development or organizational succession planning. In these organizations, employees rotate through the learning function to share their knowledge and to develop new skills from a headcount perspective; these employees are permanently housed in another department of the organization.

The ratio of employees to learning staff can also indicate a gross level of learning efficiency, especially if coupled with a significant technology investment, or effectiveness in leveraging external partners.

A higher than average ratio of employees to learning staff can suggest that the learning function is operating at or near capacity, and an increased staff headcount may be needed. In figure 9-10, the organization—though far from the maximum—is nevertheless substantially above the mean and median and may be on the verge of facing a capacity problem in the learning function continuing to meet the needs of the organization.

Figure 9-10: Ratio of Employees to Learning Staff

Operations Indicators	Your Organization		All Organizations				
	Value	Rank	Mean	Median	Min	Max	n
Ratio of employees to learning staff	472.35	27	276.88	141.83	7.19	3,333.33	185

Learning Hours Consumed and Produced

Report Location: Operations Tab

Hours of formal content available per learning staff member denotes the overall robustness of the learning portfolio, as well as the suitability of the LMS to manage existing content. Too large a figure, however, could indicate inadequate management of the inventory within the learning portfolio, or the presence of retrieval problems. Likewise, it could indicate overall poor management of the LMS, the need to integrate multiple LMSs, or that an LMS platform fails to match the needs of the organization.

Hours of formal content usage per learning staff member denotes scalability of the learning portfolio, usually through standardization or automation. It can also indicate a healthy lack of scrap in learning portfolio and efficiency in distributing content through the existing LMSs.

In figure 9-11, the hours of formal content available per learning staff member lies between the median and the mean, which suggests that the learning

Figure 9-11: Hours of Formal Content Available and Usage

Operations Indicators	Your Organization		All Organizations				
	Value	Rank	Mean	Median	Min	Max	n
Hours of formal content available per learning staff member	196.58	77	534.93	123.93	1.28	4,942.75	183
Hours of formal content usage per learning staff member	983.87	136	5,766.1	2,861.44	1.06	45,220	185

Report Location: Operations Tab

organization is managing the production of and storage learning content adequately. However, the lower than average figure for hours of formal content usage per learning staff member suggests underutilization of the existing learning portfolio and perhaps low capacity of the current LMS.

Learning Content Reuse Ratio

The learning content reuse ratio refers to the ratio of learning hours consumed to learning hours produced. Strictly speaking, a reuse ratio of 50 means that on average, for one hour of content provided (available), it was received (consumed) an average of 50 times. A more tangible (and nearly always correct) way to express the learning content reuse ratio of 50 is that every hour of content provided (available) was received (consumed) by an average of 50 employees.

So what is the big deal about this indicator? This indicator reveals the amount of learning activity occurring per unit of investment in learning content and denotes the level of efficiency in the learning function facilitated by both technology and management of the learning function. The reuse ratio is often understood as a measure of the durability of learning programs, describing their average shelf life. Similarly, the reuse ratio describes the reach of learning programs or the degree to which the learning function can, in the words of one learning executive, "develop once/ deploy everywhere."

Younger learning functions often see a higher increase in the amount of reuse of learning content than their older, more well-established counterparts. The reason for this difference is that younger organizations often experience a higher rate of growth, expand more rapidly, hire more junior-level workers, and must manage the working capital closely—often resulting in the learning function successfully reusing the most critical learning programs.

In figure 9-12, the organization is reusing its learning content on average only five times, or alternatively, an hour-long learning program is reaching only five employees. The learning management in this organization should diligently investigate why this appears to be the case and strive to bring this figure more in line with at least the 12 percent median figure.

Figure 9-12: Learning Content Reuse Ratio

Operations Indicators	Your Organization		All Organizations				
	Value	Rank	Mean	Median	Min	Max	n
Formal learning content reuse ratio	5	115	44.39	12.11	0.05	439.86	179

Distribution of Learning by Content Area

As the learning function becomes more centralized, the learning executives managing the learning function must examine core competencies and reevaluate budgets based partially on their inventories. By sheer necessity, learning executives now possess a more sophisticated understanding of what competencies exist in their learning organization and what areas could be better handled externally through a tuition reimbursement program or external service providers.

To understand where to spend and allocate learning dollars, workplace learning professionals need to know the core competencies of the learning function and how to mobilize these competencies to meet short- and long-term business needs.

Standard benchmarks for optimal percentages of learning content distribution do not exist. In lieu of a magic benchmark number, workplace learning professionals should focus on—and communicate the value of—the learning function based on the nimbleness, adaptability, and ability to shift resources rapidly to content areas to achieve business outcomes.

In general, the distribution of learning by content area should show alignment of learning content to organizational capacity and desired competency profile. In figure 9-13, the numbers suggest an imbalance toward the operational aspects of the business. The numbers also suggest a possible neglect of soft skills, particularly those in the customer facing areas of the organization.

Distribution of Learning by Delivery Medium

Since the late 1990s, the technology explosion has enabled workplace learning professionals to deliver learning through a wide variety of media. In the last seven years, learning programs delivered through instructional technology grew from 25 to nearly 40 percent. This growth reflects both an increase in the maturity of e-learning production and delivery, and a high likelihood that learning technology increasingly continues to permeate the workplace.

Although many organizations see efficiency gains as a result of e-learning maturity, this does not mean that e-learning is the correct solution in every situation. As many books on learning technology state, the method of delivery must be considered side-by-side with the strategic objective of the learning program.

Report Location: Operations Tab

Report Location: Operations Tab

91

Figure 9-13: Distribution of Learning by Content Area

Formal learning hours available by content area							
Content Area	Your Organization		All Organizations				
	Value	Rank	Mean	Median	Min	Max	n
Executive Development	20	3	4.06	3	0	31.7	179
Managerial and Supervisory	30	10	11.05	10	0	51.6	186
Sales (not including product knowledge)	15	19	6.62	4	0	50	179
Customer Service	2	112	6.59	4	0	75	170
Mandatory and Compliance	9	68	9.4	5	0	91	179
Processes, Procedures, Business Practices, and Quality	3	136	10.86	6.8	0	86.28	177
Information Technology and Systems (e.g. enterprise and desktop software)	6	93	11.56	7	0	95	176
Interpersonal Skills (e.g. communication, teamwork)	2.5	129	6.06	5	0	40	179
New Employee Orientation	1.5	124	6.02	3	0	59.15	178
Basic Skills	5.5	45	5.17	2.6	0	60	172
Profession-specific or Industry-specific (e.g. engineering, accounting, legal, medical)	3	121	16.32	9.5	0	100	176
Product Knowledge	2	106	9.54	5	0	100	171
Other	0.5	51	3.57	0	0	65.3	146

Consider that the dominant form of e-learning delivery is self-paced online. Both employees and managers favor the non-invasive, minimally disruptive, just-in-time features of self-paced online learning. It is efficient from a cost perspective (centralization, low variable costs) and from the worker's perspective because it doesn't needlessly interrupt the workflow.

There has been much talk about the use of blended learning and instructor-led online learning as being superior to other types of learning; however, blended learning may not be appropriate in as many situations as it first may seem when designing a new learning program. Keep in mind that learning for today's workers is no longer a discrete event. Learning takes place often within the context of real work. Learning for many workers is dynamic, cumulative, and something they have more control over than in the past.

In figure 9-14, the delivery mix appears to be imbalanced, favoring formal learning over other delivery methods. This organization may be neglecting significant opportunities to improve organizational learning through instructional technology or work-based learning.

Learning Usage Per Employee

Learning hours per employee is benchmarked by the widest range of organizations and is perhaps the most reliable measure of the volume of training that organizations provide to their employees each year. During the 1990s many aggressive growth organizations boasted of providing 40-50 hours of learning per employee per year. Yet, like many of the excesses of the 1990s,

Report Location: Customer Tab

Figure 9-14: Distribution of Learning by Delivery Method

| Delivery Medium | Formal hours available by delivery medium | | | | | | |
| | Your Organization | | All Organizations | | | | |
	Value	Rank	Mean	Median	Min	Max	n
Live Instructor-led Real Classroom	72	84	63.33	69	0	100	189
Live Instructor-led Virtual Classroom (online)	0	96	4.86	1	0	76	162
Live Instructor-led Remote, but Not Online (e.g. satellite, video conference, teleconference)	0	73	2.4	0	0	45	151
Self-paced Online (networked)	9	112	18.78	10.05	0	83	178
Self-paced Stand-alone (non-networked) Computer-based (e.g. CD)	9	24	4.2	0.16	0	60	158
Mobile Technology (e.g. PDA, MP3s, cell phone)	2	8	0.4	0	0	10	145
Technology Other than Computer (e.g. video and audio)	2	34	2.77	0.75	0	93.44	152
Self-paced Non-technology Delivered (i.e. print)	2	55	4.34	1	0	99	155
Other	4	25	3.57	0	0	81.14	145

this target is as quaint as a stock with a 200 P/E ratio or market capitalizations the size of a nation's gross domestic product.

More recent, the average number of learning hours across organizations grew by 15 percent, although learning expenditure per employee increased only 3 to 5 percent—indicating a very positive trend. Despite this positive trend, be sure to always compare learning hours per employee side by side with costs.

Learning hours per employee is an indirect measure of the value of learning within the organization. For an organization to invest in an hour of learning, the benefits must exceed the hourly productivity loss/opportunity costs of being away from the workplace. When considered simultaneously with the total costs of the employee, learning hours per employee can reveal the demand sensitivity of the learner's time and the utility of one hour of the learner's time, which in turn can yield the shadow price of the learner's hourly value.

In figure 9-15, the organization is providing hours of learning content far below the mean or median. At the very least, such a figure should prompt reexamination of the learning function's fundamental operations and the sponsoring management's attitudes toward the learning function.

Figure 9-15: Formal Learning Usage per Employee

| Customer Indicators | Your Organization | | All Organizations | | | | |
	Value	Rank	Mean	Median	Min	Max	n
Formal learning usage per employee	2.08	164	32.38	19.64	0.43	258.54	187

Report Location: Innovation Tab

Figure 9-16: Percentage of Formal Content Delivered Online

Financial Indicators	Your Organization		All Organizations				
	Value	Rank	Mean	Median	Min	Max	n
Percentage of formal learning delivered online	9%	112	22.96%	15.5%	0%	85%	161

Percentage of Formal Content Delivered Online

Percentage of formal learning delivered online can indirectly indicate efficiency gains in delivering or scaling formal content, and the creation of an economy of scale in formal learning. This indicator denotes the LMS infrastructure standardization level, which can reveal a potential for reduction of fixed costs. In figure 9-16, the organization is well below the mean and median, suggesting the potential for increased delivery efficiency and reduced costs, and perhaps increased delivery capacity.

This chapter details how to analyze and interpret the data generated in Level 1—the Free Key Indicators Report. As learning functions progress to using more WLP Scorecard reports, the data gathering and entry processes become more complex. The next chapter details the descriptions for all required and optional input indicators that appear in both the Scorecard and Index Reports.

Chapter 10

Creating Scorecard and Index Reports

In This Chapter

* Turning qualitative data into numerical values
* Entering data for the Scorecard and Index Reports
* Defining input indicators

Quantifying and communicating the value of learning continues to be a challenge despite the volumes of data, research, and performance indexes available to today's workplace learning professionals. The truth of the matter is that it is not just about developing great programs and measuring outcomes; it's about managing expectations and communicating results in the language of business—in ways that executives see as meaningful and valuable.

To help solve this measurement quandary, the WLP Scorecard provides two types of reports: the Scorecard Reports and the Index Reports.

A balanced scorecard, a fundamental tool in the management of business processes for a variety of industries, helps to illuminate and reinforce the power of learning in organizations. Even if organizations do not use the balanced scorecard framework to manage processes, this analytic tool enables workplace learning professionals to clarify and communicate the role of learning within a larger context.

The Index Reports include four separate reports of learning function predictors for the alignment, effectiveness, efficiency, and sustainability

Appendix A
Quick Reference

Appendix A displays a complete listing of all required and optional input indicators for the Free Key Indicators, Scorecard, and Index Reports. Use this tool for identifying, planning, and gathering data for entry into the WLP Scorecard.

dimensions. These reports provide information for all four dimensions as well as a roll-up score for the entire learning function. By analyzing all five of these scores, workplace learning professionals can compare the learning function in their organizations with the entire workplace learning and performance industry.

This chapter provides detailed descriptions of each input indicator to facilitate entry of data in the WLP Scorecard Inputs screen. After entering data in these input indicators, workplace learning professionals can generate the Scorecard or Index Reports, depending on the subscription level.

To facilitate quick data entry, all of the field input indicators are formatted consistently as illustrated in figure 10-1. For example, each input indicator description includes

- ◈ the report(s) using the input indicator
- ◈ guidance on whether the input indicator is required to generate the reports
- ◈ the path needed to navigate to the input indicator
- ◈ a full description and examples.

Workplace learning professionals in a variety of industries use these reports to illuminate and reinforce the power of learning within any

Figure 10-1: Input Indicator Overview

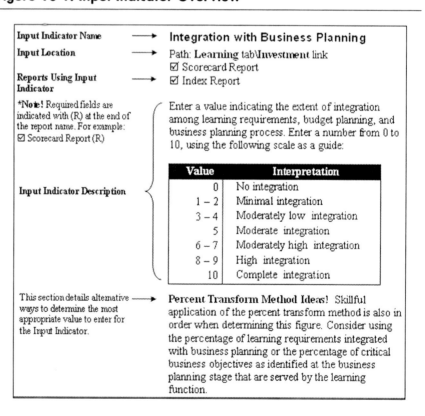

organization. Based on many interviews with these professionals, nearly everyone undertaking the process of creating a balanced scorecard ultimately finds it a worthwhile experience despite the occasional challenges. Because the balanced scorecard requires workplace learning professionals to articulate cause-and-effect relationships between activities and performance, users find themselves revisiting many of the assumptions about the learning function and the organization that were previously taken for granted.

The WLP Scorecard includes nine broad areas of data that describe and define learning functions:

1. financial
2. qualitative/impressionistic
3. learning function
4. learning function organization
5. satisfaction
6. formal learning
7. human capital
8. work-based learning
9. workforce.

Turning Qualitative/Impressionist Data into Numerical Values

Before entering data into the WLP Scorecard, let's review two types of data: **quantitative** and **qualitative.** Some researchers describe quantitative data as hard, rigorous, and objective and qualitative data as subjective and at times requiring judgment in determining a specific data value.

Both types of data are important in the WLP Scorecard. Because this tool requires users to enter a specific data value that best describes the learning function or the organization, converting qualitative information into quantitative numbers is required. There are two methods for making this conversion: rubrics and percent transform.

Rubrics Method

Some of the Input Indicators in this section include rubrics from 0 to 10 to facilitate choosing the most appropriate numerical value for entry into the WLP Scorecard. For example, the input indicator for Customer Satisfaction displays the following description:

> Enter the overall average customer satisfaction rating for quality and consistency of the organization's products and services for all

currently serviced and maintained product lines. Enter a number from 0 to 10, using the following scale as a guide:

Value	Interpretation
0	Complete dissatisfaction
1 – 2	Minimal satisfaction
3 – 4	Moderately low satisfaction
5	Moderate satisfaction
6 – 7	Moderately high satisfaction
8 – 9	High satisfaction
10	Complete satisfaction

This rubric scale enables you to select a numerical value that most represents the level of customer satisfaction with the organization's products and services. For cases in which users are gathering this data from multiple C-level managers, an average of the responses can also be used to derive the best value. For example,

- Manager A indicates 60% satisfaction
- Manager B indicates 70% satisfaction
- Manager C indicates 90% satisfaction
- Manager D indicates 100% satisfaction.

With the data, convert each into a number from 1–10:

- Sum the values = 320
- Take the average = 320/4 = 80
- Then divide by 10 and round off, resulting in a value of 8.

After this conversion, compare the value from the calculation with the rubric and confirm that the resulting value is appropriate.

Percent Transform Method

If the rubrics provided seem too vague to determine a value for entry in the WLP Scorecard, consider employing a simple rule of thumb, one that works for many kinds of qualitative/impressionistic data in the WLP Scorecard—the percent transform method.

Despite its high-sounding and clinical name, the percent transform method provides a simple way to reduce all observations to fit neatly into the rubric. To use this method, restate the question to estimate the percentage of incidence of a particular phenomenon and then back into a figure for entry in the WLP Scorecard.

Applying the Percent Transform Method:

1. Determine which number on the rubric best describes the phenomenon asked.
2. Restate the input indicator in terms of a percentage of incidence, for example:
   - The phenomenon happens X percent of the time.
   - The phenomenon happens correctly X percent of the time.
   - The phenomenon is observed in X percent of employees.
   - The phenomenon is X percent true.
   - The phenomenon is X percent fulfilled or completed
   - The phenomenon is X percent unfulfilled or incomplete.
   - The phenomenon has X percent coverage, reach or penetration.
   - The phenomenon is X percent integrated, standardized, or automated.
   - The phenomenon is fully integrated, standardized, or automated in X percent of employees or processes.
   - The phenomenon represents X percent fulfillment of expectations.
3. After restating the phenomenon, estimate a percentage based on the best information available.
4. Divide that percentage by 10 and round off.
5. Compare with the figure determined in step 1.
6. If the figure determined in step 4 represents a categorical difference as compared to the value determined in step 1, then take the average of the two and enter that value in the WLP Scorecard.
7. If the figure you arrived at in step 4 represents a slight difference, enter the figure arrived at in step 4.

Entering Data for the Scorecard and Index Reports

When entering data in the Input Indicators for the Scorecard or Index Reports, complete all required fields to generate the report. Workplace learning professionals can enter and update data in the WLP Scorecard at any time. It is recommended that users complete as much of the data as possible over time to reap the full benefit of these reports, to develop targeted action plans, and to effectively manage the learning function.

To Complete the Input Screens:
1. Open the WLP Scorecard.

Overview | Organization Profile | Input | Scorecard Reports | Index Reports | Support

2. Click the **Input** label on the Navigation Bar. The Input screen appears.

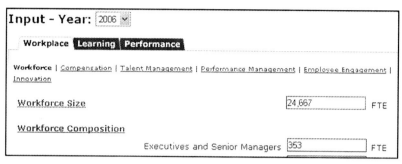

3. Select the **Workplace, Learning,** or **Performance** tabs as appropriate
4. Click the desired **Sub-Category Link.**

Workforce | Compensation | Talent Management | Performance Management | Employee Engagement | Innovation

5. Enter the data in the required input fields.
6. Closing the WLP Scorecard automatically saves all data entry items or changes.

Workplace Tab Indicators

In the Workplace tab, enter data that describes the human capital in the organization: how is it acquired, retained, classified, accessed, and sourced. Enter data that covers the characteristics of the talent management in the organization, including how the skills inventory is managed. This tab seeks information about the individual learning goals and plans, and the degree to which they are linked to organizational goals. This section also requires data describing how the organization's human capital creates value, generates assets that can be capitalized, and promotes differentiation.

Workforce Size
Path: **Workplace** tab**Workforce** link

☑ Scorecard Report (R)
☑ Index Report—(R)

Enter the average number of total employees for a year (full 12 months). Resist the temptation to enter the largest or smallest number of employees over the year, or the number of employees from a month that may seem representative, or an end-of-year or end-of-fiscal-year figure. Learning functions within banks may alternatively enter an end-of-year figure.

Workforce Size Includes:	Workforce Size Excludes:
• employees of consolidated domestic and international subsidiaries • part-time and seasonal employees • employees classified as FTEs (full-time equivalents) • corporate officers	• contracted workers and consultants • board members • employees of unconsolidated subsidiaries

The HRIS most likely contains this information. Organizations experiencing major reductions in force, reorganizations, or mergers within the last year should contact the WLP Scorecard team for assistance in determining this figure.

Workforce Composition

Path: **Workplace** tab**Workforce** link

- ☑ Scorecard Report
- ☑ Index Report

For many organizations, information about workforce composition should be available from the organization's HRIS. For this figure, enter the number of workers for each of the following employees groups:

- Executives and senior managers (VP level or above)
- Middle managers (director level)
- First-line supervisors
- Production/technical
- Administrative
- Customer service
- Sales
- IT
- Other.

An alternative way to estimate these figures is based on the *average* total number of employees across all months in the year. Some may need to back into this figure based on average percentages and available totals for workforce size. Organizations experiencing major reductions in force, reorganizations, or mergers within the last year should contact the WLP Scorecard team for assistance in determining this figure.

Hourly Employees

Path: **Workplace** tab**Workforce** link

- ☑ Index Report

Number of employees classified as nonexempt, nonsalaried, or hourly. Enter as full-time equivalents.

Employees Outside Home Country
Path: **Workplace** tab**Workforce** link

☑ Index Report

Enter the percentage of employees who perform more than 50 percent of their duties outside of the country of headquartering.

Workforce Dispersion
Path: **Workplace** tab**Workforce** link

☑ Index Report

Enter the number of countries with employees outside the country of headquartering.

Workforce Education Level
Path: **Workplace** tab**Workforce** sub-category link

☑ Scorecard Report
☑ Index Report

Enter the average number of years of college/higher education for employees. Enter as a number using the following scale as a guide:

Degree Level	Number of Years
Associate-level	1 – 2 years
Bachelor-level	4 – 5 years
Master's-level	5 – 7 years
MD/JD	7 – 10 years
Doctoral-level	7 – 12 years

For employees with some college work after high school, categorize them at the associate level. For employees described as having "some graduate school" or "some post-baccalaureate" work, assign five years as the degree level.

Obtain this information from the HRIS or by working with the HR department.

Payroll
Path: **Workplace** tab**Compensation** sub-category link

☑ Scorecard Report
☑ Index Report

Enter total salary and wages only. Do not include benefit plans and taxes. In most organizations, this figure is available from the HR or finance departments.

Total Compensation
Path: **Workplace** tab**Compensation** link

- ☑ Scorecard Report
- ☑ Index Report

Total compensation reflects the cost of employee wages and benefits allocated to the continuing operations of the organization. Total compensation includes

- salary and wages
- benefit plans
- payroll taxes
- pension costs
- bonuses
- incentive compensation
- profit sharing
- commissions.

Do not include stock options because a great deal of controversy surrounds their precise valuation. In general, to determine whether or not a form of compensation not listed above should be included in the figure, judge if the criterion is tied to ongoing operations. If so, then it should be entered into the WLP Scorecard. Both the HR and finance departments should be able to provide this figure with little difficulty. Users can also consult the organization's annual report for this figure.

Turnover
Path: **Workplace** tab**Talent Management** link

- ☑ Scorecard Report
- ☑ Index Report

Turnover refers to the percentage of employees who separated permanently from the organization voluntarily, involuntarily, or through retirement and early-retirement plans. This information should be available from the HR department. Organizations experiencing major reductions in force, reorganizations, or mergers within the last year should contact the WLP Scorecard team for assistance in determining this figure.

Tenure
Path: **Workplace** tab**Talent Management** link

- ☑ Scorecard Report
- ☑ Index Report

Tenure is the overall average number of years that employees have remained employed by the organization. This information should be available from the HR department.

Promotions
Path: **Workplace** tab**Talent Management** link

☑ Index Report

Enter the number of promotions of persons already employed by the organization. A good source for this information is the HRIS or HR department.

New Hires
Path: **Workplace** tab**Talent Management** link

☑ Index Report

Enter the number of employees hired who were not employed by the organization in a previous job. This information should be available from the HR department or HRIS.

Job Competency Documentation
Path: **Workplace** tab**Talent Management** link

☑ Scorecard Report
☑ Index Report

Enter the percentage of jobs/roles for which critical competencies/skills have been documented. The best sources for locating this information include senior HR staff and business unit leaders.

Individual Competency Profiles
Path: **Workplace** tab**Talent Management** link

☑ Scorecard Report
☑ Index Report

Enter the percentage of employee job classifications with competency profiles.

Succession Planning
Path: **Workplace** tab**Talent Management** link

☑ Index Report

Enter the percentage of key positions or roles for which at least one successor has been identified.

Individual and Organization Goal Linkage

Path: **Workplace** tab**Performance Management** link

- ☑ Scorecard Report
- ☑ Index Report

This measure determines the extent to which individual performance goals are linked to articulated organizational goals. Enter a number from 0 to 10, using the following scale as a guide:

Value	Interpretation
0	Completely unlinked
1 – 2	Minimal linkage
3 – 4	Moderately low linkage
5	Moderate linkage
6 – 7	Moderately high linkage
8 – 9	High linkage
10	Maximal linkage

Percent Transform Method Ideas! Alternative ways to identify appropriate data for this input field include restating:

- ❖ the percent of employees who have performance goals tied to organizational goals
- ❖ the percent of individual performance goals that are documented as being tied to organizational performance goals.

Individual Performance Goals

Path: **Workplace** tab**Performance Management** link

- ☑ Scorecard Report
- ☑ Index Report

Enter the percentage of employees whose job specification explicitly includes

- ❖ enumeration of performance goals/plans
- ❖ annual performance reviews.

Individual Learning Plans

Path: **Workplace** tab**Performance Management** link

- ☑ Index Report

Enter the percentage of employees whose job specifications include individual learning/development plans.

Alignment of Individual Performance Goals and Learning Plans

Path: **Workplace** tab**Performance Management** link

- ☑ Scorecard Report
- ☑ Index Report

Determine the extent to which individual employee development plans are aligned with individual performance goals. Enter a number from 0 to 10, using the following scale as a guide:

Value	Interpretation
0	Completely disjointed/no alignment
1 – 2	Minimal alignment
3 – 4	Moderately low alignment
5	Moderate alignment
6 – 7	Moderately high alignment
8 – 9	High alignment
10	Complete alignment with no exceptions

Percent Transform Method Ideas! Alternative ways to identify appropriate data for this input field include restating

- ◈ the percentage of employees with development plans aligned with individual performance goals
- ◈ the overall percentage of employee performance goals that tend to be tied to development plans.

Employee Alignment with Culture/Values

Path: **Workplace** tab**Employee Engagement** link

- ☑ Scorecard Report
- ☑ Index Report

Determine the degree of employee adoption or assumption of organization culture and values. Enter a number from 0 to 10, using the following scale as a guide:

Value	Interpretation
0	Complete lack of adoption
1 – 2	Minimal adoption
3 – 4	Moderately low adoption
5	Moderate adoption
6 – 7	Moderately high adoption
8 – 9	High adoption
10	Complete adoption

Percent Transform Method Ideas! Gather the perceptions of executives and business unit leaders when determining what to enter in this field. Alternative ways to identify appropriate data for this input field include restating

- the percentage of employees fully engaged in organizational culture or values
- the percentage of explicitly stated organizational values that have full employee engagement.

Employee Satisfaction
Path: **Workplace** tab**Employee Engagement** link

- ☑ Scorecard Report
- ☑ Index Report

Enter the average employee satisfaction with the general work environment of the organization. This figure may be obtained or inferred from annual employee surveys. Enter a number from 0 to 10, using the following scale as a guide:

Value	Interpretation
0	Complete dissatisfaction
1 – 2	Minimal satisfaction
3 – 4	Moderately low satisfaction
5	Moderate satisfaction
6 – 7	Moderately high satisfaction
8 – 9	High satisfaction
10	Complete satisfaction

Percent Transform Method Ideas! Alternative ways to identify appropriate data for this input field include restating

- the percentage of employees reporting high levels of satisfaction
- the percentage of employees reporting a level of satisfaction above a specified criterion.

Employee Satisfaction with Learning Opportunities
Path: **Workplace** tab**Employee Engagement** link

- ☑ Scorecard Report
- ☑ Index Report

Enter the level of employee satisfaction with opportunities to learn and develop job- or career-related skills and abilities. This figure might be also obtained or inferred from annual employee surveys in some organizations. During the duration of a WLP Scorecard subscription year, consider administering a brief survey to determine this figure more precisely, especially if annual employee surveys do not cover learning opportunity satisfaction. Enter a number from 0 to 10, using the following scale as a guide:

Value	Interpretation
0	Complete dissatisfaction
1 – 2	Minimal satisfaction
3 – 4	Moderately low satisfaction
5	Moderate satisfaction
6 – 7	Moderately high satisfaction
8 – 9	High satisfaction
10	Complete satisfaction

Percent Transform Method Ideas! Alternative ways to identify appropriate data for this input field include restating

* percentage of employees reporting high levels of satisfaction
* percentage of employees reporting a level of satisfaction above a specified criterion.

Absenteeism

Path: **Workplace** tab**Employee Engagement** link

☑ Index Report

Enter the average number of days of absenteeism due to illness or unexplained reasons per employee. Obtain this information from the HR department or HRIS.

Investment in Research and Development (R&D)

Path: **Workplace** tab**Innovation** link

☑ Index Report

Enter the dollar amount invested in the development of new products or services. Locate this information by consulting the finance department or an annual report. Enter this value in U.S. dollars. Convert non-U.S. currency using rate on date of entry.

Investment in R&D Includes:	Investment in R&D Excludes:
• organization-sponsored research and development • acquired research and development when reported as a separate item • software development expenses • research and development expenses from continuing operations, in the case of organizations whose primary business activity is research and development	• prospective or extractive activities • client-supported research and development or software expenses • royalties • market research and testing • acquired technology or software (including amortization) • engineering and support expenses • research and development from discontinued operations

New Products and Services
Path: **Workplace** tab**Innovation** link

- ☑ Scorecard Report
- ☑ Index Report

Enter the percentage of products and services in the current portfolio that were newly introduced into their respective markets or market segments within in the last year. Consult with the marketing department to obtain these figures to assist in creating a roll-up of new products and services readily entered into the WLP Scorecard.

Employee Time on New Products and Services
Path: **Workplace** tab**Innovation** link

- ☑ Index Report

Enter the percentage of employee time spent on products and services in the current portfolio that were newly introduced within the last year. If it is more feasible, aggregate the total amount of time spent across all relevant units throughout the organization, then divide by the number of employee in those units. Gather this information by obtaining the perceptions of executives and senior leaders.

Employee Time on Process Improvement/Innovation
Path: **Workplace** tab**Innovation** link

- ☑ Index Report

Enter the percentage of employee time spent on organizational processes of any type that were newly introduced within in the last year. If it is more feasible, aggregate the total amount of time spent across all relevant units throughout organization, then take the average. Gather this information by obtaining the perceptions of executives and senior leaders.

Employee Idea Solicitation
Path: **Workplace** tab**Innovation** link

- ☑ Index Report

Indicate if there is a formal process in the organization for employees to suggest innovations in business processes, products, or services. Enter either "Yes" or "No."

Employee Idea Conversion
Path: **Workplace** tab**Innovation** link

- ☑ Index Report

Enter the number of employee-generated ideas implemented for innovation. This may include ideas for product or service improvement/enhancement, internal process improvement, and new or improved production or delivery techniques. When entering this figure, divide the number of ideas from employees realized this year by number of ideas submitted this year. Consult with the HR department or business unit leaders.

Number of Patent Applications
Path: **Workplace** tab**Innovation** link

☑ Index Report

Enter the number of patent applications filed in the last year.

Number of Patents Received
Path: **Workplace** tab**Innovation** link

☑ Index Report

Enter the number of patents received in the last year.

Total Patents
Path: **Workplace** tab**Innovation** link

☑ Index Report

Enter the total number of unexpired patents owned by the organization.

Industry/University Partnerships
Path: **Workplace** tab**Innovation** link

☑ Index Report

Indicate the number of cooperation agreements with universities and/or business schools. Cooperation agreements include formal knowledge-sharing agreements, licensing agreements, research-to-industry programs, and others, but do not include formal employee recruiting.

Learning Tab Indicators

The Learning tab contains the most data entry categories and covers the fundamental areas in the management of the learning function and its products. This section requests data that describe the level in investment in the learning function, both in terms of actual dollars and staffing. Key aspects of the operation of the learning function are also covered:

- how well the learning function for production of learning programs is set up
- allocation of learning staff time in production and distribution of learning products

- quantity and characteristics of learning outputs
- production and usage of formal and work-based learning opportunities.

These indicators help to assess learning function processes that allow for the capture and redistribution of workplace knowledge, assess general infrastructure, provide information regarding outsourcing policies and practices, and examine the degree to which the learning function reaches beyond classroom experiences.

Total Direct Learning Investment

Path: **Learning** tab**Investment** link

- ☑ Scorecard Report
- ☑ Index Report

Deriving the expenditure on technology infrastructure could be a little tricky, depending on who paid for it, the methods of depreciation applied, and the distribution of maintenance costs.

Total direct costs for learning include formal learning, work-based learning, and the learning function's contribution to non-learning performance improvement solutions. For many organizations, gathering this figure will be easier to obtain than individual breakdowns according to formal, work-based, and non-learning solutions. However, workplace learning professionals may enter an aggregate figure for this category for ease of use if the budget is divided into sections that readily map to formal, work-based, and non-learning solutions. Each category is defined as follows:

- **Formal learning** comprises structured learning activities conducted separately from the workplace. Examples include classroom events, online lessons, or a coaching event conducted separately from work.
- **Work-based learning** refers to activities embedded in, or coincident to, an employee's normal work activity. Examples include use of knowledge repositories, job aids, knowledge sharing, and coaching while performing work tasks.
- **Non-learning solutions** include time that learning staff are involved in performance improvement activities such as organizational development, process analysis, talent management, and performance management.

Total Indirect Learning Investment

Path: **Learning** tab**Investment** link

- ☑ Scorecard Report
- ☑ Index Report

Direct Costs Include:	Direct Costs Do Not Include:
• learning and performance staff salaries including gross wages without benefits or employer-paid taxes • travel costs for learning and performance staff • administrative costs • non-salary development costs • non-salary delivery costs (such as classroom facilities, online learning technology infrastructure) • outsourced activities • tuition reimbursements	• learners travel expenses • costs of conference attendance, fees, and travel • cost of lost work time while engaged in learning formal activities • costs of internal subject matter expert time for content analysis, coaching, and knowledge sharing

In the WLP professional, total indirect learning investment costs include expenses related to formal and work-based learning only. Indirect costs for learning include

- learner travel expenses
- conference attendance, fees, travel, lodging, meals, and ground transportation
- lost work time while engaged in learning formal activities
- internal subject matter expert time for content analysis, coaching, and knowledge sharing
- reasonable opportunity costs.

Percentage of Direct Cost for Learning by Type of Solution
Path: **Learning** tab**Investment** link

- ☑ Scorecard Report
- ☑ Index Report

Enter a breakdown of the percentage of direct learning *expenditures* devoted to formal learning, work-based learning, and activities related to non-learning performance improvement solutions.

Integration with Business Planning
Path: **Learning** tab**Investment** link

- ☑ Scorecard Report
- ☑ Index Report

Enter a value indicating the extent of integration among learning requirements, budget planning, and business planning process. Enter a number from 0 to 10, using the following scale as a guide:

Value	Interpretation
0	No integration
1 – 2	Minimal integration
3 – 4	Moderately low integration
5	Moderate integration
6 – 7	Moderately high integration
8 – 9	High integration
10	Complete integration

Percent Transform Method Ideas! Alternative ways to identify appropriate data for this input field include restating

- ❖ the percentage of learning requirements integrated with business planning
- ❖ the percentage of critical business objectives identified during business planning that are served by the learning function.

Unplanned Learning Expenditure
Path: **Learning** tab**Investment** link

- ☑ Scorecard Report
- ☑ Index Report

This value represents the budget variance between planned and actual year-end learning expenditures for formal learning, work-based learning, and non-learning solutions. Calculation: (total learning expenditure for the year) – (the annual budgeted learning expenditure).

Budget Centralization
Path: **Learning** tab**Investment** link

- ☑ Scorecard Report
- ☑ Index Report

Enter the percentage of total direct learning expenditures from all areas—formal and work-based learning, and non-learning solutions—that are managed through a central operation.

External Services Expenditure
Path: **Learning** tab**Investment** link

- ☑ Scorecard Report
- ☑ Index Report

External services, also known as outsourcing or outtasking, to vendors or learning partners represent the learning function work that is completed by an external organization. For this input value, enter the percentage of total *direct* learning expenditures for external services.

Direct Expenditures Include:	Direct Expenditures Do Not Include:
• consulting services • content development and licenses • workshops and training programs delivered by external providers	• payments made in the form of employee tuition reimbursements for educational programs at educational institutions

Tuition Reimbursement Expenditure

Path: **Learning** tab**Investment** link

- ☑ Scorecard Report
- ☑ Index Report

Enter the percentage of total direct learning expenditure for employee tuition reimbursement for educational programs at educational institutions.

Learning Staff Costs (Including/Excluding Benefits and Taxes)

Path: **Learning** tab**Investment** link

- ☑ Scorecard Report
- ☑ Index Report

Enter the percentage of total direct learning expenditures for learning staff. When determining the amount of expenditures devoted to employee costs, include total salary, wages, benefits, and taxes.

For the input field *excluding* benefits and taxes, enter values only representing total salaries and wages for the learning staff.

Expenditure on Technology Infrastructure

Path: **Learning** tab**Investment** link

- ☑ Scorecard Report
- ☑ Index Report

Enter the percentage of the total direct learning expenditure for instructional technology infrastructure. When determining expenditures, include

- hardware
- software
- service plans
- licenses

- consulting fees
- maintenance
- implementation costs
- management costs.

Also, if there are any expenses relating to upgrading a legacy instructional technology system, include only the costs allocated to the learning function. Include any amortization costs borne directly or charged to the learning budget. If technology infrastructure belongs primarily to another department's budget, include only the portion allocated to the learning function.

Expenditure by Employee Group
Path: **Learning** tab**Investment** link

- ☑ Scorecard Report
- ☑ Index Report

Enter the total direct learning expenditure percentages for each hierarchical employee group listed for this indicator:

- senior managers
- middle managers
- first-line supervisors
- production/technical
- administrative
- customer service
- sales
- IT
- other.

Learning Staff Size
Path: **Learning** tab**Learning Function Staff/Talent** link

- ☑ Scorecard Report
- ☑ Index Report

Enter the number of learning function staff expressed as full-time equivalents. Although it may be tempting to enter only a simple head count of the learning function, do not use this figure as the input unless that figure equals the total FTEs. Include rotated staff only if their FTE allocation is charged to the learning function budget.

Learning Staff Time Allocation by Activity
Path: **Learning** tab**Learning Function Staff/Talent** link

- ☑ Scorecard Report
- ☑ Index Report

Enter the number of FTE internal learning staff dedicated to each of the following activities:

- administration (for example, learning management, program/project management, finances)
- needs analysis/planning/requirements/performance
- analysis/competency
- modeling
- task analysis/content analysis
- design (for example, templates, content structures, activities, information scripts, interfaces)
- development
- content
- maintenance
- delivery
- measurement and evaluation.

Learning Staff Time Allocation by Type of Solution
Path: **Learning** tab**Learning Function Staff/Talent** link

- ☑ Scorecard Report
- ☑ Index Report

Enter the percentage of learning staff time allocated to formal learning, work-based learning, and non-learning performance improvement solutions.

Learning Staff Reporting
Path: **Learning** tab**Learning Function Staff/Talent** link

- ☑ Scorecard Report
- ☑ Index Report

Enter the percentage of FTE learning staff reporting to the central learning function. Include rotating staff only if they fill a FTE allocation in the learning function.

Learning Staff Turnover
Path: **Learning** tab**Learning Function Staff/Talent** link

- ☑ Scorecard Report
- ☑ Index Report

Enter the percentage of FTE learning staff separated from the organization. Include voluntary and involuntary separations, and retirements. Do not include rotating staff unless their FTE allocations are charged to the learning function budget.

Learning Staff Tenure

Path: **Learning** tab**Learning Function Staff/Talent** link

☑ Index Report

Indicate the average number of years the learning staff members have been with the organization. Include rotated staff only if their FTE allocation is charged to the learning function budget.

Learning Staff Education Level

Input location: **Learning** tab**Learning Function Staff/Talent** link

☑ Index Report—optional

Enter the average number of years of college/higher education completed by the learning staff. To calculate this value: (sum the total years of higher education for each learning staff member) / (the number of learning staff members).

Learning Staff Time Allocation by Activity

Path: **Learning** tab**Learning Function Processes** link

☑ Scorecard Report
☑ Index Report

Enter the percentage of learning staff time allocated to formal learning, work-based learning, and non-learning performance improvement solutions.

Learning Staff Time Allocation by Type of Solution

Path: **Learning** tab**Learning Function Processes** link

☑ Scorecard Report
☑ Index Report

Percentage of learning staff time allocated to formal learning, work-based learning, and non-learning performance improvement solutions.

Standardization

Path: **Learning** tab**Learning Function Processes** link

☑ Scorecard Report
☑ Index Report

Determine and enter the extent to which learning function processes are standardized across the organization. Enter a number from 0 to 10, using the following scale as a guide:

Learning Function Standardization and Automation Percent Transform Method Tips!

To decide on the best values to enter for some of the learning function standardization and automation input indicators, do some investigation to formulate the best possible judgments. When making these judgments, remember that not all learning function processes can be standardized or automated. When entering figures for standardization and automation, consider only aspects of the learning function for which standardization and automation would apply. Do not include learning function activities that could not be standardized or automated in your determination of the figure to be entered into the WLP Scorecard.

Alternative ways to identify appropriate data for this input field include restating the percentage of

❋ learning function that is standardized

❋ learning function processes that are standardized

❋ learning and delivery that is governed by standard procedures and automation.

Value	Interpretation
0	No standardization
1 – 2	Minimal standardization
3 – 4	Moderately low standardization
5	Moderate standardization
6 – 7	Moderately high standardization
8 – 9	High standardization
10	Complete standardization

Documentation

Path: **Learning** tab**Learning Function Processes** link

- ☑ Scorecard Report
- ☑ Index Report

Determine and enter the extent to which learning function processes and standards are documented. Enter a number from 0 to 10, using the following scale as a guide:

Value	Interpretation
0	No documentation
1 – 2	Minimal documentation
3 – 4	Moderately low documentation
5	Moderate documentation
6 – 7	Moderately high documentation
8 – 9	High documentation
10	Complete documentation

Percent Transform Method Ideas! Alternative ways to identify appropriate data for this input field include restating

- the percentage of learning processes and standards that are documented
- the percentage of learning processes and standards that have a built-in protocol of documentation.

Automation

Path: **Learning** tab**Learning Function Processes** link

- ☑ Scorecard Report
- ☑ Index Report

Determine and enter the extent to which certain learning function processes are automated, such as administration or content updating. Enter a number from 0 to 10, using the following scale as a guide:

Value	Interpretation
0	No automation
1 – 2	Minimal automation
3 – 4	Moderately low automation
5	Moderate automation
6 – 7	Moderately high automation
8 – 9	High automation
10	Complete automation

Shortest Cycle

Path: **Learning** tab**Learning Function Processes** link

☑ Scorecard Report
☑ Index Report

Determine the shortest amount of time required for internal employees or outsourcing partners to design, develop, and deploy one hour of formal content (for example, an hour of primarily informational e-learning content). This value should be calculated under normal circumstances for content managed by the learning function. Enter this value in the number of days, including any fraction. For example half a day should be entered as 0.5; three and one-quarter days should be entered as 3.25, and so on.

Longest Cycle

Path: **Learning** tab**Learning Function Processes** link

☑ Scorecard Report
☑ Index Report

Determine the longest amount of time required for internal employees or outsourcing partners to design, develop, and deploy one hour of formal content (for example, to develop a certification program or simulation). This value should be calculated under normal operating circumstances for content managed by the learning function. Enter this value in the number of days. If the value is less than one day, then enter it as a fraction of an 8-hour day: for example, half a day should be entered as 0.5, three and one-quarter days as 3.25, and so on.

Total Formal Hours Available

Path: **Learning** tab**Output (Formal Learning)** link

☑ Scorecard Report
☑ Index Report

Perform a one-time count of the total number of hours of formal learning content available. This value, entered in hours, should include live classes, workshops, seminars, online course catalog content, video, and print. Although many learning functions determine this figure with relative ease, highly decentralized learning functions face a greater challenge determining this value.

New Formal Hours

Path: **Learning** tab**Output (Formal Learning)** link

☑ Scorecard Report
☑ Index Report

Perform a one-time count of the total number of hours of new formal learning content available in the last year. This value, entered in hours, should include live classes, workshops, seminars, online course catalogs, video, and print. Do not include updated content hours in this figure.

Updated Formal Hours

Path: **Learning** tab**Output (Formal Learning)** link

☑ Scorecard Report
☑ Index Report

Enter the total number of hours of existing formal content updated in the last year. This value, entered in hours, should include live classes, workshops, seminars, online course catalogs, video, and print.

Formal Hours Retired

Path: **Learning** tab**Output (Formal Learning)** link

☑ Scorecard Report
☑ Index Report

When auditing formal learning content, determine the total number of hours rendered inactive and no longer available for employee use. Include all formal content, whether archived, disposed of, or destroyed.

Formal Hours by Content Area

Path: **Learning** tab**Output (Formal Learning)** link

☑ Scorecard Report
☑ Index Report

For organizations submitting data for previous years' *ASTD State of the Industry* reports, the following should be readily available. Determine and enter the percentage of formal learning content by the following content areas:

- executive development
- managerial and supervisory

- sales (not including product knowledge)
- customer service
- mandatory and compliance (for example, safety, security)
- processes, procedures, business practices, and quality
- information technology and systems (for example, enterprise and desktop software)
- interpersonal skills (for example, communication, team work)
- new employee orientation
- basic skills
- profession specific or industry specific (for example, engineering, accounting, legal, medical)
- product knowledge
- other.

New Formal Hours by Content Area

Path: **Learning** tab**Output (Formal Learning)** link

☑ Scorecard Report
☑ Index Report

Enter the percentage of formal learning hours available by the content areas listed below (the total should equal 100 percent):

- executive development
- managerial and supervisory
- sales (not including product knowledge)
- customer service
- mandatory and compliance (for example, safety, security)
- processes, procedures, business practices, and quality
- information technology and systems (for example, enterprise and desktop software)
- interpersonal skills (for example, communication, team work)
- new employee orientation
- basic skills
- profession specific or industry specific (for example, engineering, accounting, legal, medical)
- product knowledge
- other.

Formal Hours by Delivery Method

Path: **Learning** tab**Output (Formal Learning)** link

☑ Scorecard Report
☑ Index Report

Another stalwart of the data collected for the *ASTD State of the Industry Report* and for the ASTD BEST Award submissions, these figures are closely monitored by elite-performing learning functions. This input indicator focuses on the distribution of technology versus non-technology delivery methods. Enter the percentage of formal learning hours available via each of the following delivery methods:

- live instructor-led real classroom
- live instructor-led virtual (online) classroom
- live instructor-led remote, but not online (for example, satellite, video conference, teleconference)
- self-paced online (networked)
- self-paced stand-alone (non-networked) computer-based (that is, CD-ROM)
- mobile technology (for example, PDA, MP3, cell phone)
- technology other than computer and mobile (for example, videotape, audio CD)
- self-paced nontechnology delivered (that is, print)
- other.

Knowledge Repositories/Expert Knowledge

Information management is key in every organization. There are two primary traditions of providing essential information: instruction and sharing. *Instruction* is information that's taught. When a learning need requires instruction, training is provided.

Information sharing can be done formally or informally. When learning is more appropriately addressed with information, knowledge management may be the solution. So what exactly is knowledge management? Knowledge management is the explicit and systematic management of intellectual capital and organizational knowledge as well as the associated processes of creating, gathering, organizing, retrieving, leveraging, and using intellectual capital for the purposes of improving organizations and the people in them.

Through these processes, organizations capture and store data and information in a central or distributed electronic environment—often referred to as a knowledge base or a knowledge repository.

Customization of Formal Content
Path: **Learning** tab**Output (Formal Learning)** link

- ☑ Scorecard Report
- ☑ Index Report

Determine and enter the percentage of formal learning hours available that are customized for the organization. Include hours of existing formal learning content that have been adapted for the organization, and templated (that is, standard format that requires only insertion of content) formal learning content created uniquely and exclusively for the organization. Customized learning content does not include generic "off-the-shelf" content from external providers.

Knowledge Repositories
Path: **Learning** tab**Output (Work-Based Learning)** link

- ☑ Scorecard Report
- ☑ Index Report

Enter the total hours of non-course-based, searchable, informational content that is created, maintained, or sponsored by the learning function. Although the majority of this content is likely to be stored electronically, it is possible that some of this information may be housed manually or in electronic retrieval systems.

New Hours of Expert Knowledge Entered into Repositories
Path: **Learning** tab**Output (Work-Based Learning)** link

- ☑ Scorecard Report
- ☑ Index Report

Enter the total number of new hours of expert knowledge that have been captured and entered into knowledge repositories. This information should be searchable and available to employees in the organization.

Knowledge Sharing
Path: **Learning** tab**Output (Work-Based Learning)** link

- ☑ Scorecard Report
- ☑ Index Report

Enter the number of hours of knowledge sharing planned, sponsored, or facilitated primarily by the learning function.

Maturity of Management of Formal Learning
Path: **Learning** tab**Infrastructure** link

- ☑ Scorecard Report
- ☑ Index Report

This value represents the maturity of the system used for managing formal learning within the organization. Enter a number from 0 to 10, using the following scale as a guide:

Value	Interpretation
0	Nascent, just born
1 – 2	Minimal maturity, infant stage
3 – 4	Moderately low maturity, childhood stage
5	Moderate maturity, adolescent stage
6 – 7	Moderately high maturity, young adult stage
8 – 9	High maturity, adult stage
10	Complete mature, seasoned adult stage

Maturity of Work-Based Learning Infrastructure
Path: **Learning** tab**Infrastructure** link

- ☑ Scorecard Report
- ☑ Index Report

Enter the level of maturity for the system used to collect, analyze, and report on the performance of the learning function in the organization. Enter a number from 0 to 10, using the following scale as a guide:

Value	Interpretation
0	Nascent, just born
1 – 2	Minimal maturity, infant stage
3 – 4	Moderately low maturity, childhood stage
5	Moderate maturity, adolescent stage
6 – 7	Moderately high maturity, young adult stage
8 – 9	High maturity, adult stage
10	Complete mature, seasoned adult stage

Percent Transform Method Ideas! It may be somewhat difficult to determine a simple percent transform method for this qualitative measure since this scale is bounded at the low end by an absolute zero and includes a highly metaphorical rubric. Consider a percent transform criteria that includes progress toward a defined level of maturity of a work-based learning infrastructure.

Infrastructure Standardization
Path: **Learning** tab**Infrastructure** link

- ☑ Scorecard Report
- ☑ Index Report

Determine and enter a value representing the extent to which systems, both electronic and human based, for managing learning are consistent across the organization. Enter a number from 0 to 10, using the following scale as a guide:

Value	Interpretation
0	Completely inconsistent
1 – 2	Minimal consistency
3 – 4	Moderately low consistency
5	Moderate consistency
6 – 7	Moderately high consistency
8 – 9	High consistency
10	Complete consistency with no exceptions

It is highly unlikely for most organizations to rate the learning function at either extreme of this scale—meaning either "completely inconsistent" or having "complete consistency with no exceptions."

Percent Transform Method Ideas! Alternative ways to identify appropriate data for this input field include restating

- learning function systems are consistent X percent of the time
- learning function systems are consistent in X percent of key processes
- learning function systems are consistent in X percent of learning programs.

Measurement Maturity

Path: **Learning** tab**Infrastructure** link

☑ Scorecard Report
☑ Index Report

This input reflects the maturity of systems for collecting, analyzing, and reporting on the performance of the learning function in the organization. Enter a number from 0 to 10, using the following scale as a guide:

Value	Interpretation
0	Nascent, just born
1 – 2	Minimal maturity, infant stage
3 – 4	Moderately low maturity, childhood stage
5	Moderate maturity, adolescent stage
6 – 7	Moderately high maturity, young adult stage
8 – 9	High maturity, adult stage
10	Complete mature, seasoned adult stage

Number of Providers

Path: **Learning** tab**Outsourcing** link

☑ Scorecard Report
☑ Index Report

Enter the total number of current external providers that furnish any goods or services to the learning function. Include only external providers who supply invoices for goods or services, not any vendors where compensation is paid out of a petty cash account.

Longevity of Relationships

Path: **Learning** tab**Outsourcing** link

☑ Scorecard Report
☑ Index Report

This value indicates the average number of years that all current vendors have been retained. Calculation: (number of years with each current provider) / (the total number of current providers).

Management of External Providers

Path: **Learning** tab**Outsourcing** link

- ☑ Scorecard Report
- ☑ Index Report

Enter the percentage of outsourced services managed centrally by the learning function.

Learning Activities Outsourced

Path: **Learning** tab**Outsourcing** link

- ☑ Scorecard Report
- ☑ Index Report

Enter the percentage of outsourced, outtasked, or products/services contracted to third-party vendors for the following learning function activities:

- planning, analysis, competency modeling
- content design, development, acquisition, maintenance, and delivery
- learning management/administration
- measurement and evaluation
- infrastructure
- other.

Formal and Work-Based Learning

Path: **Learning** tab**Integration** link

- ☑ Scorecard Report
- ☑ Index Report

Determine the extent of integration of formal and work-based learning opportunities. Enter a number from 0 to 10, using the following scale as a guide:

Value	Interpretation
0	No integration
1 – 2	Minimal integration
3 – 4	Moderately low integration
5	Moderate integration
6 – 7	Moderately high integration
8 – 9	High integration
10	Full integration with no exceptions

Percent Transform Method Ideas! Alternative ways to identify appropriate data for this input field include restating

◈ the percentage of formal learning programs that are integrated into work-based learning

◈ the percentage of work-based programs that have been designed to complement or reinforce the performance objectives of formal learning (and vice versa)

◈ the percentage of formal learning programs that have work-based components that support the same set of performance objectives.

Work-Based Learning and Work

Path: **Learning** tab**Integration** link

☑ Scorecard Report
☑ Index Report

Determine the extent to which knowledge repository access and knowledge sharing opportunities are embedded in workflow. Enter a number from 0 to 10, using the following scale as a guide:

Value	Interpretation
0	No embeddedness
1 – 2	Minimal embeddedness
3 – 4	Moderately low embeddedness
5	Moderate embeddedness
6 – 7	Moderately high embeddedness
8 – 9	High embeddedness
10	Full embeddedness

Percent Transform Method Ideas! Alternative ways to identify appropriate data for this input field include restating

◈ the percentage of business processes that afford work-based learning opportunities

◈ the percentage of employees having immediate access to knowledge repository/sharing opportunities at the workplace.

For data related to work-based learning, you are the expert. If the CEO were to approach you and ask, "What are the characteristics of our top-performing customer service representatives? What sets them apart from all the rest?" You would be able to list several characteristics right off the top of your head. The CEO consulted you as an expert and would respect your answers. With your unique professional skills and perspective, you are the best judge of work-based learning and whether the data you might enter into the WLP Scorecard reflects the truth in your organization.

Enterprise Data

Path: **Learning** tab**Integration** link

- ☑ Scorecard Report
- ☑ Index Report

Determine the level of integration of learning databases with other enterprise databases. Enter a number from 0 to 10, using the following scale as a guide:

Value	Interpretation
0	No integration
1 – 2	Minimal integration
3 – 4	Moderately low integration
5	Moderate integration
6 – 7	Moderately high integration
8 – 9	High integration
10	Full integration with no exceptions

Percent Transform Method Ideas! Use common sense in determining whether it really makes sense for certain enterprise databases to be integrated with learning databases. Exclude irrelevant enterprise databases from your judgment. Alternative ways to identify appropriate data for this input field include restating

- the percentage of learning databases that regularly send data to enterprise databases
- the percentage of enterprise databases that are set up to receive data from learning databases.

Formal Learning and Competencies

Path: **Learning** tab**Integration** link

- ☑ Scorecard Report
- ☑ Index Report

Determine the extent of mapping of formal learning opportunities to job/role competencies, for example, by agency of a learning management system. Enter a number from 0 to 10, using the following scale as a guide:

Value	Interpretation
0	No mapping
1 – 2	Minimal mapping
3 – 4	Moderately low mapping
5	Moderate mapping
6 – 7	Moderately high mapping
8 – 9	High mapping
10	Full mapping

Formal Learning and Individual Learning Plans

Path: **Learning** tab**Integration** link

- ☑ Scorecard Report
- ☑ Index Report

Determine the extent of mapping of formal learning opportunities to individual employee competency gaps/learning needs, for example, by agency of a learning management system. Enter a number from 0 to 10, using the following scale as a guide:

Value	Interpretation
0	No mapping
1 – 2	Minimal mapping
3 – 4	Moderately low mapping
5	Moderate mapping
6 – 7	Moderately high mapping
8 – 9	High mapping
10	Full mapping

Percent Transform Method Ideas! Alternative ways to identify appropriate data for this input field include restating

- the percentage of formal/work-based learning opportunities that include performance objectives explicitly tied to meeting competency gaps
- the percentage of individuals identified as having competency gaps/learning needs and for which meeting those needs is explicitly tied to formal/work-based learning opportunities.

Work-Based Learning and Individual Learning Plans

Path: **Learning** tab**Integration** link

- ☑ Scorecard Report
- ☑ Index Report

Determine extent of mapping of work-based learning opportunities to individual employee competency gaps/learning needs, for example, by agency of a learning management system. Enter a number from 0 to 10, using the following scale as a guide:

Value	Interpretation
0	No mapping
1 – 2	Minimal mapping
3 – 4	Moderately low mapping
5	Moderate mapping
6 – 7	Moderately high mapping
8 – 9	High mapping
10	Full mapping

Percent Transform Method Ideas! Alternative ways to identify appropriate data for this input field include restating

⬧ the percentage of formal/work-based learning opportunities that include performance objectives explicitly tied to meeting competency gaps

⬧ the percentage of individuals identified as having competency gaps/learning needs and for which meeting those needs is explicitly tied to formal/work-based learning opportunities.

Formal Hours Used
Path: **Learning** tab**Usage (Formal Learning)** link

☑ Scorecard Report
☑ Index Report

For this value, calculate the total formal learning hours for content accessed or completed by learners. Calculation: (the number of hours available) × (the number of employees who accessed or completed the learning content). For example, if 100 new employees participated in an eight-hour workshop on consultative selling techniques, the formal hours used equals 800.

Formal Hours Used by Employee Group
Path: **Learning** tab**Usage (Formal Learning)** link

☑ Scorecard Report
☑ Index Report

Enter the number of formal learning hours accessed or completed for each of the following employee groups. To determine these figures, add the total hours across all content for each employee group. Enter as total number of hours for each of the following employee groups:

⬧ executives and senior managers
⬧ middle managers

- first line supervisors
- production/technical
- administrative
- customer service
- sales
- IT
- other.

Formal Hours by Delivery Method
Path: **Learning** tab**Output (Formal Learning)** link

- ☑ Scorecard Report
- ☑ Index Report

Another stalwart of the data collected for the *ASTD State of the Industry Report* and for the ASTD BEST Award submissions, these figures are closely monitored by elite-performing learning functions. This input indicator focuses on the distribution of technology versus non-technology delivery methods. Enter the percentage of formal learning hours available via each of the following delivery methods:

- live instructor-led real classroom
- live instructor-led virtual (online) classroom
- live instructor-led remote, but not online (for example, satellite, video conference, teleconference)
- self-paced online (networked)
- self-paced stand-alone (non-networked) computer-based (that is, CD-ROM)
- mobile technology (for example, PDA, MP3, cell phone)
- technology other than computer and mobile (for example, videotape, audio CD)
- self-paced non-technology delivered (that is, print)
- other.

Knowledge Repository Access
Path: **Learning** tab**Usage (Work-Based Learning)** link

- ☑ Index Report

Enter the total number of requests to knowledge repositories that are created and/or maintained by the learning function.

Knowledge Repository Time
Path: **Learning** tab**Usage (Work-Based Learning)** link

- ☑ Scorecard Report
- ☑ Index Report

Determine the total number of hours employees spent viewing and interacting with knowledge repository content. Enter the total time logged by all employees in all online knowledge repositories that are created and/or maintained by the learning function.

Knowledge Repository Time by Employee Group

Path: **Learning** tab**Usage (Work-Based Learning)** link

- ☑ Scorecard Report
- ☑ Index Report

To gather this data, consult the organization's learning management systems and business leaders to develop the general scope of usage among employee groups within their span of accountability. For this section, enter the total number of hours logged viewing knowledge repository content for each of the following employee groups:

- executives and senior managers
- middle managers
- first line supervisors
- production/technical
- administrative
- customer service
- sales
- IT
- other.

Knowledge Sharing Time as a Novice

Path: **Learning** tab**Usage (Work-Based Learning)** link

- ☑ Scorecard Report
- ☑ Index Report

Enter the average number of hours spent per employee as recipients in knowledge sharing, including participation in communities of practice, expert consultation, and coaching.

Knowledge Sharing Time as an Expert

Path: **Learning** tab**Usage (Work-Based Learning)** link

- ☑ Scorecard Report
- ☑ Index Report

Enter the average number of hours spent per employee as a *provider* in knowledge sharing, including participation in communities of practice, expert consultation, and coaching.

Time on Challenging Work Assignments
Path: **Learning** tab**Usage (Work-Based Learning)** link

- ☑ Scorecard Report
- ☑ Index Report

Enter the average percentage of employee time spent on challenging work assignments, deliberately assigned as a learning opportunity.

Time on Other Discretionary Learning
Path: **Learning Usage (Work-Based Learning)** link

- ☑ Scorecard Report
- ☑ Index Report

Indicate the average number of employee hours spent on unstructured, self-directed learning activities, including Internet/intranet searches, external bulletin board participation, participation in online user groups, review of journals or trade publications, and accessing online libraries or information databases.

Performance Tab Indicators

This section focuses on the *effects* of workplace learning. Many of the data entry fields in the Performance tab represent the measurements that learning executives use to describe the overall effect of the learning on performance improvement. In this tab, workplace learning professionals assess the strategic outcomes of performance improvement efforts, productivity improvement, business outcomes, and levels of satisfaction among major learning function customers.

Competence Gap
Path: **Performance** tab**Compatibility** link

- ☑ Index Report

Indicate the extent of gap between the current and desired competence levels to meet current business needs. Enter a number from 0 to 10, using the following scale as a guide:

Value	Interpretation
0	No gap
1 – 2	Minimal gap
3 – 4	Moderately low gap
5	Moderate gap
6 – 7	Moderately high gap
8 – 9	High gap
10	Complete disjoint

Human Capital Readiness Percent Transform Method Ideas!

Two readiness measures may require workplace learning professionals to apply the percent transform method. For example, consider readiness to indicate:

* the percentage of the organization that is fully mobilized to meet strategy
* the percentage of likely challenges the organization is able to meet.

Seek out people within the organization most likely to provide an accurate judgment of readiness. As a rule of thumb, the more senior the managers, the more likely their estimates, as it relates to their accountability, will be accurate.

When seeking out the person best able to provide these figures, consider applying the following test:

* Consider who in your organization is likely to give the most reliable figure if asked about readiness by a member of the press or someone sitting on the Board of Directors. Military organizations are particularly adept at estimating and describing readiness, as readiness is one of the fundamental products military organizations produce.

Percent Transform Method Ideas! Consider using some measures from an annual employee survey, such as knowledge of job, as general guides for this input.

Human Capital Readiness

Path: **Performance** tab**Compatibility** link

☑ Scorecard Report
☑ Index Report

Determine the readiness of the organization's workforce to meet future business needs. Specifically, enter a figure that describes the level to which current competence matches desired competence for future business needs. Use the following scale as a guide:

Value	Interpretation
0	Complete unreadiness
1 – 2	Minimal readiness
3 – 4	Moderately low readiness
5	Moderate readiness
6 – 7	Moderately high readiness
8 – 9	High readiness
10	Maximal readiness

Reduction in Time to Competence/Performance

Path: **Performance** tab**Compatibility** link

☑ Scorecard Report
☑ Index Report

Determine and enter the average percentage reduction in total hours of time to competence/desired proficiency across all employee groups.

Individual Productivity Improvement

Path: **Performance** tab**Productivity** link

☑ Scorecard Report
☑ Index Report

Determine overall improvement in individual output across all employees. Enter a number from 0 to 10, using the following scale as a guide:

Value	Interpretation
0	No improvement
1 – 2	Minimal improvement
3 – 4	Moderately low improvement
5	Moderate improvement
6 – 7	Moderately high improvement
8 – 9	High improvement
10	Maximal improvement

Business Unit Productivity Improvement

Path: **Performance** tab**Productivity** link

☑ Scorecard Report

☑ Index Report

Determine improvement in business unit productivity across all business units. Enter a number from 0 to 10, using the following scale as a guide:

Value	Interpretation
0	No improvement
1 – 2	Minimal improvement
3 – 4	Moderately low improvement
5	Moderate improvement
6 – 7	Moderately high improvement
8 – 9	High improvement
10	Maximal improvement

Customer Satisfaction

Path: **Performance** tab**Business Outcomes** link

☑ Scorecard Report

☑ Index Report

Most organizations possess a plethora of customer satisfaction data for the organization's product suite. The challenge lies in distilling (possibly) reams of customer satisfaction data into a single, definitive figure for entry.

Enter the overall average customer satisfaction rating for quality and consistency of the organization's products and services for all currently serviced and maintained product lines. Enter a number from 0 to 10, using the following scale as a guide:

Value	Interpretation
0	Complete dissatisfaction
1 – 2	Minimal satisfaction
3 – 4	Moderately low satisfaction
5	Moderate satisfaction
6 – 7	Moderately high satisfaction
8 – 9	High satisfaction
10	Complete satisfaction

Percent Transform Method Ideas! Alternative ways to identify appropriate data for this input field include restating

- ❖ the percentage of customers reporting high levels of satisfaction
- ❖ the percentage of customers reporting a level of satisfaction above a specified threshold.

Productivity Percent Transform Method Tips!

Productivity is an academic construct historically used to develop mathematical models for demand and pricing. Despite its mask of precision, productivity can be described in numerous, perhaps contradictory, ways. Determine how the organization conceives of and measures productivity, and determine the amount of productivity increases that senior management considers acceptable, normal, and exceptional.

Possible restatements for use with the percent transform method include

- ❖ the percentage of improvement over the previous year (using the same measures of productivity that your senior management uses)
- ❖ the percentage of productivity goal increases achieved.

Revenue

Path: **Performance** tab**Business Outcomes** link

- ☑ Scorecard Report
- ☑ Index Report

Most workplace learning professionals locate this information from the finance department or via an annual report for the organization. When determining the total revenue generated by the business, include all recognized customer, operating, investment, rent, and accrued, unbilled revenue. For governmental organizations, enter the budget figure in place of revenue.

Income/Profit

Path: **Performance** tab**Business Outcomes** link

- ☑ Scorecard Report
- ☑ Index Report

Enter the net profit or net income *before taxes*. Consult with the finance department or refer to the organization's annual report to locate this information. Since many organizations maintain several financial measures describing profit in varying levels of detail and complexity, enter the simplest and most precise number possible.

Some organizations having difficulty locating this value can leverage the following calculation: (sum of revenue and gains) − (sum of expenses and losses). For organizations with more sophisticated accounting systems, include any effects related to discontinued operations, extraordinary items, total income taxes, and minority interest.

For all stock-issuing organizations, do not include payments of stock dividends as an expense. Banks should include securities gains and losses. Governmental organizations should enter 0.

Revenue from New Products/Services

Path: **Performance** tab**Business Outcomes** link

- ☑ Scorecard Report
- ☑ Index Report

In this entry, try to be as consistent as possible in applying the criteria for recognizing revenue from new products and services as ordinary revenue in the organization. Include revenue from products and services that were newly introduced in the last budget year. Also include revenue from products and services that may have been developed and released in a budget year prior to the most previous budget year that did not recognize revenue until the current year. As with the straight revenue figure, include all recognized customer, operating, investment, rent, and accrued unbilled revenue.

Organizations reporting in a currency that has been revalued by their nation's central banking system in the previous year, or whose currencies have experienced high volatility due to inflation or other reasons, should contact the WLP Scorecard team for assistance in entering this figure.

Organizational Readiness

Path: **Performance** tab**Business Outcomes** link

- ☑ Scorecard Report
- ☑ Index Report

Determine the organizational readiness for future organization changes, market changes, and environmental changes. Enter a number from 0 to 10, using the following scale as a guide:

Value	Interpretation
0	Complete unreadiness
1 – 2	Minimal readiness
3 – 4	Moderately low readiness
5	Moderate readiness
6 – 7	Moderately high readiness
8 – 9	High readiness
10	Maximal readiness

C-Level Satisfaction

Path: **Performance** tab**Perceptions** link

- ☑ Scorecard Report
- ☑ Index Report

Enter a figure that describes the top level and senior executives' satisfaction with the learning function's performance. Enter a number from 0 to 10, using the following scale as a guide:

Value	Interpretation
0	Complete dissatisfaction
1 – 2	Minimal satisfaction
3 – 4	Moderately low satisfaction
5	Moderate satisfaction
6 – 7	Moderately high satisfaction
8 – 9	High satisfaction
10	Complete satisfaction

C-Level and Business Unit Leader Tip

For both C-level and business unit leader satisfaction, be prepared for brutally honest feedback. In obtaining this data, brutal honesty is critical since these two measures of satisfaction often have more direct bearing on learning function sustainability than any other single factor. Using percent transforms as suggested above might be reasonable substitutes for using the applicable rubrics in some cases, yet we advise against doing so. We suggest that the figures you enter into the WLP Scorecard be as simply stated as the rubrics are. You may even want to survey CEOs and business leaders using the actual rubrics attached to these two measures.

Business Unit Leader Satisfaction

Path: **Performance** tab**Perceptions** link

- ☑ Scorecard Report
- ☑ Index Report

Enter a figure that describes the business unit leader/manager satisfaction with the learning function activities provided for their department/division. Enter a number from 0 to 10, using the following scale as a guide:

Value	Interpretation
0	Complete dissatisfaction
1 – 2	Minimal satisfaction
3 – 4	Moderately low satisfaction
5	Moderate satisfaction
6 – 7	Moderately high satisfaction
8 – 9	High satisfaction
10	Complete satisfaction

Learner Satisfaction (Formal)

Path: **Performance** tab**Perceptions** link

- ☑ Scorecard Report
- ☑ Index Report

Enter a figure that describes learner satisfaction with formal learning opportunities (most commonly, classroom or online courses). Enter a figure that describes the average across all programs. Avoid entering a figure that might overstate satisfaction, such as learning satisfaction with the most popular learning programs. Enter a number from 0 to 10, using the following scale as a guide:

Value	Interpretation
0	Complete dissatisfaction
1 – 2	Minimal satisfaction
3 – 4	Moderately low satisfaction
5	Moderate satisfaction
6 – 7	Moderately high satisfaction
8 – 9	High satisfaction
10	Complete satisfaction

Learner Satisfaction (Work-Based)

Path: **Performance** tab**Perceptions** link

- ☑ Scorecard Report
- ☑ Index Report

Be prepared for some straight talk in the feedback received from learners! Enter a figure that describes learner satisfaction with work-based learning opportunities—coaching, knowledge sharing, reference content, and access to experts. As with satisfaction of formal learning, average the satisfaction across all opportunities and avoid weighting the average by including only popular programs. Enter a number from 0 to 10, using the following scale as a guide:

Value	Interpretation
0	Complete dissatisfaction
1 – 2	Minimal satisfaction
3 – 4	Moderately low satisfaction
5	Moderate satisfaction
6 – 7	Moderately high satisfaction
8 – 9	High satisfaction
10	Complete satisfaction

Now that we've reviewed all of the input indicators available for generating the Scorecard or Index Reports, the next chapter focuses on generating the Scorecard Report and analyzing the data to determine what needs to be managed in the learning function.

Chapter 11

The Scorecard Reports:
Mapping the Learning Function with Powerful Decision-Making Tools

---
❋

In This Chapter

- Generating and customizing the Scorecard Report
- Exporting data and charts
- Positioning the Scorecard Report findings with the CEO
- Defining the balanced scorecard dimensions
- Interpreting report results

❋

After entering the data for a learning function in the WLP Scorecard, workplace learning professionals can create four separate Scorecard Reports: Financial, Operations, Customer, and Innovation. Each Scorecard Report corresponds to a balanced scorecard management dimension. Customized Scorecard Reports are also available according to organizational characteristics such as size, region, and industry.

In a Scorecard Report, results are displayed as a standard set of learning metrics mapped to Financial, Operations, Customer, and Innovation management dimensions. Many of the learning metrics are ratio measures, or per-unit measures. In the same way that financial ratios capture behaviors that contribute to organizational performance, the ratios displayed in each of the four Scorecard Reports depict how well organizational resources are being used in to improve performance, create impact at the business unit level, and achieve short-term performance goals.

Generating and Interpreting the Scorecard Reports

Users can access the Scorecard Reports using the four tabs at the top of the screen. Each tab represents the four dimensions of the balanced scorecard—Financial, Operations, Customer, and Innovation. Click the Customize tab to customize a report.

Benchmarking Forum members see an additional tab labeled BMF for additional customization options.

To Generate the Scorecard Reports:

1. Open the WLP Scorecard.
2. Click the **Scorecard Reports** label on the navigation bar. The report appears on the screen.
3. Select the **Year:** drop-down menu to select the appropriate report year, if needed.
4. Click the **Financial, Operations, Customer,** or **Innovation** tabs at the top of the screen to navigate to the desired indicators.
5. Use the descriptions of the indicators below to analyze the data in the **Your Organization** columns and benchmark the results compared to the data in the **All Organizations** columns.
6. To download the report, cut and paste the report data into a spreadsheet or word processing document.
7. To display a chart for an indicator, click the indicator name. A chart comparing the learning organization score with the mean of all organizations appears.

Figure 11-1: The Financial Dimension Scorecard Report & Chart

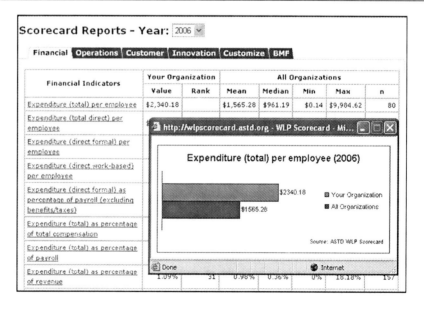

Tip! Charts are available for each metric displaying a value for your organization. The chart compares your organization's score to the mean score of all organizations in the database. Copy the chart by right-clicking in the chart area and selecting Copy from the shortcut menu. Paste the chart information into any document.

Tip! Each table displayed in the Scorecard Reports can be cut and pasted into a spreadsheet or word processing file. To complete this process:

- Click and drag to select the table to copy.
- Right-click in the table.
- Select **Copy** from the short-cut menu.
- Paste the table into an active spreadsheet or word processing file.

The WLP Scorecard automatically calculates and generates a comprehensive set of learning metrics and displays them in a table consisting of six columns. The two leftmost columns contain values for your organization. The four rightmost columns contain a set of descriptive statistics related to each metric—including the mean, median, minimum, maximum, and the number of organizations in the database contributing data for that metric.

Figure 11-2: The Operations Dimension Scorecard Report

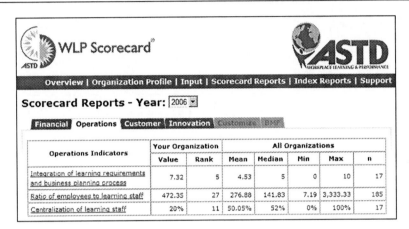

Operations Indicators	Your Organization		All Organizations				
	Value	Rank	Mean	Median	Min	Max	n
Integration of learning requirements and business planning process	7.32	5	4.53	5	0	10	17
Ratio of employees to learning staff	472.35	27	276.88	141.83	7.19	3,333.33	185
Centralization of learning staff	20%	11	50.05%	52%	0%	100%	17

Working With Reports

In the Customize section, select types of organizations and a subset of indicators to generate a customized report (figure 11-3).

To Customize the Scorecard Reports:
1. Open the WLP Scorecard.
2. Click the **Scorecard Reports** label on the navigation bar. The report appears on the screen.
3. Select the **Year:** drop-down menu to select the appropriate report year, if needed.
4. Click the **Customize** tab at the top of the screen.
5. The Customize Reports screen appears.
6. Select
   - the type of organizations you want to be compared to using the drop-down menus
   - one or more indicators that you want to compare—financial, operations, customer and innovation.
7. Click the **Generate Report** button at the bottom of the page to create and display a customized Scorecard Report.

Tip! Hold the **CTRL** key to select multiple indicators.

Table 11-1: The Scorecard Reports Data Descriptions

Your Organization Column	Description
Value	A calculated number describing the quantity of an indicator or metric.
	Example: Based on the "ratio of employees to learning staff" value in figure 11-2, there are 472.35 employees in the organization for each full-time equivalent learning function staff member.
Rank	The location of a particular value in the set of all values for a particular indicator or metric.
	Example: In this example, "ratio of employees to learning staff" has a rank of 5 out of 27, making it one of the higher values in the distribution.

All Organizations Column	Description
Mean	The mean score is considered the most robust, or least affected by the presence of extreme values (outliers), of all types of central tendency measures, because each number in the data set has an impact on its (mean) value.
	The mean is represented by the following formula: **Mean = Sum of all numbers / by the # of values that make up that sum**
	The mean is a good measure of central tendency for roughly symmetric distributions but can be misleading in skewed, or nonsymmetric, distributions because it can be influenced a great deal by extreme values. Therefore, other statistics, such as the median, may be more informative and appropriate for distributions that are quite often skewed.
	Example: In figure 11-2, the mean value for the "ratio of employees to learning staff" is approximately 276. This benchmark indicates that for all organizations that responded for this indicator in the WLP Scorecard, they have approximately 276 employees in the organization for each full-time equivalent learning function staff member.
Median	The median is the middle of a distribution arranged by magnitude: half of the scores are above the median, and half are below. The median is less sensitive to extreme scores than the mean, which makes it a better measure than the mean for highly skewed distributions. For example, the median income of a demographic group is usually more informative than the mean income.
	Example: In figure 11-2, 50 percent of all organization learning functions entering data in the WLP Scorecard for the "ratio of employees to learning function staff" entered ratio values above 141 and 50 percent of the responding organizations entered values below the median.
Min	The minimum value of all valid entries for that indicator or metric.
	Example: In figure 11-2 the min. value is 7.19.
Max	Indicates the maximum value of all valid entries entered by all organizations who responded.
	Example: In figure 11-2, the maximum value entered for the "ratio of employees to learning staff" is 3,333—meaning that one organization using the WLP Scorecard has approximately 3,333 employees for each full-time equivalent learning function staff member.
n	The number of organizations that entered data for the input indicator.
	Example: Figure 11-2 indicates that as of the time this report was viewed, 185 organizations entered data for the "ratio of employees to learning staff" indicator. The number of organizations appearing under the "all organizations" section of the WLP Scorecard report may change daily—hence possibly changing the mean, median, min, and max values displayed in the report.

Figure 11-3: The Customize Reports Screen

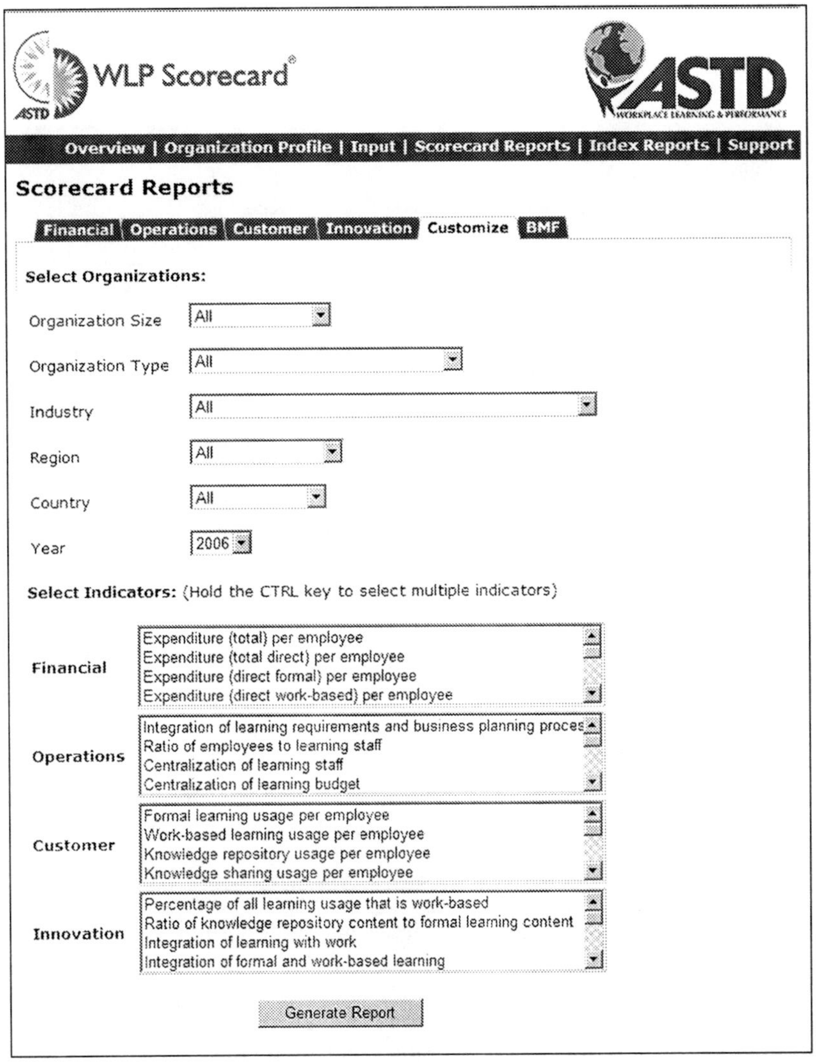

Interpreting the Scorecard Reports Results

These days, selling training is an upward battle for workplace learning professionals lacking a concrete idea of how it is going to impact the organization. Senior management demands solid results—or at least a promise of positive results. Metrics provide the means to quantify results.

Measuring learning—and more important measuring what matters—is different for every organization. Senior management wants to know how training is going to help the organization to increase revenue, lower costs, maximize productivity and profitability, and keep pace with (or outpace) the competition.

Using Scorecard Reports: A Learning Manager's Perspective

Learning leaders often contact ASTD when studying the most recent *ASTD State of the Industry Report.* Eager to better understand how the efficiency and the effectiveness of their learning functions stack up to others, the leaders ask for guidance on interpreting their learning function figures when compared with the *State of the Industry Report* results.

During one such conversation, the workplace learning professional queried, "We've been looking at the *State of the Industry Report* and want to follow up on some of the figures. According to the report, companies spend $950 per employee per year on average for workplace learning. According to our calculations, our organization spends only $400 per year. Are we out of line? Help me understand what these numbers mean."

The first step is to clarify the immediate questions. Identify any other measures of value, and discover any deeper issues posing challenges for the learning manager.

In other words, when using the WLP Scorecard, determine what set of learning and business measures tell the most compelling story of where the learning function has been in the past year. Paint the best picture of where the learning function should go in the next year, and then determine how to get there.

By reporting on a wide-range of learning metrics according to the four key areas of managerial effort, the Scorecard Reports provide answers to the questions "Just what do we want from our learning programs" and "How do we know whether we're getting there?"

(Sidebar continues on page 146)

Using Scorecard Reports: A Learning Manager's Perspective (continued)

The next step is to put the learning manager's numbers into perspective. Compare the learning function numbers to the full range of figures reported for the measures of interest. Clarify what a typical range might be. The learning manager usually begins to feel relieved at this point—either his or her figures fall within the typical range or there is a ready explanation if they don't.

By reviewing a set of descriptive statistics like those displayed in the Scorecard Report, the learning manager expands the sense of what is normal and gains a greater confidence in current resource allocations.

After achieving a baseline understanding of this core information, the next step is to analyze organization size, industry, and type, and then to make comparisons according to a finer mesh. At this point, learning managers often have an "a-ha" moment, calling upon their knowledge of the industry sector and gaining new insights into what industry competitors might be doing.

In analyzing the Scorecard Report data, if a learning manager determines that industry competitors spent 25 percent more per employee or could produce one hour of content at two-thirds the price, then he or she has gained a richer understanding of the learning function and raised a new set of compelling questions.

Although the WLP Scorecard helps to illuminate data that was already available, workplace learning professionals need to do a bit of probing and reframing. Often they need guidance on how to interpret the report findings. The WLP Scorecard leads to a greater understanding of the story behind the numbers by reporting a standard set of learning metrics on the managerial dimensions of financial, operations, customer, and innovation, and by allowing users to make comparisons according to industry characteristics.

Figure 11-4: The Customized Scorecard Report

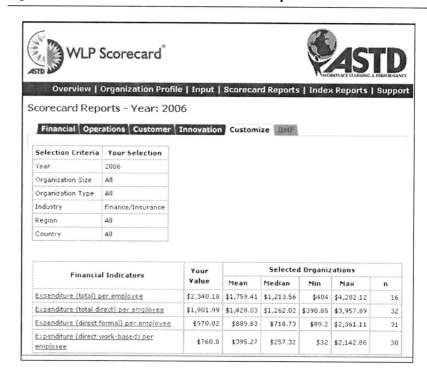

Although each organization is different, management often dictates what matters to them. Similarly, workplace learning professionals need to clearly communicate what the learning function needs in terms of time, resources, and funding to achieve those results.

The challenge is establishing a link between the learning activities that took place weeks ago and the successes that departments or the organization celebrate today. Workplace learning professionals need to narrow down a few specific metrics that are valued by senior management, and to establish realistic targets for measurement and performance using those metrics.

Balanced scorecards are one solution to create this link in a systematic way. The WLP Scorecard connects learning investments and activities to business outcomes. Since the WLP Scorecard uses a standard set of workplace learning, performance, and business metrics, it provides a complete performance measurement system. By reporting both common business metrics *and* learning-centric metrics, rather than on learning-centric metrics alone, the WLP Scorecard provides a common language for learning professionals, learning executives, and non-learning executives to communicate about workplace learning and performance.

The WLP Scorecard facilitates comparison of the cost-effectiveness of learning and performance activities, not just levels of expenditure. WLP Scorecard users can explore what organizations spend, and what levels and types of expenditures are most effective.

As shown in figure 11-5, the WLP Scorecard includes four dimensions and major managerial categories that define the activities requiring managerial attention. A performance measurement system focuses on metrics and indicators that describe each of these categories. Notice that the major managerial categories of total learning expenditure and internal operations are further broken down into more precisely defined areas of managerial attention. Each of these areas contains sets of metrics and indicators that describe activity in more detail for measurement and fine tuning.

The Scorecard Reports provide learning indicators mapped to these four perspectives—financial, operations, customer, and innovation. The power of this tool can only be harnessed by fully understanding each of these four dimensions as described in the next sections. This is an ideal starting point for workplace learning professionals to develop a balanced scorecard tailored to the organization and to report the learning function activity in a way that both learning professionals and senior management value.

The Financial Dimension

The first step in communicating learning in the balanced scorecard framework is to evaluate the financial aspects of the learning function. This process helps to determine whether the learning function's financial performance is supporting the right organizational and financial goals.

Financial Dimension Indicators

The Scorecard Report displays four categories of financial measures including:

Total Expenditure:
* expenditure (total) per employee
* expenditure (total) as percentage of total compensation
* expenditure (total) as percentage of payroll
* expenditure (total) as percentage of revenue
* expenditure (total) as percentage of income/profit
* expenditure by employee groups.

Direct Expenditure:
* expenditure (total direct) per employee
* percentage of direct expenditure on external services
* percentage of direct expenditure on tuition reimbursement
* percentage of direct expenditure by type of solution
* percentage of direct expenditure on technology infrastructure

(Sidebar continues on page 148)

Figure 11-5: The WLP Scorecard Dimensions and Managerial Categories

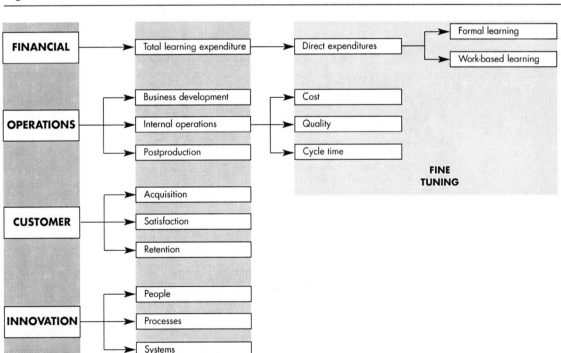

147

Financial Dimension Indicators (continued)

Direct Expenditure:
* percentage of direct expenditure on learning staff (including benefits/taxes)
* percentage of direct expenditure on learning staff (excluding benefits/taxes).

Direct Expenditures for Formal Learning:
* expenditure (direct formal) per employee
* expenditure (direct formal) as percentage of payroll (without taxes and benefits)
* direct cost per formal learning hour available
* direct cost per formal learning hour used.

Direct Expenditures for Work-Based Learning:
* expenditure (direct work-based) per employee
* direct cost per hour of work-based learning used.

When non-learning executives develop balanced scorecards to manage their businesses, they typically begin by identifying those financial measures believed to be the most descriptive of the health and profitability of the organization. Most often these include residual income, economic value added (EVA), operating profits, net profits, operating profit after taxes, earnings before interest and taxes (EBIT), return on net assets (ROA), earnings before interest, taxes, depreciation and amortization (EBITDA), return on equity (ROE), cash flow return-on-investment, and return on capital employed (ROCE).

Although these financial measures may not directly apply to the learning function, it is important that learning executives understand how the learning function financial measures affect the financial performance of any organization.

Learning function financial measures include four categories of measures: total expenditure, direct expenditure, direct expenditures for formal learning, and direct expenditures for work-based learning (figure 11-6).

If the learning function is not currently using a balanced scorecard, a good starting point is to find at least one measure from each of the four financial dimension areas to create and tailor a financial metrics scorecard that management views as essential. Beware not to communicate a one-dimensional perspective of total expenditures but rather illustrate the expenditure outlays throughout the learning function. Find and communicate the measures that

Figure 11-6: The WLP Scorecard Financial Dimension

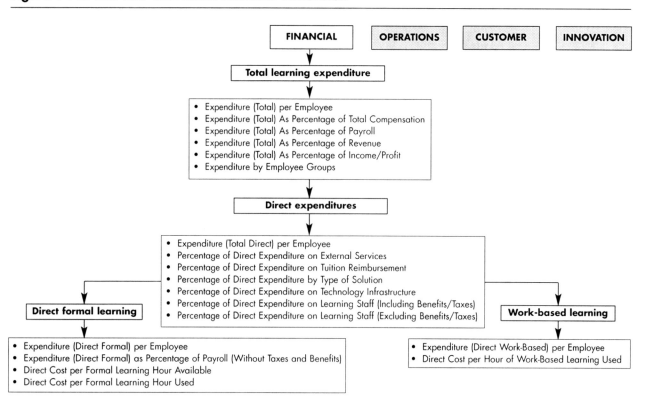

best describe the financial *profile* of learning function when it's at peak performance.

The Operations Dimension

Besides aligning strategy and initiatives, another key benefit of the scorecard method is that it introduces measurements with a focus beyond financial measurement. The operations dimension, often referred to as the internal business perspective, measures the implementation and execution of business strategy (see figure 11-7).

Figure 11-7: The WLP Scorecard Operations Dimension

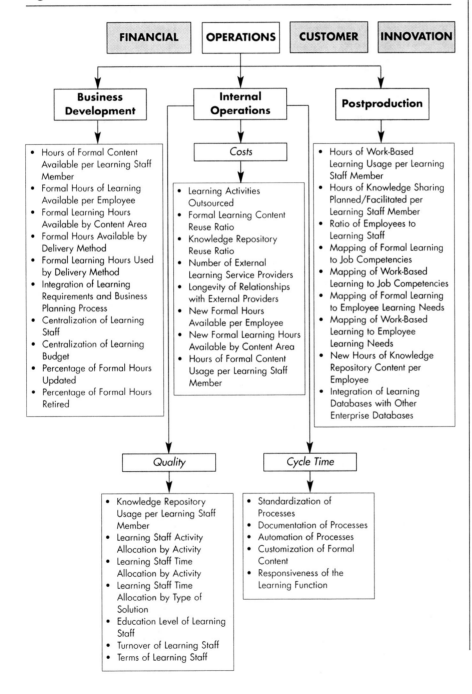

Operations Dimension Indicators

The Scorecard Report provides various operations metrics including

* integration of learning requirements and business planning process
* ratio of employees to learning staff
* centralization of learning staff
* centralization of learning budget
* education level of learning staff
* turnover of learning staff
* tenure of learning staff
* learning staff activity allocation by activity
* learning staff time allocation by activity
* learning staff time allocation by type of solution
* hours of formal content available per learning staff member
* hours of formal content usage per learning staff member
* hours of work-based learning usage per learning staff member
* knowledge repository usage per learning staff member
* hours of knowledge sharing planned/facilitated per learning staff member
* formal learning content reuse ratio
* knowledge repository reuse ratio
* standardization of processes
* documentation of processes
* automation of processes
* customization of formal content
* responsiveness of the learning function
* number of external learning service providers
* longevity of relationships with external providers
* learning activities outsourced
* formal hours of learning available per employee
* few formal hours available per employee
* percentage of formal hours updated
* percentage of formal hours retired
* formal learning hours available by content area

(Sidebar continues on page 150)

Operations Dimension Indicators *(continued)*

* new formal learning hours available by content area
* formal hours available by delivery method
* formal learning hours used by delivery method
* mapping of formal learning to job competencies
* mapping of work-based learning to job competencies
* mapping of formal learning to employee learning needs
* mapping of work-based learning to employee learning needs
* new hours of knowledge repository content per employee
* integration of learning databases with other enterprise databases.

Business Development Indicators

The Scorecard Report provides various business development indicators including

* hours of formal content available per learning staff member
* formal hours of learning available per employee
* formal learning hours available by content area
* formal hours available by delivery method
* formal learning hours used by delivery method
* integration of learning requirements and business planning process
* centralization of learning staff
* centralization of learning budget
* percentage of formal hours updated
* percentage of formal hours retired.

Figure 11-8: Example of the Operations Dimensions Cycles

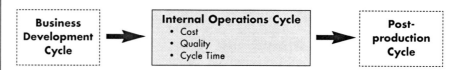

A key difference between this dimension and the other three is that an operation has a discrete beginning and end. Good operations represent complete cycles of activity and tend to be repeated with little or no variation in performance. Since operations are typically quantifiable, the costs associated with them are usually very easy to determine. Operations are often closely tied to an organization's hard assets, because most operations consume hard assets at predictable rates. Of all the dimensions, the operation dimension is the most manageable and receives the preponderance of managerial attention within most organizations.

Perhaps the biggest challenge in defining operations is precisely delineating where value-creating operations begin and end. One of the great strengths of the balanced scorecard methodology is its recognition and accommodation of this troublesome phenomenon. The balanced scorecard method takes the traditional notion of an operations cycle and adds a smaller cycle to both the beginning and the end.

The WLP Scorecard operations cycle is composed of three cycles: business development, internal operations, and postproduction (figure 11-8). Together these three cycles make up the unique internal value chain and are flexible enough to extend the boundaries of the overall operation cycle such that the processes can be brought into measurable and manageable states. To fully understand all metrics and aspects of the operations dimension, let's take a detailed look at each cycle and its metric.

Business Development

Business development, the first step in the operations dimension, refers to what is broadly called market research—that is, discovering the needs and wants of selected population segments, identifying the overall size of markets, estimating product demand, and setting up pricing and revenue models.

First, develop the blueprints for building a business machine to create value, define operational procedures, and demarcate what is out of bounds. In developing business for the learning function, the workplace learning professional must create the demand for learning products and set up systems to allocate resources to meet those demands. During this process, leveraging instructional design skills and performing analyses will ensure that training is the right solution for the alleged performance deficits. This critical step in learning operations management requires that workplace learning professionals use or acquire competencies within the learning function.

Most non-learning executives populate this area of a balanced scorecard with traditional marketing metrics (that is, new product revenue, expected market share, or time to market).

Workplace learning professionals need to measure this area in terms of available competencies, skills inventory, capacity, usage, and adaptability. Remember, this process seeks to set up boundaries and parameters—and the means to accomplishing these goals requires management of working capital and building an efficient learning function quickly.

Internal Operations

Internal operations—probably the most labor-intensive step in the operations dimension—focuses on designing the measures and performance objectives by which learning programs, and ultimately organization-wide performance, are produced. Measures in this area reflect the need for consistency, efficiency, timeliness, and predictability in both the production and the delivery of learning programs.

For almost a century, internal operations have been managed almost exclusively by financial statements. This has given rise to an effective, elegant analytical framework for managing and measuring internal operations that provides a standard for operational excellence. This framework has three components: cost, quality, and cycle time.

Cost

Cost is as important to managing the learning function as it is to any other business unit. The most enduring learning function metrics tend to focus on cost ratios such as expenditure per employee.

More progressive organizations invest in activity-based costing systems that capture the contribution of human capital more efficiently than traditional cost measures. If available, these types of measures should be used for any learning function.

Based on years of ASTD research, the cost indicators available in the WLP Scorecard represent the activities most closely the tied to learning function cost centers and are, therefore, most predictive of future learning costs.

Quality

Quality has been foremost in the management of organizational operations for decades. Historically, management determined an acceptable level of defects because quality was thought to be highly correlated with costs. In other words, the lower the quality, the lower the costs. Over the past 30 years, however, the total quality management movement has shifted organizational thinking from a view of providing products and services of a minimum acceptable level of quality to a more holistic view where all parts of the organization are committed to high levels of quality throughout the production cycle.

Business Development

According to the 2006 *ASTD State the Industry Report*, over 40 percent of performance improvement resources in top-performing learning organizations are devoted to non-learning solutions.

Cost: Most non-learning business functions measure cost by using historical information, identifying the short- and long-term goals of the organization, and, most of all, applying a lot of common sense.

Cost Indicators

The Scorecard Report provides various cost indicators including

* learning activities outsourced
* formal learning content reuse ratio
* knowledge repository reuse ratio
* number of external learning service providers
* longevity of relationships with external providers
* new formal hours available per employee
* new formal learning hours available by content area
* hours of formal content usage per learning staff member.

Quality Indicators

The Scorecard Report provides various quality indicators including

* knowledge repository usage per learning staff member
* learning staff activity allocation by activity
* learning staff time allocation by activity
* learning staff time allocation by type of solution
* education level of learning staff
* turnover of learning staff
* tenure of learning staff.

Cycle Time Indicators

The Scorecard Report provides various cycle time indicators including

* standardization of processes
* documentation of processes
* automation of processes
* customization of formal content
* responsiveness of the learning function.

This focus on total quality has created more of a balance between process level, individual employee, and customer experience. As a result, the defect rates, amount of scrap, rework rates, and ratio of inventory have readily gained status as core measures in any quality program. Statistical process control methods enable organizations to determine when processes are in or out of control and at what point the process needs to be adjusted to meet product specifications.

More frequently these hard methods of measurement are being supplemented by softer measures of customer experience (that is, customer experiences of purchasing, accessing, or servicing products). Customers now perceive products and services as a bundled pair so much so that an unpleasant experience, either before or after the purchase, can ruin a customer's perception of quality just as easily as if the product itself were defective.

For many organizations, especially those in the service industry, quality measures are highly customer-centric and address areas such as satisfaction, responsiveness, time to resolution, and even pleasantness of customer experience. Similarly, quality measurements in the learning function are no longer a matter of receiving top scores on smile sheets. As with non-learning business functions, quality needs to strike a balance between process level measures and individual level measures.

Knowledge repository usage and learning staff time allocation are process-level measures that affect both the timeliness and the integrity of outputs. Education, turnover, and tenure of the learning staff describe quality in terms of inputs.

As a best practice, workplace learning professionals should compare the quality indicators in the Scorecard Reports in conjunction with the customer dimension data. In all cases, resist any temptation to describe the quality of the learning function *primarily* in terms of others' perceptions.

Cycle Time

Many business operations are repeatable events that have a clear beginning and end, and a finite number of well-defined tasks with precise criteria for demarcating initiation and completion. Those events typically consume a predictable amount of time and resources, and the resources required may decrease as these processes become more efficient.

Some of the most familiar cycles relate to sales, order fulfillment, manufacturing stages, and production. To deliver value, most organizations rely on short cycle times to produce more goods or meet customer expectations in a timely manner.

Throughput is the amount of resources, including time, that is consumed during a cycle. Although some learning executives in the world's top learning organizations have made good use of manufacturing cycle effectiveness—a ratio of processing time to throughput time—they confess that it is an imperfect measure that is not well suited to the learning function.

Learning executives using cycle time to measure learning function activity should keep this measure very simple. For example, learning program development may be taking longer for some initiatives if clearly defined milestones and completion points were not defined early in the process, or if these have not been used previously as traditional metrics.

The WLP Scorecard provides measures to help manage many aspects of learning operations including standardization, documentation, automation of processes, and clarity of beginning and end points. These measures describe the capacity for learning operations to support increasing amounts of throughput.

Customization of formal content and responsiveness of the learning function balance out the above three measures of the structural integrity of the learning function, with softer measures of the capacity and nimbleness of a structure should it need to be expanded.

Postproduction

When buying a new car, most salespersons will likely encourage the buyer to purchase a warranty. For an additional cost, the dealer agrees to repair or replace the vehicle should any manufacturing defect arise. Buyers often feel uncomfortable with such an offer, and respond by saying, "I thought this was a good car! Don't you stand behind anything you sell?" Unrattled, the salesperson will enthusiastically say, "Of course I stand behind our product. If I didn't stand behind it, I would sell you this car and hope I never saw you again. If it lost an axle on the freeway, well, shame on us! But instead I'm willing to stand behind this product for the next 100,000 miles, which is why I am offering you this warranty."

The salesperson is providing a familiar example of postproduction, which refers to the extension of the operational boundaries beyond the main transaction and final delivery of the product or service. The nature of postproduction varies widely depending on industry, and may include

- maintenance
- warranty
- repair
- recycling and disposal
- returns and replacement
- exchanges
- refunds and account credits
- payment processing

Postproduction Indicators

The Scorecard Report provides various postproduction indicators including

* hours of work-based learning usage per learning staff member
* hours of knowledge sharing planned/facilitated per learning staff member
* ratio of employees to learning staff
* mapping of formal learning to job competencies
* mapping of work-based learning to job competencies
* mapping of formal learning to employee learning needs
* mapping of work-based learning to employee learning needs
* new hours of knowledge repository content per employee
* integration of learning databases with other enterprise databases.

* invoicing
* account servicing and billing
* collections
* disputes and complaint resolution
* product or service plan upgrades
* buy-back/consignment.

So how is this relevant to the WLP profession? The well-known saying, "If you put a good person against a bad system, the system will always win," often holds true. Even the most sophisticated, big-ticket learning program will be of no consequence if the learner goes back to a workplace situation where learning is not supported and nurtured.

Historically, trainers often cited a learner's home organization or department as dysfunctional or toxic if there proved to be a lack of learning transfer to the job. After many lessons learned, today's workplace learning professionals understand their critical role and responsibility to extend the learning experience back on the job for all learners.

The products and services of the learning function are delivered to internal customers to improve performance. These internal customers use the learning function products and services to enhance the value proposition of their own products and services, a significant part of which is realized *after* their products and services are delivered.

Postproduction performance in non-learning operations usually consists of a balance between traditional operational metrics (that is, quality adherence, cycle time, and cost), and customer-facing metrics such as satisfaction or upsells.

Like other business units, the learning function is under pressure to push the boundaries of learning and must be held accountable for lasting learning effects after a program's end. Learning executives must ensure and demonstrate that learning is not just a one-shot event. Postproduction metrics capture how well the learning function sustains and reinforces the effects of learning programs to achieve performance goals.

The Customer Dimension

Depending on the organization, learning functions may have one type of customer (that is, other business units) or a diverse customer base including internal employees, contracted partners, and end users of the company's products. Those organizations heavily influenced by total quality management devote a great deal of effort to managing customer expectations, even before any goods and services are ever exchanged. No matter whether customers are internal or external, the processes of acquiring, satisfying, and retaining customers are of utmost importance (figure 11-9).

Figure 11-9: The WLP Scorecard Customer Dimension

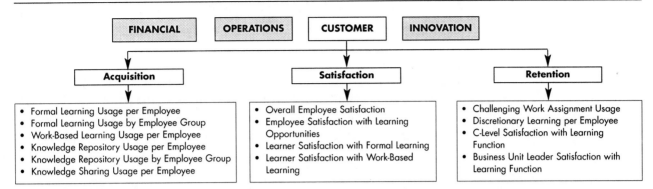

Outside the learning function, managers diligently try to grow the customer base of an organization by identifying new customers and then extracting the most value possible from those customers. Although customer satisfaction receives a lot of attention, it is only one piece of the customer dimension in creating value for any organization. When non-learning executives construct a balanced scorecard in the customer dimension, they typically look at customer activity in three areas:

❋ **Acquisition:** Customer acquisition refers to efforts to increase market share or deliver an organization's value proposition to new or increased market segments. Depending on the products, the value proposition may be communicated through price, quality, brand image, or other unique features.

❋ **Customer Satisfaction:** Customer satisfaction, the second aspect of the customer dimension, is the focus of a great deal of effort in most organizations, and rightly so. Customer satisfaction has both immediate and potential long-term economic benefits that can be measured easily. High customer satisfaction, aside from the financial benefits, is also a noble goal that transcends the buyer/seller relationship and improves the quality of lives.

❋ **Retention/Loyalty:** Few businesses can sustain themselves with a base of one-time customers. Customer retention and loyalty refer to the efforts to generate return business from existing customers and to prevent them from migrating to a competitor. Good customers make economic sense, as any sales manager knows. Companies will try to generate an ongoing cash flow from customers through loyalty programs, after-market service programs, or product enhancements.

Non-learning managers often construct balanced scorecard measures around customer acquisition, satisfaction, and loyalty/retention in markets where they are competing for a top position. The measures chosen reflect the organizational performance goals needed to win, place, or show and not be outpaced by the competition.

Customer Dimension Indicators

The Scorecard Report provides various customer dimension indicators including

Acquisition:
❋ formal learning usage per employee
❋ formal learning usage by employee group
❋ work-based learning usage per employee
❋ knowledge repository usage per employee
❋ knowledge repository usage by employee group
❋ knowledge sharing usage per employee.

Satisfaction:
❋ overall employee satisfaction
❋ employee satisfaction with learning opportunities
❋ learner satisfaction with formal learning
❋ learner satisfaction with work-based learning.

Retention/Loyalty:
❋ challenging work assignment usage
❋ discretionary learning per employee
❋ C-level satisfaction with learning function
❋ business unit leader satisfaction with learning function.

In the short term, innovation drives value through rapid exploitation of new markets. In the long term, it creates value accumulating assets that can become capitalized.

Even though learning function managers have a much smaller, sometimes more dedicated, customer base, they must nevertheless understand their customers in the same way: There are always potentially more customers, and they are ready to spend money even if you don't know they exist.

Satisfaction for this customer base consists of what the learning function has done for them lately. Retaining customers is often considerably harder that acquiring them the first time. For these reasons, the learning function must design its customer performance success plan around the areas of acquisition, satisfaction, and loyalty/retention.

Customer satisfaction is determined by individual learner expectations and experiences, and should be fairly straightforward. As a best practice, be sure to focus on the satisfaction of business leaders and senior managers. These professionals sponsor future learning programs and facilitate if the learning is allowed to be applied back on the job. On-the-job learning transfer and application requires an alignment of individual learner satisfaction and business unit leader/senior manager satisfaction.

Innovation Dimension Indicators

The Scorecard Report provides various innovation dimension indicators including

People:
* percentage of all learning usage that is work-based
* ratio of knowledge repository content to formal learning content
* percentage of learning staff time spent on non-learning solutions
* number of hours of knowledge sharing planned/facilitated per learning staff.

Processes:
* integration of learning with work
* integration of formal and work-based learning
* percentage of formal learning delivered online
* automation of learning function processes.

Systems:
* maturity of system for collecting, analyzing, and reporting data
* maturity of system for managing formal learning
* maturity of system for managing work-based learning
* infrastructure standardization across the enterprise.

The Innovation Dimension

Today, nearly every organization must continually reinvent itself to survive or compete. Few organizations maintain operational excellence, stability in their customer bases, or sustained profitability (or sustained readiness) without embarking on substantial initiatives to develop unique, core internal capabilities.

Because organizations need continuous innovation, shouldn't the learning function, one of the main drivers of innovation, follow suit? Elite-performing learning professionals sit strategically at the planning table with C-level executives, where they are consulted with and expected to plan and execute innovative learning solutions so the organization will realize performance goals.

Both inside and outside the learning function, innovation is managed at three levels: **people, process,** and **organizational systems.** Therefore, balanced scorecard measures identify critical success factors that relate to the skills inventories at all three levels (figure 11-10). Some measures in the innovation dimension apply to most business units in any organization. As a best practice, align the learning function measures with those used by the organization as a whole as much as possible.

* **People** refers to the human capital aspect of innovation. It captures activities often associated with breakthroughs and innovative work over time. These activities support and are often coincident with highly creative behavior and compelling products.

Figure 11-10: The WLP Scorecard Innovation Dimension

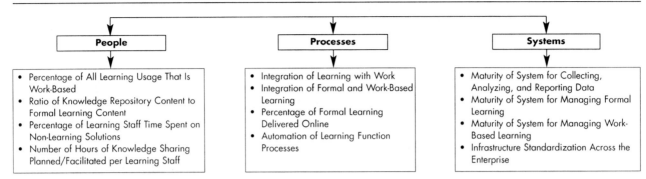

◈ **Processes** refer to both human and nonhuman agents that support information exchanges, accumulation of knowledge, and visualizations of creative thinking.

◈ **Systems** refer to feedback systems that allow creativity to be embedded in organizational structure, assimilated into organizational culture, and shared by all those who could potentially benefit from it. Organizational systems also refer to management practices that encourage and support creativity appropriately—neither suffocating nor granting too much freedom.

Practical Tips for Applying the WLP Scorecard

The classification of WLP Scorecard indicators into the four dimensions, although rigorous and scrupulous, may not be applicable to every learning function or organization. It is very possible that a measure classified in the operations dimension might be more appropriate in the customer dimension. In these cases, let common sense prevail.

Balance Short- and Long-Term Perspectives

The balanced scorecard approach is not just another way to reassemble financial measures so that they appear softer. It is a tool to help define current processes while discovering new processes—both of which enable workplace learning professionals to create more relevant performance goals.

The balanced scorecard approach does not confine users to a 30-day or quarter mentality as most financial statements do. Successful business management requires the ability to shift adeptly between short- and long-term perspectives. When selecting performance goal measures, look for processes that transcend accounting periods because achieving the desired future financial performance may take several years. Use the balanced scorecard methods to connect short-term financial objectives in the financial perspective with longer-term strategic objectives in the other dimensions.

Focus on All Dimensions

The majority of companies and organizations that use the balanced scorecard method put a disproportionate amount of attention on operations and financial measures because hard numbers either readily exist or are easy to obtain. At all costs, avoid repeating the mistakes of the accounting profession by turning metrics into rigid performance targets that serve only to create a roadmap for looting the organization.

Be Strategic

Details are not the same as fundamentals, so don't head straight for the details. The strength of the balanced scorecard approach is that it gives a perspective of the future while referring that perspective back to the here and now. Users can't look to the future—or the past—if they are looking down at their feet. The balanced scorecard aims to illuminate links between performance goals and measures so that the process of creating value becomes clear, and the contribution of the learning function becomes indisputable.

Select the Right Number of Measures

For each dimension of the balanced scorecard—financial, operations, customer, and innovation—try to settle on no more than seven to nine core measures, even though additional measures might be easily applicable. The purpose of mapping the learning function to the balanced scorecard is to create transparency and simplicity, and to facilitate greater understanding of learning function and its contributions to non-learning managers who stand to benefit the most from its successes.

This chapter details how to generate and customize the Scorecard Reports and how to interpret the data for select indicators to make managerial decisions and drive learning function performance. The next chapter illustrates how generate and interpret the Index Reports—the highest level of reporting that allows users to measure and manage the learning function strategically and over a longer-term view than with Scorecard Reports.

Chapter 12

The Index Reports: Creating a WLP Value Plan by Linking Learning to an Organization's Profit Plan

---
In This Chapter

- Generating the Index Reports
- Understanding Index Report overview
- Understanding the WLP Indexes
- Developing a Business Profit and WLP Value Plan

The highest level of reporting, the Index Reports, allows users to measure and manage the learning function strategically over a longer-term view than with Scorecard Reports. The Index Reports map a standard set of learning function measures and predictors to four WLP indexes: alignment, efficiency, effectiveness, and sustainability. These indexes allow users to visualize the areas of the learning function that contribute most to its strength and fitness. Each report flags areas in the learning function that might indicate a weakness within the organization. Each report also contains a feature enabling workplace learning professionals to perform a sensitivity analysis and determine how changes in indicators affect the index score.

Communicating in the Language of Business

Workplace learning professionals need to communicate in the language of business. The information available in the Index Reports is no exception. Following is a conversation with a CEO that typifies the level of detail needed to communicate the learning function value.

Tip! Appendix A includes a quick reference grid indicating all of the required data needed to generate the Index Reports.

159

Using Index Reports: A Conversation with the CEO

This is the approach that one learning executive took.

CEO: Tell me what's happening with all that money that I've allocated to your learning budget.

Learning Executive: We measure and manage workplace learning and performance according to four areas: alignment, effectiveness, efficiency, and sustainability. I'll take just a second to tell you about each of those areas.

In the area of **effectiveness,** we have improved performance in several key business processes. As a result, we have increased overall revenues by almost 10 percent and revenue from new products by over 20 percent. In benchmarking the results of these efforts, we have increased individual employee productivity and customer satisfaction levels to rival those of the highest performing companies. All of these achievements were accomplished **efficiently,** by spending a little more than the industry average per employee, but by delivering much more content just at the time of need, so our delivery costs are well below the industry average.

CEO: Go on.

Learning Executive: We are confident that we can **sustain** our current level of impact in all strategic initiatives, and we still have the capacity to support the new strategic direction over at least two more business cycles with our current level of investment. In centralizing our learning staff and standardizing how we develop and deliver our course offerings, we are using the same number of resources to support and sustain more learning initiatives. In benchmarking our learning organization with top competitors, it should come as no surprise that our level of **alignment** is on par with the level of other top performers. As the learning function is becoming a closer partner with other business units, we are creating more customized content to support the sales staff who are working with our best-selling newer products.

CEO: It sounds like you are managing the resources well. But I've always thought the learning function, as you call it, was pretty tightly wound with the rest of the business. You seem to be wavering.

Learning Executive: We are partnering and working well with other business units, but we could be doing better.

CEO: All right, I have a homework assignment for you. You seem to be doing well overall, but I need to know more regarding what is worrying you about alignment. I want you to identify the areas of greatest strength regarding alignment as well as the biggest risks. Think you can have something for me when we meet next week?

Learning Executive: Yes.

One week later...

Learning Executive: Last week we talked about the overall performance of the learning function and agreed to take a closer look at how well all efforts and money invested in learning are aligning with the rest of the organization. Specifically you asked me to identify the areas of greatest strength and risk related to alignment.

The areas of strength include linking individual performance goals with organizational performance objectives and adapting classroom training to meet pressing needs.

We are most at risk in ensuring that key employee groups get the right learning programs hard-wired into their job development plans. In the past we've done too much firefighting, and as a result we have had unplanned learning expenditures outside the normal range for companies like ours.

CEO: I see...you clearly have done your homework.

Learning Executive: I have a good staff and a good management tool.

CEO: Alright. I have extra funding for the learning function if there is something that really needs fixing. How soon can you tell me what areas we should improve, and what would happen if we brought those areas up to snuff with the rest of the field?

Learning Executive: In fact, I did a little investigating to prepare for our meeting. If we improve our efforts of lining up key employee group learning plans with their performance goals, and bring them up to the level of the best in class, we can both bring our alignment to above the industry average and cover the greatest amount of risk.

CEO: How much money is required and do you need to hire outside consultants to help find these problem areas and recommend what to do?

Learning Executive: There is no need to hire consultants or spend any additional money. I've chatted with my colleagues in HR and business unit leaders, and we have identified what needs to be done, the expected effect, and the required effort. Once we take care of this area, the entire learning function will be above the norm in each of those four areas of management that I mentioned.

CEO: Well, you've done an excellent job. It sounds like you're running a good ship, and that's exactly why I hired you as a learning executive.

Generating the Index Reports

After entering all learning function data required to generate the Index Reports, users can create a comprehensive WLP Index Report along with four separate diagnostic reports by selecting the Index Reports label on the navigation bar to view report details.

To Generate the Index Reports:

1. Open the WLP Scorecard.
2. Click the **Index Reports** label on the navigation bar. The Index Reports screen appears.
3. Click the **Year:** drop-down menu to select the desired report year.
4. Click the **WLP Index, Alignment, Efficiency, Effectiveness,** or **Sustainability** tabs at the top of the screen to view the desired report.

WLP Index Reports Overview

The WLP Index Report displays six tabs:

* The **WLP Index tab** combines the four index dimensions to display an overall index for each dimension and an overall index rollup score.
* The **four index tabs** measure the alignment, efficiency, effectiveness, and sustainability of the learning function compared to all organizations in the database.
* The **BMF tab,** available to Benchmarking Forum members only, displays the BMF Member Index Report Ratings for the year.

Analyzing the WLP Index Report Tab

Together, the first five tabs display values enabling comparison of the learning function to the entire workplace learning and performance industry. The WLP Index Score for alignment, effectiveness, efficiency, and sustainability is presented in a square graphic, with the score for your learning function in the upper left section of the square. The average score for all organizations in the database is in the red-shaded section to the lower right.

A comprehensive WLP Index Score also appears in a similarly designed square graphic, containing the overall WLP Index Score in the upper left section of the square and the average score for all organizations in the red-shaded section to the lower right.

Need help interpreting the data in the report? Table 12-1 describes each dimension in the WLP Index tab and provides an example of how to interpret the data as represented in figure 12-1.

Table 12-1: The WLP Index Screen Descriptions

WLP Index Reports Overview	Description
WLP Index Report	Displays a combination score based on alignment, efficiency, effectiveness, and sustainability scores. The WLP Index represents the overall quality of the learning function.
	Example: The organization has an overall WLP Index Score of 53, slightly below the industry average of 57. At first glance, this organization compares adequately with all other learning organizations. However, this organization may have achieved a score of 53 by consistently being somewhat below the mean in all areas of the learning function, or may have many areas where improvement could be made. A closer look at the Alignment, Effectiveness, Efficiency, and Sustainability Indexes should reveal particular areas of strength and weakness, and help direct the learning executive's attention to the appropriate areas.
Alignment Report	Measures the extent to which the learning function is aligned with organizational goals and other aspects of the organization.
	Example: The organization's Alignment Score of 67 is well above the industry mean Alignment Score of 52, suggesting that this organization has many areas of strength that support alignment. The learning executive ought to determine which areas of alignment most contribute to this score, as well as the areas that might be pulling down this score, and the areas that pose the greatest risk to the Alignment Score remaining well above the mean. An Alignment Score of 67, if unchanged, compared with an industry mean score of 52 indicates a learning function that will likely accompany organizational strategy and fulfill strategic objectives in the next two to four quarters.
Efficiency Report	Measures the efficiency of the learning function.
	Example: In this example, the organization's Efficiency Score of 30 is well below the mean score of 54. Although there might be individual areas of great strength, further analysis will likely show that most of the learning function areas are performing poorly, and need immediate attention. An Efficiency Score remaining at 30 when compared with an industry mean score of 54 indicates a learning function at great risk for reorganization or relegation in the next one to six quarters.
Effectiveness Report	Measures organizational productivity, human capital, financial performance, employee retention, and satisfaction.
	Example: The organization has an Effectiveness Score of 66, which is slightly above the mean of 61. Such a score may suggest that this organization has many areas of strength that are nevertheless counter-balanced by areas of weakness, whose result is a score nearer to mediocrity than excellence.
	As with this Alignment Score example above, the learning executive ought to determine which areas of effectiveness most contribute to this score, as well as the areas that might be pulling down this score, and the areas that pose the greatest risk to the Effectiveness Score remaining well above the mean. An Effectiveness Score of 66 as compared with an industry mean score of 61 may also indicate a learning function whose effects might be expected to support organizational strategy and value creation in the upcoming two quarters.
Sustainability Report	Measures the extent to which the learning function can sustain its current level of success.
	Example: The organization's Sustainability Score of 49 is below the mean score of 62. As with the Efficiency Score example, there might be a few individual areas of great strength that are nevertheless cancelled out by the majority of learning function areas that are performing poorly, requiring immediate attention. A Sustainability Score of 49, if left unchecked, as compared with an industry mean score of 62, may also indicate a learning function at risk for budget cuts, resource reductions, or diminution of effects in the upcoming two to eight quarters.

Figure 12-1: The WLP Index Reports Screen

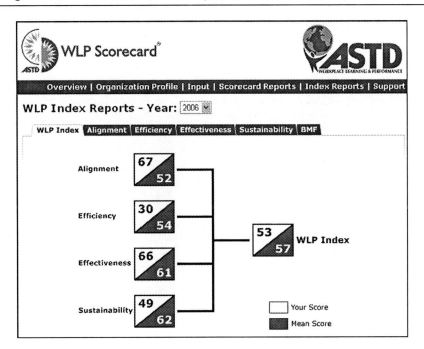

Analyzing the Diagnostic Reports

In each of the diagnostic reports, the WLP Scorecard will identify indicators that are likely to the exert the greatest impact on your WLP Index Score and consequently may be priorities to strengthen the alignment, effectiveness, efficiency, or sustainability of the learning function.

To understand how exactly to interpret the data available in the four diagnostic report screens, take a look at table 12-2. It describes the report screen elements and how these features provide learning executives with powerful tools to determine which learning function areas require attention—and the impact that changes in resources invested in these areas are likely to exert. Each example is based on figure 12-2.

Performing a Sensitivity Analysis

After reviewing each indicator, workplace learning professionals should perform a powerful sensitivity analysis. Modify the scores on any indicators to determine the impact that a different set of indicator scores has on the Index Score.

Table 12-2: WLP Dimension Tab Descriptions

Alignment Report Elements	Description
Current Alignment	Displays the current index score for the selected diagnostic report. **Example:** The organization's current Alignment Score is 67, well above the industry mean Alignment Score of 512.
New Alignment	Displays a new index score for the selected diagnostic report after performing a "sensitivity analysis" by entering a new value in the "Change Your Score" column. **Example:** The current value of 67 will change to the new value(s) entered into any of the Change Your Score fields.
Indicator	Displays the name of the indicator.
Value	All WLP Scorecard values range from 0 to 100, with 0 representing the lowest score and 100 the highest score. **Example:** The Value for this organization's Individual and Organization Goal Linkage is 8.
WLP Elite Value	Represents the mean value for the top scoring organizations in the WLP Scorecard database for the particular indicator. This score typically represents values observed in the top 10 to 20 percent performing learning organizations. **Example:** The WLP Elite Value for Individual and Organization Goal Linkage is 5, while the value for this organization's Individual and Organization Goal Linkage is 8.
WLP IndicatorWatch	The WLP IndicatorWatch enables you to quickly determine which areas of the learning function require managerial attention. The horizontal bulb depicts your learning function's strength in each indicator. • Red denotes an indicator that is substantially and negatively impacting the index score. • Yellow denotes an indicator that is moderately and negatively impacting the index score. • Green denotes an indicator that strengthens the index score. **Example:** The value for this organization's Individual and Organization Goal Linkage is 8, above the WLP Elite Value of 5 for Individual and Organization Goal Linkage. The green WLP IndicatorWatch denotes that this measure strengthens the Alignment Index Score.
Change Your Score	Enter a value in the **Change Your Score** column to perform a sensitivity analysis to determine the impact a different set of indicator values has on the Index Score.

Figure 12-2: The Alignment Diagnostic Report Screen

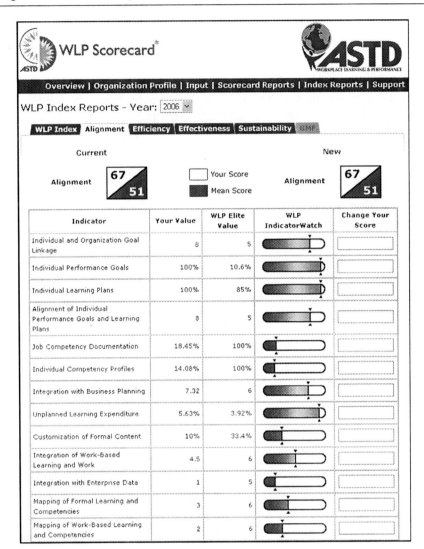

To Perform a Sensitivity Analysis:
1. Open the WLP Scorecard.
2. Click the **Index Reports** label on the navigation bar. The Index Reports screen appears.
3. Click the **Year:** drop-down menu to select the desired report year.
4. Click the appropriate diagnostic report tab—**Alignment, Efficiency, Effectiveness,** or **Sustainability**—at the top of the screen to view the diagnostic report.
5. Select an indicator to apply new values.
6. Enter a new value in the **"Change Your Score"** column for the desired indicator.
7. After entering the new value, click outside the data entry box.
8. The WLP Scorecard will calculate an updated Index Score and display the updated Index Score in the **"New" square graphic.**

As shown in figure 12-3, this organization's current "Alignment of Individual Performance Goals and Learning Plans" value of 4.5—below the WLP Elite Value of 8—denotes a yellow display in the WLP IndicatorWatch.

To determine the effect of improving this value from 4.5 to the WLP Elite Value of 8, enter an 8 in the Change Your Score field. By making this change, the organization improved its overall Alignment Index Score from 63, slightly below the industry mean, to 67, slightly above the industry mean.

Using the Index Reports to Develop a Business Profit and WLP Value Plan

By comparing the Your Value score, the WLP Elite Value scores and the WLP IndicatorWatch bulb in this report, workplace learning professionals can visually identify the specific areas of the learning function that contribute most to its strength and fitness.

Figure 12-3: Example of a Sensitivity Analysis Using the WLP Index Report

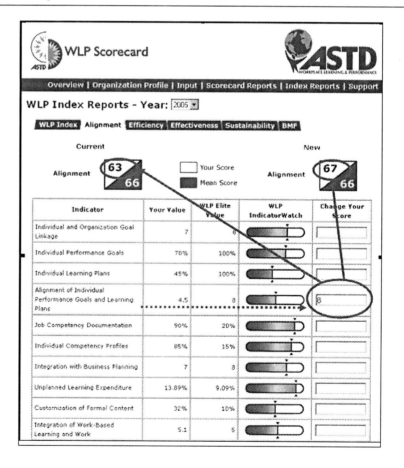

Because diagnostic reports flag areas in the learning function that indicate weakness or room for improvement, the next section details the information provided in each diagnostic report, including the suggested steps of how to use the report data to develop a profit plan around learning—known as the WLP Value Plan—and how to simultaneously link the organization's overall profit plan with the WLP Value Plan.

By creating a WLP Value Plan, workplace learning professionals can step into the world of non-learning counterparts and become a partner in developing the organization's overall profit plan. The WLP Value Plan provides a comprehensive performance measurement and management system that articulates the organization's plan for creating wealth and identifies the metrics that reveal the wealth-creating areas of the learning function.

Table 12-3 provides an overview of the recommended steps and key information needed to develop a business profit plan and WLP Value Plan.

Table 12-3: Developing a Profit and WLP Value Plan Overview

Diagnostic Report	Steps
Effectiveness Index	**Goal:** To create a core profit plan around learning and connect the organizational profit plan directly to the learning function and its activities. This is the minimum but essential analysis that every learning executive needs to undertake to run the learning function like a business. 1. Determine sales/revenue goals. 2. Determine operational expenses. 3. Determine expected operating profit. 4. Determine cost of investing in capital assets and working capital. 5. Evaluate the range of scenarios.
Efficiency Index	**Goal:** Determine an operating platform that ensures everyone gets what they need to succeed and learning programs achieve operational excellence. 1. Determine operating cash flow. 2. Determine resource needs (in cash) to fund changes in operating assets/working capital. 3. Determine cost of investment in long-term/long-lived assets. 4. Determine cost of capital.
Sustainability Index	**Goal:** Manage return on learning activity to maximize accumulation of learning assets, human capital, and drive reinvestment in value-creating learning activity. 1. Determine expected return. 2. Determine asset utilization. 3. Evaluate externally and internally.
Alignment Index	**Goal:** Harmonize layers of workplace learning and performance, and managing variance. For the learning function to align with the organization, learning solutions need to respond to organizational needs at three levels: high-level strategic needs, business unit operational needs, and individual employee development needs. To effectively manage learning function alignment, select several alignment measures at each of the three levels of alignment.

The four dimensions of WLP Index Reports—in addition to illuminating the effects of learning investments on business results—provide the structure that learning managers need to connect business strategy directly to the learning function. These powerful tools enable learning managers to

◈ use the Effectiveness Index and indicators to connect the organizational profit plans directly to the learning function and create a **core profit plan** around learning
◈ use the Efficiency Index and indicators to ensure that the learning function has an **operating platform** with the resources required to execute the learning strategy and fulfill key objectives
◈ use the Sustainability Index and indicators to **manage return** and drive further accumulation of learning assets and human capital, and reinvestment in the learning function
◈ use the Alignment Index and indicators to **manage variances,** and establish and assure **alignment at all performance levels.**

The "Establish and Maintain Alignment" stage of business strategy occurs throughout the execution of the Business Profit Plan and the WLP Value Plan processes, and it corresponds to the Alignment Index. The role of the Alignment Index in the WLP Value Plan is to construct a governance mechanism that manages many of the functions established in the "Determine Operating Platform" and "Manage Return" stages of the Business Profit Plan, and the Efficiency and Sustainability Indexes in the WLP Value Plan.

Understanding the Business Profit and WLP Value Plan Processes

To run learning like a business—to set up a measurement and management strategy—learning managers must configure the learning function to plug into the business strategy. There must be an unbroken connection among the articulation of business strategy, the overall organization profit plan, and the WLP Value Plan.

Business strategy, and the means for managing the execution of strategy, is typically developed in three stages:

1. Determine revenue or profit goals.
2. Develop the operating platform for achieving the revenue or profit goals.
3. Set expectations for return-on-investment of resources.

Together, these steps form the overall organizational profit plan, which frequently is nearly identical to the organization's budget. The profit plan, however, is not just a set of numbers or expectations. It is the blueprint for both measurement and management of all business functions—including the learning function.

As illustrated in figure 12-4, each stage of the overall organization profit plan is usually achieved through a set of steps appearing in the shaded area of the Business Profit Plan section.

Corresponding to these stages and steps are the WLP Indexes of Effectiveness, Efficiency, and Sustainability. The Effectiveness Index corresponds with the "Determine Profit/Revenue Goals" stage of business strategy, whereas the Efficiency Index corresponds to the "Determine Operating Platform" stage, and so on.

The WLP Value Plan is informed by—and accompanies—the corresponding stages that non-learning managers use to develop a Business Profit Plan. The WLP Value Plan step, in the gray shaded area to the right, is divided into two categories:

◈ business side of learning function
◈ WLP side of learning function.

Both categories represent areas that require learning managers to determine a measurement strategy.

The remainder of this chapter details the stages and steps to create the Business Profit Plan using the four WLP Indexes.

Figure 12-4: Overview of the Business Strategy Stages and the Steps to Create a Business Profit Plan and a WLP Value Plan

		WLP VALUE PLAN	
BUSINESS STRATEGY	BUSINESS PROFIT PLAN	BUSINESS SIDE OF LEARNING FUNCTION	WLP SIDE OF LEARNING FUNCTION
		WLP INDEX	

BUSINESS STRATEGY

- Determine PROFIT/INCOME goals
- Determine OPERATING PLATFORM
- Manage RETURN

BUSINESS PROFIT PLAN

Determine PROFIT/INCOME goals:
1. Determine sales/revenue goals
2. Determine operational expenses
3. Determine expected operating profit
4. Determine cost of investing in capital assets and working capital
5. Evaluate the range of scenarios

Determine OPERATING PLATFORM:
1. Determine operating cash flow
2. Determine resource need in cash to fund changes in operating assets/working capital
3. Determine costs of investment in long-term/long-lived assets
4. Determine cost of capital

Manage RETURN:
1. Determine expected return
2. Determine asset utilization
3. Compare with external benchmarks and internal stakeholder expectations

4. Manage performance variance

WLP INDEX

EFFECTIVENESS

EFFICIENCY

SUSTAINABILITY

ALIGNMENT

BUSINESS SIDE OF LEARNING FUNCTION

1. Determine LF contribution to sales/revenue
2. Determine cost impact
3. Audit learning function assets
4. Reposition assets/Determine the need for additional assets
5. Evaluate assumptions

1. Determine LF impact on overall cash flow
2. Determine LF impact on overall working capital
3. Determine LF impact on overall long-term investment strategy
4. Evaluate LF investment opportunities' effect on overall cashflow

1. Determine learning activity that most supports return
2. Determine best allocation for learning programs across asset types
3. Validate internally and externally against business measures

WLP SIDE OF LEARNING FUNCTION

1. Determine the role of learning on the value prep of revenue producing products and services product and service
2. Determine gaps between LF assets and produce/service strategy needs
3. Determine gaps between LF competencies
4. Determine plan to fill gaps using both financial and nonfinancial means (CID, learning job redesign, process redesign)
5. Build some slack into the LF

1. Determine efficiency gains opportunities
2. Determine where efficiency gains can be made with and without additional investment
3. Connect LF competencies to organization strategy needs
4. Select measures for simultaneously managing costs and efficiency variances

1. Link learning function outputs to measures of return
2. Link learning impact to business performance, revenues
3. Validate internally and externally against learning measures

Establish and maintain ALIGNMENT

1. Assure individual alignment
2. Assure learning function alignment
3. Set up communication structure between organization and LF

Steps to Developing the Profit and Learning Value Plan: Effectiveness

Step 1: Determine sales/revenue goals.
Step 2: Determine operational expenses.
Step 3: Determine expected operating profit.
Step 4: Determine cost of investing in capital assets and working capital.
Step 5: Evaluate the range of scenarios.

Focusing on Sales/Revenue Goals:

Learning executives must understand what factors most influence sales and revenues in the organization. Based on past experience, the most effective CLOs understand the markets as well as the market risks in their industries. They can describe their product lines and new product initiatives in remarkable detail, and often can communicate the value proposition of those products as convincingly as any vice president of marketing. These CLOs also possess a detailed understanding of

* the influence of competitor's strategy
* regulations
* broad trends
* major risks
* biases
* decision habits
* preferences of the key decision makers within the organization.

By leveraging this understanding, the most successful CLOs can determine how to shape the learning function to positively affect the amount of sales revenue the organization can generate.

The Effectiveness Index: The Core of the Profit Plan and the WLP Value Plan

In any organization, value begins with profit, which in turn begins with revenue, even though successful learning programs can impact both the revenue and expenses. Therefore, to begin creating an overall organization profit plan and the corresponding WLP Value Plan, managers need to look toward the future and make projections about the favorability of markets, the level of competition, the behavior of customers, the robustness of supply chains, and the need for additional capital. As in all profit plans, each of these projections contains assumptions about the future performance of an organization's key business functions, most of which can be articulated through accounting measures.

For today's intangible asset–heavy organizations, each of the projections carries assumptions about the organization's talent capacity, performance of human capital, and the need for additional personnel. Value cannot be created in today's organizations without a significant contribution from human capital—and business challenges cannot be met without high levels of human performance. The learning function must now join in the conversation with managers of other business functions when forecasting future revenues and profits. Consequently, the WLP Value Plan begins with determining the impact of workplace learning on the performance of all other key business functions (see figure 12-5).

Step 1: Determine Sales/Revenue Goals

The logical place to begin developing the value plan for the learning function is the same place senior managers typically begin building their profit plan—expected sales or revenue. Understanding sales or revenue forecasts entails much more than just looking at graphs and talking about meeting arbitrary targets to increase sales or revenue by X percent.

By beginning with sales and revenue forecasts, workplace learning professionals gain a good sense of what kind of income and profit is reasonable and then can clarify assumptions about critical cost measures, such as the cost of goods sold.

The information obtained from the WLP Effectiveness Diagnostic Report plays into any organization's sales and revenue estimates. To create a WLP Value Plan, workplace learning professions need to clarify how the learning function contributes to projected sales and revenue.

The WLP Effectiveness Index Report provides insight into the effects of workplace learning on individual and group productivity. The goal at this point in the value plan is to connect improvements in individual and group productivity facilitated by the learning function to sales and revenue

Figure 12-5: The Effectiveness Diagnostic Report

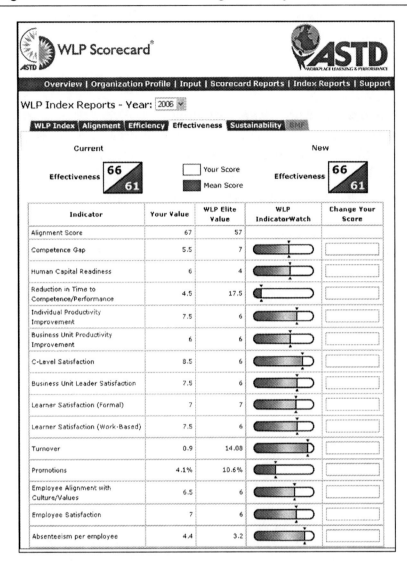

projections. Several report predictors relate to the larger organization to accomplish this goal including

- individual productivity improvement
- business unit productivity improvement
- revenue per employee
- new products and services.

The following section details how to interpret the Effectiveness Diagnostic Report indicators to develop the WLP Value Plan.

Individual Productivity Improvement

Effective learning is rarely temporary. Rather, it is systematic and targets the required aspects of a learner's development to successfully perform on a project or in a role. How learners perform back on the job after a learning event varies widely. An acceptable level of improved individual productivity is necessary to drive business unit and organizational productivity. High levels of individual productivity improvement, therefore, indicate a likelihood of organizational productivity improvement; in particular, productivity improvement that can be measured readily and tracked back to the effective learning.

Business Unit Productivity Improvement

One hallmark of learning function effectiveness is achieving increasing levels of productivity with groups of employees. Learning functions that are well distributed throughout business units are capable of accommodating diverse learning plans between and within individual business units to accomplish this goal.

Revenue per Employee

This fundamental effectiveness measure indicates the point when an organization drives productivity through its employees as well as the capacity for extracting revenue returns from investments in learning.

Higher revenue per employee portrays the ability of the learning function to extract value, and how much value it extracts from organizational and human capital, among other things.

New Products and Services

Few organizations are exempt from the pressures to innovate, adapt, and grow. Offering new products and services is fundamental for any organization to remain competitive. An effective learning function supports nearly every aspect of new product and service development and deployment—including learning new production skills, readying a salesforce, and educating customers. A higher number of new products and services, when considered with other figures, can determine the effectiveness of the learning function in transforming innovation into valuable products and services.

Step 2: Determine Operational Expenses

During the previous step, it isn't unusual for some managers to disagree about what kind of sales or revenue goals are reasonable. Fortunately, the next step—determining operating expenses—requires much less latitude of judgment and is usually derived more quickly.

Operating expenses are divided into two main categories:

- **Fixed costs** can be very large and usually represent investments in assets that are expected to last the duration of a major initiative.

For example, a lease on a building—whether the building is utilized at 10 or 100 percent of capacity—costs the organization the same. While it may not be worth the learning executive's time to understand the details of all organizational fixed assets, it is critical to understand which aspects of the learning function contribute to an organization's total fixed assets. When developing the WLP Value Plan, workplace learning professionals need to understand the degree to which learning expenditures constitute fixed costs and articulate the level of fixed costs required for the learning function to perform at its optimum.

◈ **Variable costs** increase or decrease according to the levels of sales or revenue to which they are tied and are usually expressed as a percent of sales. For example, raw materials are 30 percent of sales or labor is 15 percent of sales. Although the variable costs of learning functions are also relatively small when compared with those of the entire organization, learning assets are often characterized by increasing returns. As a result, it is possible that as the learning function expands to serve more learners, variable costs will decrease.

When developing the learning function value plan and linking it to the overall organizational profit plan, be sure to consider how increased sales and revenue goals could impact the fixed and variable costs of the learning function. Determine which learning resources are needed to support the organizational performance goals. The following section details how to interpret the Effectiveness Diagnostic Report indicators to develop the WLP Value Plan.

Human Capital Readiness

An important aspect of a *truly* strategic learning function is the ability to accumulate and deploy human capital to anticipate and meet future challenges. High human capital readiness is associated with organizations that can

◈ resist deleterious effects of industry shocks
◈ meet a changing environment without depleting resources
◈ influence the industry space to the point of exerting industry leadership.

High human capital readiness indicates adequate human capital accumulation and an aptitude for future human capital deployment, and it indicates the successful appropriation of individual knowledge capital to the organization.

Turnover

Though not strictly part of learning function metrics, organizational turnover has a strong bearing on the effectiveness of the learning function. Low turnover creates stability and obviates the need for repeating learning activities. Groups with low turnover assimilate new knowledge quickly and create a more nimble, highly responsive learning function.

Absenteeism per Employee

Low absenteeism per employee has multiple causes but is nevertheless commonly associated with an effective learning function. Low absenteeism per employee indicates a higher likelihood of employee engagement, which is an implicit objective and a desired result of effective learning programs. A rate of high absenteeism per employee can indicate other deficits in learning function effectiveness, particularly when considered with other measures of employee engagement.

Step 3: Determine Expected Operating Profit

Conceptually, this step is easy for non-learning managers. To determine operating profit or operating income, subtract operating expenses from sales or revenue, as appropriate. Because there are numerous ways to describe operating profit, find out what measures your organization uses to describe, calculate, and manage operating profit.

At this step in the process:

 - Determine the learning function's contribution to revenue through new products and services.
 - Evaluate how the accumulation of intangible assets—such as satisfaction and alignment with organizational culture and values—contributes positively to productivity and less directly to sales or revenue.

Sometimes contributions feed back more resources into the learning function proportionate to the increase in sales or revenue. Don't be surprised if it is difficult relating the precise financial contribution to operating profit. Learning executives need to clearly communicate the connection between how the learning function impacts both the revenue and expense side of the equation. The following section details how to interpret the Effectiveness Diagnostic Report indicators to develop the WLP Value Plan.

C-Level Satisfaction

Senior management support is a critical component in nearly every organization demonstrating an effective learning function. Satisfaction among C-level management can indicate the learning function's effectiveness.

High satisfaction often precludes a substantial investment of attention and resources into the learning function. High satisfaction also creates an environment that drives learning function effectiveness.

Business Unit Leader Satisfaction

Business unit leaders can substantially impact learning program success because of their influence on senior management's perceptions and future learning investment decisions. Based on their approval and level of enthusiasm toward a learning program, these business unit leaders also affect subordinates. It is rare that a learning program can expect long-term success without high levels of business unit leader satisfaction.

Learner Satisfaction (Formal)

Learner satisfaction heavily impacts the general perception of any learning opportunities—formal or work-based—within an organization. High learner satisfaction indicates ongoing susceptibility to the positive effects of formal learning, and an ongoing willingness to exchange valuable time on the job with time spent in formal learning.

Learner Satisfaction (Work-Based)

High satisfaction with work-based learning indicates that learners have a propensity to fully participate in future learning programs and to accept environmental or technological enhancements to their work functions.

Employee Alignment with Culture and Values

Successful organizations often have a unique, vibrant culture that impacts organization performance incalculably. An effective learning function actively engages employees in the organization's culture and values, at all phases of an employee's growth. High employee alignment with culture and values is, therefore, both an input and an output of effective learning.

Employee Satisfaction

Employee satisfaction represents a broad response to past formal and work-based learning opportunities and indicates whether future responses to formal and work-based learning opportunities are likely to be successful. High employee satisfaction relates to how much employees value learning programs. Much of an employee's satisfaction comes from taking an active role in improving those aspects of his or her work experience.

Customer Satisfaction

Customer satisfaction affects most organizations' bottom line, directly and indirectly. High customer satisfaction is the result of numerous processes that contribute to the value of that product or service, and it will drive customers to prefer that brand. Customer satisfaction indicates the extent to which systematic learning programs have resulted in product or service differentiation. When combined with revenue data, customer satisfaction can indicate the price premium that has resulted from the investment in learning.

Percentage of Revenue from New Products and Services

Innovative products and services owe part of their originality to contributions from effective learning functions that support the establishment of various revenue streams. A high percentage of revenue from new products and services is a more direct indicator of the effectiveness of investments in systemic learning programs to extract profits due to timely market entry, market positioning, product or service differentiation, or other ability to command a premium price.

Step 4: Determine the Cost of Investing in Capital Assets and Working Capital

The previous three steps set up a rudimentary income statement and determined the level of contribution from the learning function to sales and revenues, operating expenses, and finally operating profits. By gathering information from stakeholders in other business units, workplace learning professionals can then construct a system for following the flow of investments in the learning function through learning programs and activities, and finally to outcomes that affect operating profits.

This process helps describe the links between learning programs/activities to organizational and financial performance. Perhaps most important, this process enables workplace learning professionals to track changes in the resources allocated to the learning function to the performance of the learning function, and then to tangible business results. Creating a system for measuring these changes enables these professionals to manage activities much more strategically and with much greater precision.

At this step in the process, non-learning executives develop an investment plan for two kinds of assets: short-term consumable assets and long-term capital assets. Non-learning executives also need to evaluate financing opportunities for both types of assets.

Short-term assets are usually consumed in the accounting periods immediately following the acquisition, and are treated as working capital. **Long-term capital** assets, often tied to strategy, are capitalized, then depreciated or amortized over several years. Because long-term asset investments will likely involve additional financing, non-learning executives use special methods to evaluate investment opportunities and long-term assets. These methods include net present value (NPV) and internal rate of return (IRR).

NPV is the more common of these two methods. IRR, a more complicated technique, tends to yield results that are consistent with net present value, although sometimes it is a preferred measure when specific thresholds of return are required. These are not the only criteria used to aid in the decisions of whether and how to invest long-term assets, but both NPV and IRR carry a lot of weight in financial decisions.

Learning executives need to determine if the learning function possesses all of the assets needed to support and meet the organizational goals—or whether additional investment is needed to achieve desired results such as reductions in time to proficiency and the preparation of managers and other personnel to occupy positions to execute the new strategy. Both the learning function and the value-producing organizations need to be ready to meet the challenges of their new performance goals. The following section details how to interpret the Effectiveness Diagnostic Report indicators to develop the WLP Value Plan.

Reduction in Time to Competence/Performance

One of the most powerful indicators of learning function effectiveness is the level to which it facilitates an organization to create economies of scale within its own production functions. Reduction in time to competence indicates that the learning function has been successful in attenuating or reducing the size of production cycles, or promoting desired levels of proficiency much earlier in the production cycle.

Promotions

In an increasing number of organizations, the learning function is being relied upon to prepare selected staff for promotions. In such organizations, a high number of promotions can indicate the learning function's mid- and long-term effectiveness in shaping promotable personnel and preparing them for higher levels of responsibility within the organization.

Organizational Readiness

Organizational readiness represents the potential adaptability to environmental shocks, market and regulatory environment changes, attacks from competitors, and the evolution of the industry. Organizations capable of adapting to these changes also require a learning function that itself is optimally ready to adapt and respond to strategic and tactical needs brought about by changes that the organization experiences.

Step 5: Evaluate the Range of Scenarios

When reaching this last step in developing the WLP Value Plan—which supports the organizational profit plans—workplace learning professionals will have learned much about organizational strategy, the assumptions that go into the strategy, and the unique ways in which the value of the learning function can mobilize intangible assets to create value for the entire organization.

Not only does this process equip users with powerful tools to manage the learning function and improve organizational performance, but it also builds partnerships with managers and other business units, and facilitates the use of a common vocabulary to communicate with one another.

However, the work in determining the profit plan is not complete. Nobody can predict the future accurately. The most carefully laid profit plans, and indeed the most carefully laid WLP Value Plans, will not match future realities. Assumptions made today, based on the best information available, may prove to be completely erroneous as the future unfolds.

At this stage, non-learning executives typically subject their profit plan to a number of scenarios to determine where estimates are either overstated or understated. Some managers create numerous scenarios with the rigor of scientific research, changing only one variable at time. Most managers will go the simpler route of performing a sensitivity analysis: that is, creating similar profit plans according to worst-case, best-case, and most-likely-case scenarios. A sensitivity analysis provides a range of likely outcomes and allows managers to set aside additional resources should the future bring substantial deviations from the original profit plan.

Risk management is a fundamental part of judicious planning, and learning executives should perform a similar analysis with their value plans at this stage. Most learning executives follow their non-learning executive counterparts and perform best-, worst- and most-likely case scenario analyses for their learning functions.

In addition to the standard forms of scenario planning, the learning executive should consult the WLP Scorecard for two additional pieces of information: the alignment score and competence gap. The following section details how to interpret the Effectiveness Diagnostic Report indicators to develop the WLP Value Plan.

Alignment Score

The level of learning function alignment affects nearly every aspect of learning function effectiveness indirectly. High alignment is critical for any systematic learning initiative to be effective, although determination of the precise areas of the learning function affected can in some cases require a review of several periods of data.

Competence Gap

The competence gap refers to the discrepancy between existing skills inventories and skills inventories the organization needs to meet objectives. A long-term result of an effective learning function is a small or gradually decreasing competence gap.

Developing a Range of Scenarios: Since even the most likely scenarios can represent a considerable range, more and more learning executives are using "most likely plus" and "most likely minus" scenarios. The "most likely plus" scenario describes a more favorable, though less probable outcome, and represents an outcome that is reasonable to obtain should the organization perform exceptionally. On the other hand, the "most-likely minus" scenario describes a scenario that reflects suboptimal performance or failure of a high-risk project.

The Efficiency Index: The Reality Check that Ensures Everyone Gets What They Need to Succeed

Much work goes into constructing both the overall organization profit plan and the corresponding profit plan around learning. Yet even a seemingly bulletproof profit plan needs a reality check. Every business function requires and consumes resources to produce goods and services, whether distributed immediately or booked into inventory. The learning function is no exception. An important part of managing the efficiency of the learning function is to assure that it has enough resources to achieve performance objectives, yet also has safeguards against consuming resources that could be put to good use in other areas of the organization (figure 12-6).

At this point in the process, after the overall organization profit plan has been determined, non-learning executives need to determine whether there are enough resources in reserve to fund *operations*. If resources are not sufficient, then the organization will have to consider alternative means of obtaining the funds.

Steps to Developing your Profit Plan and Learning Value Plan: Efficiency

1. Determine operating cash flow.
2. Determine resource need in cash to fund changes in operating assets/working capital.
3. Determine cost of investment in long-term/long-lived assets.
4. Determine cost of capital.

Figure 12-6: The Efficiency Diagnostic Report

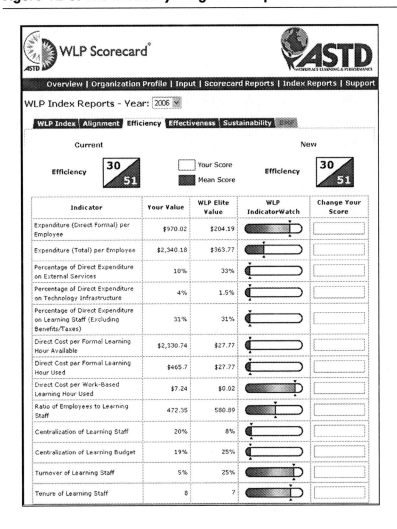

Indicator	Your Value	WLP Elite Value	WLP IndicatorWatch	Change Your Score
Expenditure (Direct Formal) per Employee	$970.02	$204.19		
Expenditure (Total) per Employee	$2,340.18	$363.77		
Percentage of Direct Expenditure on External Services	10%	33%		
Percentage of Direct Expenditure on Technology Infrastructure	4%	1.5%		
Percentage of Direct Expenditure on Learning Staff (Excluding Benefits/Taxes)	31%	31%		
Direct Cost per Formal Learning Hour Available	$2,330.74	$27.77		
Direct Cost per Formal Learning Hour Used	$465.7	$27.77		
Direct Cost per Work-Based Learning Hour Used	$7.24	$0.02		
Ratio of Employees to Learning Staff	472.35	580.89		
Centralization of Learning Staff	20%	8%		
Centralization of Learning Budget	19%	25%		
Turnover of Learning Staff	5%	25%		
Tenure of Learning Staff	8	7		

At this stage in the value plan, the learning executive should determine and evaluate the cost drivers of the learning function, decide whether those costs are justified, and establish how the production and delivery of learning problems programs affects operating cash flow in the organization.

By evaluating the efficiency of the learning function, the learning executive must get into the habit of understanding efficient learning delivery and production within in the wider context of an *operations platform*. The WLP Scorecard illuminates where efficiency improvements may also positively affect the cash position of the organization.

Well-designed and -delivered learning products consume resources both inside and outside the learning function. Efficiency gains can either free up or consume greater amounts of resources, especially if an efficiency gain is associated with an increase in learning function scale. Understanding how learning function efficiency affects the *working capital* of other business units enables workplace learning professionals to partner with business unit leaders and to manage both resources and relationships with greater precision than afforded in the past. The following section details how to interpret the Efficiency Diagnostic Report indicators to develop the WLP Value Plan.

Step 1: Determine Operating Cash Flow

The first step that non-learning executives take when creating a profit plan is to determine the need for cash and the current operating cash flow. During this stage, learning executives need to communicate with non-learning managers to understand the measures used to describe operating cash flow.

In recent years, controversy surrounded the issue of which measures most accurately reflect cash flow, especially in high-growth, highly leveraged companies. Earnings-based measures have become very popular measures of cash flow—for example, EBIT (earnings before interest and taxes) and its most high-profile derivative, EBITDA (earnings before interest, taxes, depreciation, and amortization). Critics of EBITDA point out that it does not account for fluctuations in working capital and tends to overstate earnings so it is better used in evaluating profitability than cash flow.

Fortunately, decisions on how to measure business unit or enterprise-wide cash flow do not fall on learning executives, and most of the time, operating cash flow can easily be located on a cash flow statement.

Learning executives need to evaluate the implications of learning function efficiency on the amount of cash that flows through the learning function. Do not automatically assume that increases in learning function efficiency will necessarily increase cash flow or make more cash available for use in other areas. Learning function efficiency is not a monolithic phenomenon but rather is distributed among people and systems. The following WLP Scorecard efficiency measures highlight which aspects of the learning function contribute most to efficiency, and where efficiency gains can be achieved without negatively impacting cash flow.

Percentage of Expenditure on Learning Staff

Percentage of expenditure on learning staff, a common benchmark that denotes one of the largest expenditures managed by learning executives, is sometimes used as a leading indicator of learning function costs and, consequently, can illuminate future learning function costs or changes in efficiency due to staff changes.

Expenditure per Employee (Direct Formal)

Expenditure per employee ratios, a common and enduring benchmark, indicate the amount of learning resources allocated to each individual learner and can fluctuate somewhat year to year depending on the industry. Expenditure per employee can connect learning function vulnerability to changes in learning budgets or expectedly high demand for learning resources. Considered with work-based expenditure per employee ratios, formal expenditure per employee ratios can help determine optimal allocation of learning programs according to whether they are formal or work-based.

Expenditure per Employee (Total)

Another common and enduring benchmark, expenditure per employee ratios indicate the amount of learning resources allocated to each individual learner and can fluctuate somewhat year to year depending on industry. Expenditure per employee can indicate learning function vulnerability due to changes in learning budgets or expectedly high demand for learning resources. Considered with other figures, expenditure per employee ratios can help determine break-even points for learning programs, which in turn help drive learning function efficiency.

Percentage of Expenditure on External Services

A common benchmark that denotes level of outsourcing, percentage of expenditure on external services can be disproportionately higher in smaller organizations, or in large organizations with heavy capital investments. Percentage of expenditure on external services can indicate potential future costs savings. When compared with other organizations within the applicable sector, it indicates responsiveness of the learning function to strategic change.

Cost per Formal Learning Hour Used

Cost per formal learning hour used, another fundamental indicator of efficiency, represents the dollar cost of providing one hour of instruction to one person within the organization. This benchmark reveals information about capacity and the learning function's ability to scale. A common rule of thumb is that the ratio of cost per formal learning hour used to cost per formal learning hour provided or available should be in the rough vicinity of 1:10, although in many of the largest, elite-performing organizations the ratio approaches 1:20. Cost per formal learning hour used can indicate whether current levels of efficiency can be maintained or perhaps increased by marginal increases in number of learners served by learning programs.

Cost per Hour of Work-Based Learning Used

Akin to cost per *formal* learning hour used—cost per hour of work-based learning used—represents the dollar cost of providing one hour of work-based learning content to one person in the organization. This benchmark can be compared with the cost per formal learning hour used to determine whether learning resources are being deployed in a manner that maximizes use of time, whether certain methods of delivery are being used for maximal effect, and whether the learning function has achieved optimal balance of formal and work-based learning.

Hours of Formal Content Available per Learning Staff Member

The hours of formal content available per learning staff member indicator often shows the durability and reusability of an organization's learning content and illuminates the continuing amount of resources needed to create and manage formal learning content.

Hours of Formal Content Usage per Learning Staff Member

One of the benefits of formal content delivery is that it can reach many learners at once. High formal content usage per learning staff member indicates an ability to reach groups of learners with a given amount of resources. Combined with other metrics, it can indicate changes in fixed and variable costs, or marginal improvements in formal learning due to increases in learning function reach or scope.

Formal Hours Available/Provided Online

The formal hours available online metric has the advantage of being available anytime, anywhere to all users in an organization. If an organization offers a large number of formal hours of online content to learners, the learners will generally spend fewer hours away from the job. Online formal learning content also permits immediate evaluation and feedback, and it can help detect additional learning needs much sooner than traditional classroom-based formal learning.

Formal Hours Used Online

Formal hours used online indicates the adequacy of the technological infrastructure delivery capacity, delivery efficiency, and substitutability of online formal learning content for traditional classroom-based learning content. Increases in formal hours used online can indicate potential reductions in time to competence, and scalability of future formal content to be placed online.

Step 2: Determine Resource Need in Cash to Fund Changes in Operating Assets/Working Capital

Upon determining operating cash flow and its contributions to the learning function, learning executives will have a good sense of where short-term efficiency gains can be made without additional funding. Likewise, the non-learning executive will be able to determine which operational initiatives require additional working capital. The following WLP Scorecard measures indicate the amount of working capital currently available in the learning function for deployment directly on learning products, and indirectly on organizational performance.

These measures facilitate decision making about current learning function working capital, and how potential deficits could be met both within the learning function and through resources from other departments. Learning executives need to be prepared to handle objections to increasing the amount of funding directed toward the learning function. It often takes the roar of a lion to increase funding available to grow learning function operating assets, but all it takes is the squeak of a mouse to freeze or reduce funding.

Year-to-Year Efficiency Gain

Year-to-year efficiency gain refers to a likelihood of sustained and continuous improvement in the output and production features of the learning function. High efficiency gains tend to indicate a well-managed, highly engaged learning function.

Percentage of Expenditure on Technology Infrastructure

This common benchmark denotes the level of investment in learning technology. In particular, it indicates the learning function's contribution to the overall IT infrastructure and the amount to which technology has been efficiently leveraged in the past. This percentage can indicate future increases in learning function capacity, changes of efficiency in delivery, and the ability to scale globally.

Ratio of Employees to Learning Staff

Similar in principle to ratios of formal content available per learning staff member, this ratio denotes how much attention and how many resources can be devoted to organizational learning needs at a given time. Ratio of employees to learning staff can indicate the efficiency of future large scale learning programs, the resources needed for potential large-scale programs, as well as future costs related to increasing learning staff size.

Centralization of Learning Staff

A highly centralized learning staff can create a more synergistic learning organization that is better able to produce and deliver quality content given a constant amount of learning organization resources.

Hours of Work-Based Learning Usage per Learning Staff Member

This indicator refers to the level of success staff can achieve by introducing and managing work-based learning activities within the organization. A high amount of work-based learning usage per learning staff member can indicate later period increases in employee time on task, or greater distribution of proficient performance throughout a large group.

Hours of Knowledge Sharing Planned/Facilitated per Learning Staff Member

Frequently, facilitating effective knowledge sharing is a more difficult task than facilitating formal learning. Yet the positive effects of knowledge-sharing activities include the ability to scale quickly throughout one or more workgroups, often organically. Well-planned knowledge-sharing activities need comparatively little ongoing management by the learning function. For these reasons, higher hours of knowledge sharing planned/facilitated per learning staff member can indicate increases in efficiency.

Documentation of Processes

Thorough documentation of processes (both learning processes and business processes related to the learning function) reduces the need to "reinvent the wheel," allowing learning managers to assemble a collection of best practices, and evaluate records of past learning programs and their results for the purposes of continuously improving both the learning function and business processes.

Responsiveness of the Learning Function

Highly nimble learning functions are better able to provide targeted learning and just-in-time solutions, using fewer resources to achieve desired results. In some cases a highly responsive learning function achieves efficiency benefits by providing more compact learning programs at an earlier phase in employee development, thereby obviating the need for larger, more costly programs at a later employee development phase.

Step 3: Determine Cost of Investment in Long-Term/ Long-Lived Assets

The third step in assessing resource needs for both the organization and the learning function is fundamentally no different from the previous step. The only difference is that both learning and non-learning executives take a longer-term view of needs. Many of the techniques used in the previous section apply to this stage as well. Learning and non-learning executives, however, must shift focus from tactics to strategy. In the previous stage, deficits in resources available for meeting the profit plan and value plan performance goals were normally addressed by allocations of cash. For the longer-lived assets required to meet the current profit and value plan goals, an organization sometimes has more options available to raise needed cash.

When determining longer-term learning function asset needs, the learning executive needs to connect the current set of competencies within the learning function with the organization's overall investment strategy. Determining which options are best suited happens during Step 4, when determining the cost of capital.

Outside the learning function, cash investments in longer-term assets are approved with the expectation that a specific amount of the expenses will be able to be capitalized. Although investments in longer-term learning assets may not carry the same expectations, learning executives proceed as if held to similar expectations. Learning executives should evaluate the following WLP Scorecard measures as assets that can be capitalized or can be described as having the same asset dynamics as capital assets. The following WLP Scorecard metrics denote areas of long-term learning function assets that have the potential of becoming capital learning assets.

Tenure of Learning Staff

Similar to low turnover, greater tenure of learning staff allows the learning function to standardize work processes, maintain high productivity, retain unique skills, and maintain consistent output. High tenure is a key ingredient of optimal resource allocation among staff within a learning function. When tenure reaches a certain level, efficiency gains can be realized within a learning function.

Knowledge Repository Usage per Learning Staff Member

Knowledge repository usage per learning staff member refers to the ability of the learning staff to capture expert knowledge in a usable format *and* to render it usable to learners within the organization. In short, it is the ability of the learning function to broker expert knowledge within the organization. A high number of hours may help indicate future efficiency gains, reduction in time to expertise, or an increase in number of experts within the organization (or persons with highly strategic expert knowledge).

Knowledge Repository Reuse Ratio

This ratio indicates the amount of formal learning content successfully applied in events over time among separate groups of learners. Knowledge repositories often contain vast stores of expert knowledge. Some of this expert knowledge is applicable beyond a single production or management technique, or a single organizational unit. Greater access of expert knowledge that can apply to many situations within a knowledge repository can reduce the need for costly and time-consuming programmed learning activities or larger scale formal learning programs and increase time on task for especially complex work activities.

Cost per Formal Learning Hour Available/Provided

A fundamental indicator of efficiency, cost per formal learning hour available/provided represents the dollar cost of providing one hour of instruction regardless of the number of persons benefiting from the hour of learning content. This benchmark reveals information about the future ability of an organization to deliver learning content efficiently given the current amount of resources allocated to it.

Centralization of Learning Budget

Centralized learning budgets provide several benefits including

- reducing administrative resources and tracking efforts
- reducing number of redundant or non-strategic learning activities
- basing resource allocation decisions on a single set of non-conflicting goals
- increasing the likelihood that the learning function is being managed according to the culture of the wider organization—giving it greater visibility and modularity with the scheme of the entire organization's budgeting
- creating efficiency gains in managing the learning function budget.

Step 4: Determine Cost of Capital

Management of learning function efficiency goes hand-in-hand with cash flow management. Increasing learning function efficiency sometimes requires additional investment, but it pays off by freeing up other resources and increasing future cash flows. Therefore, the fourth and final step is to evaluate financing options to meet any deficits in both short- and long-term function assets—and any additional costs associated with raising additional capital.

When acquiring additional learning function capital, learning and non-learning executives must determine the effects such investment might have on current cash flow and expected cash flow throughout the duration of the profit plan. Potential efficiency gains should be weighed against any potential constrictions of cash flow. Any surprises related to learning function cash flow should be the result of better-than-expected revenues achieved through improved performance, rather than unexpected, unplanned learning expenditures.

The following metrics for the WLP Scorecard relate to areas in the learning function where the cost of capital can be determined with a reasonable amount of accuracy. Most of these metrics relate to longer-term assets that nevertheless need to be available for potentially extensive periods of deployment throughout the duration of the profit plan. It is also very likely that the organization is still paying costs in the current profit plan for acquisitions made in each of these areas in previous years. Close monitoring of these metrics enables financial prudence and better management of costs related to efficiency-enhancing investments and learning function efficiency.

Turnover of Learning Staff

The benefits of having a stable learning staff are numerous and affect every aspect of the learning function. Low turnover increases the learning function's ability to standardize work processes, maintain high productivity, retain unique skills, and maintain consistent output. High turnover may create a ceiling in the level of efficiency the learning function may achieve, owing to a disproportionately high amount of resources being directed toward onboarding new learning staff.

Formal Learning Content Reuse Ratio

This benchmark indicates the amount of formal learning content successfully applied in events over time, among separate groups of learners. A higher formal learning content reuse ratio indicates the ability of an organization's learning function to anticipate the need for future allocations of resources, produce durable learning content, and deploy learning programs throughout the organization continuously over long periods of time.

Standardization of Processes

A high degree of standardization of processes, also referred to as templating, allows for effective production techniques to be encoded in actual production processes, requiring minimal search effort by the learning staff. Greater standardization also reduces the likelihood of producing defective or misaligned learning programs, and helps create a standard learning environment that reduces the cognitive load on learners.

Automation of Processes

A fundamental aspect of efficiency, pervasive process automation facilitates precise management of resources and production, reduces variable costs, and potentially increases the reach of the learning function without increasing variable costs.

Management of External Providers

More and more organizations are finding management of external learning service providers to be as much of a challenge as managing the learning function activities that remain within the organization. Because many outsourcing decisions are made with the aim of increasing learning function efficiency, adequate levels of external learning service partners are needed to realize the efficiency benefit of outsourcing elements of the learning function.

Steps to Developing Your Profit Plan and Learning Value Plan: Sustainability

1. Determine expected return.
2. Determine asset utilization.
3. Evaluate externally and internally.

The Sustainability Index: What Keeps You in the Game?

Learning is a lifelong application. The benefits of learning extend for months and sometimes years after a learning program is completed. Frequently, the benefits of learning even accumulate and grow in value over time. Yet for the learning function to capitalize on such valuable assets over time, it must do more than operate efficiently. To drive accumulation of human capital and create a sturdy talent inventory, the learning function must continue to generate a return and justify reinvestment.

No business can be sustained for long without being able to generate a return. As profits dry up so do high-quality investments and additional resources for future growth. The sustainability dimension of the WLP Scorecard corresponds to the point in the profit planning process where non-learning managers determine strategy to maximize investor returns (figure 12-7).

In some organizations, the notion of investor can be applied to stakeholders, or anyone who benefits from involvement in the organization beyond just receiving wages. Yet for all organizations, this stage of the profit planning defines the notion of value as it is seen to the outside world. The WLP Scorecard connects the value proposition of the learning function to the value proposition of key business initiatives, and communicates this value proposition to business leaders in any organization.

Step 1: Determine Expected Return

The simplest way of expressing return is the ROI methodology, which Jack Phillips modified for application in learning functions. ROI is a ratio of financial outputs to inputs over a determined period of time and is

Figure 12-7: The Sustainability Diagnostic Report

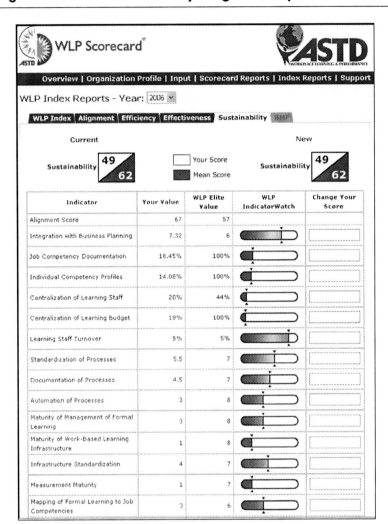

expressed as a percentage. Under Phillips's methodology, ROI analysis can be specified to individual projects and accounts for less tangible or non-positive benefits, such as cost savings or risk reduction.

Business leaders calculate and discuss ROI because it is a straightforward conceptualization of desired return. Despite its usefulness and clarity, many managers regard ROI as a very rough estimate of investor returns, lacking the precision of other ratios of return.

When defining a profit plan, managers may prefer different measures of returns to facilitate more standard and comparable components of value. For example, some analysts prefer return-on-assets (ROA) because it provides insight into how an organization's current assets are able to return a profit. Others prefer economic value added (EVA)—a modification of residual income—because it is a dollar value and promotes greater consistency. EVA considers the cost of capital, risk, and is more applicable to individual business units than ROI. As a result of this popularity, EVA has spurred the integration of a number of management techniques into practices of value-based management.

Another popular way of describing return is return-on-equity (ROE). ROE is a favorite because it can be broken down into three components, which considered together shed a lot of light on what contributes most to investor returns:

- **Profitability:** net income divided by sales or revenue
- **Turnover:** a more specific description of ROA and amount of sales or revenue the business generates from its capitalized assets
- **Leverage:** the percentage of value-driving assets that are debt financed.

Regardless of the methods used to calculate and communicate return, workplace learning professionals need to determine which WLP Scorecard measures best support the organization's ability to sustain a return. These professionals need to connect the learning function to other business functions that increase profitability, maximize asset turnover, make use of debt-financed business resources, and create sustainability for both the learning function and the organization's financial health.

Alignment Score

The learning function's level of alignment is an important yet intangible aspect of sustainability. Within the context of sustainability, the alignment score relates the degree to which the learning function is integrated into the larger organization. It is given responsibility for critical organizational goals. A high level of alignment indicates a strong connection to critical and fundamental organizational processes, as well as the likelihood of the learning function to achieve and maintain "top-of-mind" status among business leaders.

Integration with Business Planning

Any business function or process that is not tied to fundamental business planning has a low chance of enduring more than one business cycle. The learning function is no exception. The learning function that maintains close ties with business planning is less vulnerable to resource reallocations or catastrophic budget reductions. A high degree of integration with business planning indicates a learning function that is less likely to be deployed in reactionary ways, and more likely to become an ongoing partner in the formulation and execution of organizational strategy.

Centralization of Learning Staff

A highly centralized learning staff is more likely to act as a cohesive group and perform synergistically. A centralized learning staff is less likely to invest in redundant learning programs and is better able to communicate and cooperate with business lines and senior management.

Centralization of Learning Budget

A centralized learning budget has the advantage of transparency among business line owners, senior management, and learning executives. This transparency allows learning resources to be treated rigorously and in accordance with the organization's strategic objectives. For these reasons, a highly centralized budget may create a propensity for senior management to approve larger, less restricted, or wider scoped budgets. Centralized budgets can be evaluated with demanding excessive management attention. Highly centralized budgets can be tied more readily to other organizational performance measures and can increase the likelihood of the learning function becoming institutionalized and a fundamental part of the organization's structure and functioning.

Standardization of Processes

Standardization of learning processes is a fundamental aspect of reusability. It allows learning resources to be applied without using excessive learning function resources and permits recurring activities and operations to be managed by exception. Standardized processes are often characterized by durability, by virtue of the manageability and broad application to fundamental organizational operations.

Automation of Processes

Automation of learning processes frees up learning function resources and permits recurring activities and operations to be managed by exception. A high degree of automation encodes organizational best practices into regular workflow, retains accumulated knowledge, and indicates that critical aspects of the learning function are performing optimally while not consuming excessive organizational resources.

Infrastructure Standardization

A high amount of infrastructure standardization promotes greater reuse and modularity, allowing for adequate planning and delivery of work-based learning programs over multiple occasions.

C-Level Satisfaction

Senior management determines a substantial portion of the learning function's budget and, therefore, must be satisfied that their investment of resources in the learning function achieves adequate results. A high level of satisfaction among senior managers denotes confidence in the learning function and in the learning executives' abilities to achieve favorable strategic and tactical results. High C-level satisfaction indicates a lower likelihood of decreased learning budgets or mandates of reduction in scope and activity.

Business Unit Leader Satisfaction

Business unit leaders assume high accountability for their decisions to invest in learning for their lines of business. They usually have first-hand knowledge of whether a learning program achieved the desired results. In essence, business unit leaders are the customers of the learning function. Their level of satisfaction frequently determines whether learning investments will continue, whether the learning function will be consulted as a strategic partner, and whether learning programs are likely to exert the desired effect on their businesses in the long-term.

Learner Satisfaction (Formal)

Learner satisfaction is not a perfect measure of the success of a learning program. A pattern or sustained trend of learner dissatisfaction, however, will likely impact the desired results of a learning program adversely; it may create resistance or complacence about future learning programs. Conversely, high satisfaction increases the goodwill of the learning function and may help offset short-term opportunity costs associated with participation in a formal learning program.

Learner Satisfaction (Work-Based)

Learner satisfaction is not a perfect measure of the success of a learning program. A pattern or sustained trend of learner dissatisfaction will likely impact the desired results of a learning program adversely; it may create resistance or complacence about future learning programs. Conversely, high satisfaction, particularly with work-based learning, enhances the workplace experience and creates greater goodwill toward the learning function.

Step 2: Determine Asset Utilization

After senior managers determine how they will measure return, they can then allocate assets to generate revenue. Frequently these assets are allocated directly to managers of profit centers within the organizations. Although ROI provides a vivid snapshot of return, it is not precise enough to help managers decide which profit centers deserve the most valuable assets, nor does it yield metrics that adequately describe the performance of those assets.

The previous step focused on analyzing expected returns and determined the ways in which the learning function could best achieve an acceptable amount of return. Learning executives need to focus on aligning the learning function value plan with business initiatives that impact profitability, asset turnover, and utilization of debt-financed assets.

After drafting road maps for capturing revenue, senior managers start down that road and give the wheel to business line managers. These line managers are then responsible for ensuring that the assets and capital allocated become fully engaged in supporting the organization's profit plan. Charged with the responsibility to use these assets to generate revenue and ultimately a return, business line managers focus on asset utilization.

Measures of asset utilization are often described as turnover ratios including long-term asset turnover (or fixed asset turnover) working capital, inventory, and accounts receivable. Although a detailed analysis of aspects of asset utilization is out of the scope for this work, learning executives need to understand how profit centers are managed and, in particular, what asset utilization measures are used to describe favorable performance behavior.

Job Competency Documentation

A high amount of job competency documentation facilitates accumulation of a skills inventory. As a result, learning functions can develop more precise skills gap analysis and, therefore, can develop more effective learning programs. Learning functions able to exploit these benefits become producers and managers of valuable organizational assets.

Individual Competency Profiles

A high number of individual competency profiles and talent management programs are important in developing a skills inventory. High numbers of individual competency profiles promote job matching, team or group assignment, and facilitate identification of high-potential employees. Adequate job competency documentation and individual competency profiles complement standard HR functions, leading to more integrated employee development over a longer duration of an employee's tenure in the organization.

Learning Staff Turnover

Experienced learning staff members acquire extraordinary amounts of knowledge about the organization's learning function and the organization's critical success factors. Retaining the learning staff over several business cycles keeps expert knowledge in the organization, creates stability within a learning function, and solidifies the learning organization's strategic role within the larger organization.

Documentation of Processes

Documentation of processes creates a record of learning activities and enables workplace learning professionals to refer to, evaluate, and improve future learning programs. High levels of process documentation help to drive permanency of the learning function and increase the accessibility of learning to all consumers.

The WLP Scorecard provides learning metrics that link the learning function, business unit performance, revenue, and ultimately return—those areas likely to have the greatest impact on business units and stakeholder returns.

Choosing the right metric is crucial to making this analysis work. Learning executives should consider using return measures that can be broken down into assets at the organizational level and into asset utilization categories at the business unit level.

This generic method—successfully implemented in many industries to link strategy and the technical core of the business—is not applicable for every organization. Focus on combining the right metrics to link high-level return goals with systems for managing and measuring the use of productive assets.

Work-based Learning Infrastructure

Work-based learning will be useless if it has limited ability to scale due to an inadequate infrastructure. Organizations lacking a work-based learning infrastructure often have "one-shot training programs" with short-term results. A high degree of infrastructure indicates a stable commitment of resources throughout the organization to not only enhance the workplace but also to provide multiple, mutually supportive learning events.

Mapping of Formal Learning to Job Competencies

The results of successful formal learning programs often include additions to an organization's skills inventory. Learning functions that make the effort to increase important organizational assets, and that can demonstrate success in doing so, are more likely to garner adequate resources and be consulted for future organizational initiatives.

Mapping of Work-Based Learning to Job Competencies

Additions to an organization's skills inventory are often the results of a successful work-based learning program. Successful work-based learning programs encourage senior management to consult the learning function when attempting to improve some aspect of the workplace. Learning functions that make important contributions to the workplace environment will demonstrate success and are often allocated adequate resources and support to continue their efforts.

Mapping of Formal Learning to Employee Learning Plans

Evaluation of successful formal learning programs often reveals information about individual learner characteristics and how those characteristics could be developed to the maximal benefit to the organization. Learning functions that make the effort to feed such knowledge back into individual learning plans will frequently be regarded as a strategic partner in major personnel and HR initiatives, thereby gaining a scope outside the strict bounds of the learning function.

Mapping of Work-Based Learning to Employee Learning Plans

As with formal learning programs, the evaluation stages of successful work-based learning programs often reveal information about individual learner characteristics and how those characteristics could be developed to the maximal benefit of the organization. Learning functions that make the effort to feed such knowledge back into individual learning plans will often be regarded as a strategic partner in major personnel and HR initiatives.

Step 3: Evaluate Externally and Internally

The last step in developing a profit plan is to conduct a healthy reality check against external benchmarks and stakeholder expectations. In the language of psychological testing, benchmarking is a form of external validation, whereas comparison with stakeholder expectations is a form of internal validation. For many businesses the most essential internal validation comes from expectations and perceptions of internal learning function consumers.

The WLP profession has gained considerable benchmarking expertise in the last several years for organizations of all sizes and across multiple industries, including nonprofit and governmental organizations. Eagerness to measure learning efforts has driven the creation of impressive measurement systems whose full usefulness has yet to be determined.

At this final stage, non-learning executives validate the profit plan. Likewise, workplace learning professionals need to examine the usefulness of information in the WLP Value Plan.

Maturity of Management of Formal Learning

Maturity of formal learning management is associated with a durable and adaptable learning function—one that has created and managed several formal learning programs. A high level of measurement maturity indicates confidence in future formal learning programs. It also indicates the expectation that future formal learning programs will create results that can be managed by business leaders to achieve their own business unit objectives.

Measurement Maturity

Measurement maturity reflects a high perceived value of learning and a commitment among learning executives to make learning relevant to all organization stakeholders. A high degree of measurement maturity reflects successful efforts to capture the effect of learning in organizational objectives, and indicates the likelihood for the learning function and learning products to obtain adequate ongoing attention and for the learning function to create manageable learning products.

Exploring the Alignment Index: Harmonizing Layers of Work and Managing Variance

Let's begin this discussion about alignment by acknowledging that alignment is a massive topic—the number of books recently published on alignment and the volumes of discussion threads alone can attest to this fact.

Twenty years ago, the mention of "learning function alignment" might have aroused suspicion and jeers that the speaker suffered from some form of "academentia." As the training field has blossomed into the WLP profession, the learning function's scope has also expanded considerably. It has permanently moved away from its former tactics-only role brought in during the middle of a business process, to a more strategic role, where the learning function becomes integrated into high-level strategy.

Organizations that have successfully integrated the learning function into higher levels of organizational strategy have realized business value through cost reduction, optimization of the learning portfolio, tighter alignment of the learning function with strategic objectives, and implementation of best learning practices.

Organizations that excel in linking learning and performance are doing so by forging partnerships between the learning function and other business units—thereby increasing the dollar investment in the learning function. Others excel by applying their comprehensive understanding of best practices to organization-wide learning. Combining an increasing content reuse ratio with smaller than predicted increases in average learning expenditure per employee often reflects greater alignment of the learning function with concrete performance objectives.

Alignment is not about techniques and reliance on a few favorite tricks. Creating and maintaining alignment in the learning function requires active management and a very keen sense of adaptability. Although measurement plays an important role in managing all areas of the learning function, simply monitoring dials and gauges is not going to bring about alignment.

Managers wishing to establish and maintain optimal alignment must focus on two features:

- Alignment is a **multilayered phenomenon** and must be managed differently according to level.
- Alignment requires monitoring specific areas of **variance** within the learning function.

Alignment and Its Role at Three Layers

ASTD research, based on the reports of numerous learning executives and their non-learning counterparts, indicates that for the learning function to maximize its strategic value and align with the organization as a whole, learning solutions need to address organizational needs at three levels:

1. High-level strategic needs
2. Business unit operational needs
3. Individual employee development needs.

Successful learning function leaders cite focusing on a few learning function measures at each of the three alignment levels rather than a single one-size-fits-all measure as the key to achieving alignment success.

Because well-aligned learning functions usually yield consistent measures at all three levels, learning executives need to know where misalignment is occurring or is likely to occur. Focusing on multiple metrics prevents a false confidence that alignment can be described by just one metric. As with so many areas of modern management, alignment is an iterative process,

Figure 12-8: The Alignment Diagnostic Report

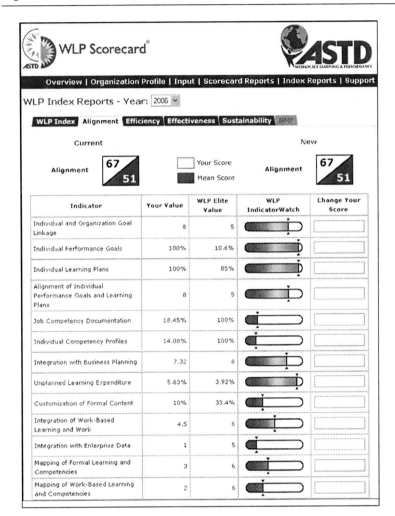

requiring careful monitoring of activity between the levels of alignment, and the learning function activity as it corresponds outside the learning function. Learning executives need to get into the habit of managing alignment with a loose hand, and devoting measurement efforts to discover where exceptions in alignment of the learning function occur. This next section explores the three layers of alignment and the Alignment Diagnostic Report indicators to help with this measurement (see figure 12-8).

Individual Layer Alignment

The key to aligning the learning function with business strategy is connecting the individual to value-creating work. In most businesses, good alignment is not a matter of luck. Rather, it is the result of a deliberate design beginning at the individual level. Workplace learning professionals responsible for designing and developing the profit and WLP Value Plan for the learning function develop a keen understanding of the particular workings of organizational strategy. As a result, these professionals can partner with

HR to develop jobs, job environments, and learning programs that feed directly into strategic objectives. The WLP Scorecard contains sensitive measures that convey these characteristics of individual level learning as it relates to alignment.

Individual Performance Goals

Assisting individual employees in meeting their performance goals is a critical objective of learning programs. It serves as an intermediate step in aligning a learning program to ensure maximal impact on organizational and strategic goals. A high incidence of individual goals helps to focus learning activities and employee efforts on achieving organizational objectives and reduces "busy" activity.

Individual Learning Plans

Constructing individual learning plans for all employees is a major task. Yet the higher the number of employees having individual learning plans, the more likely these employees have entered into the scope and reach of the learning function. Consequently, individual learning plans can both denote the level of penetration of the learning function within the organization and predict the likelihood of successfully encompassing employees not yet adequately reached by the learning function.

Alignment of Individual Performance and Learning Plans

High linkage of individual performance and learning plans, one of the fundamental components of alignment, ensures that learning programs support measurable and tangible performance objectives. Additionally, high linkage can create greater visibility for the learning function at the strategic phase and thereby support greater alignment.

Individual Competency Profiles

Constructing individual competency profiles can be an even more laborious task than constructing individual learning plans. Yet organizations having a high number of individual competency profiles benefit from an enhanced ability to assemble and manage skill inventories. They also provide staffing and learning programs that better meet the strategic objectives. Many learning executives highly value and seek these precise levels of alignment between the learning function and organizational goals.

Learning Function Layer

At the business unit level, alignment is determined by how adaptable the learning function's core assets are to meeting strategic needs. Although formal learning is often well suited for delivery to business units, this delivery method is at times more expensive and has high opportunity costs of employee time away from the job.

For optimal alignment at the business unit level, a learning function's formal content must bring about a stream of benefits as close to the unit goals as possible. If the learning executive has designed the WLP Value Plan in concert with the organization's profit plan, formal learning content will be well positioned to support the expected business unit performance levels.

The WLP Scorecard provides three measures of formal learning content and alignment of the learning function. These measures provide insight into the ways that formal learning content can be best managed, including evaluating the cost and benefits of customization versus updating, and managing supplier relationships.

Customization of Formal Content

Customization of formal content not only describes the level of adaptability of the learning function but also the degree to which formal learning has been designed to be adaptable. Both features contribute to increasing alignment of the learning function.

Percentage of Formal Hours Updated

Alignment refers not only to the concurrence of the learning function to strategic objectives but also to the adaptability of the learning function as strategy becomes implemented throughout the organization. Adequate amounts of updated formal learning hours reflect a high degree of learning function responsiveness to organizational needs and changes, as well as a commitment to remaining aligned.

Percentage of Formal Hours Retired

Retired learning content indicates a vigorous and aligned learning function that has created learning products that have been successfully implemented and consumed. Retired content is sometimes viewed as a lagging indicator of alignment. It is useful, however, as a leading indicator insofar as it portrays freed up learning resources that are currently available to be employed elsewhere in the organization.

Organization Layer

Strategic alignment is designed top down but is implemented bottom up. Nevertheless, the larger organization plays a very important role in strategic alignment. If organizational culture is allowed to run amok, it is bound to stymie attempts at aligning any business function—including the learning function—despite even the most brilliant business strategy.

Organizations build and maintain the structure to communicate information and regulate behavior to achieve goals. Some organizations facilitate bureaucratic and tacit mechanisms for collecting and channeling the energy of the business. An organization of business functions aligned harmoniously with strategy is like a waterwheel that collects water running chaotically down a river and converts the flow into energy.

Measurement of alignment at the organizational level aims to determine how well the broad structure of the business harnesses chaotic energy then focuses it into robust and reliable business processes. As it relates to the learning function, measurement of organization level alignment denotes how well the organization structures capture learning activity and focus it into performance activity.

These measures address the question: Does the organization allow water to just flow on by, or does it capture the energy of the flowing water and convert it into something that creates value? By providing measures of linkage between individual capabilities and organizational goals, the WLP Scorecard enables management at a higher level, with greater impact, all for the same amount of managerial effort.

In addition to these metrics, the WLP Scorecard provides two other key metrics for use in measuring the learning function alignment with the organizational objectives. The first of these, **employee satisfaction with learning opportunities,** depicts the ability of organizations to feed back employee satisfaction into business processes and other fundamental organizational mechanisms. Not surprisingly, many top learning executives remark that satisfaction among learners begets greater satisfaction among other aspects of work. Organizations that can capture energy related to satisfaction obtain a potential advantage over their competitors.

The second measure, **unplanned learning expenditure,** is more concrete, and it is perhaps the most widely used alignment metric.

Individual and Organizational Goal Linkage
One of the fundamental components of alignment—individual and organizational goal linkage—requires diligent and ongoing formative evaluation. High levels of individual and organizational goal linkage increase the likelihood that learning programs will reach desired objectives. It showcases that the contribution of the learning function is reaching desired objectives.

Unplanned Learning Expenditure
Unplanned learning expenditures are often a reliable indication that misalignment is occurring within the organization. Unplanned learning expenditures frequently point to redundant learning efforts. They can illuminate "rogue" activity within the organization. A low amount of unplanned learning expenditures suggests adequate front-end alignment and careful management of the learning budget.

Integration of Work-Based Learning and Work

A fundamental component of alignment, a high level of embeddedness of work-based learning in the actual workplace, can indicate successful adaptation of work-based learning programs to organizational objectives and seamlessness between work-based learning activities and actual work activities.

Integration with Enterprise Data

Integration with enterprise data indicates the degree to which the learning function has achieved visibility in the highest levels of the organization. Tying learning function effects to organizational goals forces the learning function to operate strategically rather than simply producing "learning products."

Employee Satisfaction with Learning Opportunities

Employee satisfaction with learning opportunities is a common indicator of many desirable workplace conditions. High levels of employee satisfaction with learning opportunities are useful in determining how well the learning function aligns broadly with the larger organization and how well individual employee performance contributes to efforts to align the learning function to workplace performance objectives.

Alignment Is Also About Managing Variance

A sound measurement strategy makes the invisible visible. It directs attention, the scarcest resource of all, to the areas of the organization that most deserve that attention. With the help of the WLP Scorecard, workplace learning professionals can set up areas within the learning function that run on autopilot most of the time. Of course, not every business function (including the learning function) can be set up to manage itself. A crucial component of managing the learning function—one that even the best learning executives occasionally struggle with—is realigning the learning function when there is slippage or occasional derailment.

The learning function is very complex. Like an expensive sports car, it needs attention, especially after an afternoon drive at the high performance level for which it was designed. Even if the learning function is performing well and has plenty of capacity to spare, learning executives must ensure that the learning function does not stray from organizational strategy as detailed in the profit plan. An important part of management includes monitoring and processing inputs to yield alignment and superior performance.

Sometimes superior performance happens in spite of anyone's best management efforts. In this rare case, deviation from strategy and planning is not necessarily a bad thing, but rather needs to be understood and possibly integrated into the business.

In business terms, deviation from plans is usually called **variance.** Budget holders and financial managers understand variance very narrowly, either as favorable or unfavorable monetary deviations from key line items in financial statements. Financial managers are most concerned with variances that pertain to the strategy set up in the profit plan. In particular, they express concern for those areas of strategy most likely to carry substantial risks such as revenue, cost, market share, competitive risk, changes in demand, and unforeseen shocks.

Learning executives do not need to be as concerned with variances—and there are many of them—that happen outside the learning function. Some variances within the learning executive's control can critically affect alignment of the learning function and items on financial statements. The WLP Scorecard illuminates these specific areas and takes the guesswork out of which fluctuations in learning activity deserve attention.

Fortunately, variances in the learning function alignment are more likely to affect the learning function internally than other financial areas of the business. That does not mean, however, that variances deserve any less attention or should be treated as trifles. If the value plan is set up to coincide with the organization's profit plan, then workplace learning professionals can connect areas of the unfavorable alignment to potential negative financial impacts. Conversely, if the learning function is falling out of alignment with the rest of the organization due in part to negligence of senior management, then workplace learning professionals need to make a stronger case that the learning function deserves more attention by showing the consequences of a misaligned learning function in terms they best understand.

Rather than affecting the whole, variance in alignment of the learning function is most likely to have an effect on specific aspects of effectiveness or sustainability, and may create fluctuations in the financial statement items to which they are connected.

This next section discusses the WLP Scorecard sections that highlight unfavorable variances affecting the effectiveness and sustainability of the learning function.

Managing Variance: Effectiveness

Misalignment often diminishes learning function effectiveness and appears as variance in internal customer levels of satisfaction. Lower than expected satisfaction is not a cause of misalignment, yet misalignment almost always causes decreased satisfaction across the board. A single episode or brief period of dissatisfaction by a business unit leader or among learners is not sufficient to declare the whole learning function out of alignment. Detecting a level of misalignment requires attention and the learning executive must see consistency in measures of dissatisfaction.

As it relates to the profit plan, unfavorable variances that mitigate the effectiveness of learning function are most likely to impact variable costs (as determined in step two of the WLP Value Plan).

Business Unit Leader Satisfaction

Business unit leaders assume substantial accountability for their decisions to invest in learning programs for their lines of business. They usually have first-hand knowledge of whether a learning program is achieving the desired results. In essence, business unit leaders are the customers of the learning function, and their satisfaction frequently determines whether learning investments will continue in the future, and whether the learning function will increase its influence within that business unit.

Learner Satisfaction (Formal)

Although there is no consensus about whether it is always a reliable indicator of alignment, high learner satisfaction is nevertheless closely related to learners' successful achievement of performance goals, as well as favorable perceptions of how relevant formal learning programs are helping them fulfill performance expectations.

Learner Satisfaction (Work-Based)

Although there is no consensus of learner satisfaction serving as a reliable indicator of alignment, high learner satisfaction is closely related to the learner successfully meeting performance goals, as well as favorable perceptions of how relevant work-based learning programs are in helping them fulfill performance expectations. Additionally, high learner satisfaction with work-based learning, and about the workplace in general, sometimes feed back into one another, creating incentives among learners to maximize their work-based learning experiences.

Managing Alignment: Sustainability

Unfavorable variances affect the sustainability of the learning function, beginning at the top. Senior management satisfaction—by virtue of having the most control over funds and their allocation—is a key measure for detecting misalignment and, more important, evaluating the sustainability of the learning function.

Senior management satisfaction and integration with business planning represent two coarse measures and will tend to be stable in most cases. Fluctuations are most likely to appear at the end of a reporting cycle or at the beginning of a budget cycle, when summative learning function performance reports become available.

The WLP Scorecard also contains several sensitive measures that detect areas of gradual decoupling of the learning function with organizational strategy. Learning executives often find these measures useful in fine-tuning areas of alignment or in rebalancing competencies.

From the perspective of the profit plan and thus financial statements, mis-alignment is likely to affect areas of asset utilization within the learning function, and very possibly outside the learning function, where it can exert an influence on other dimensions of asset utilization—for example, working capital, accounts receivable, fixed assets, and current inventory. If mis-alignment in the learning function is sufficient to jeopardize sustainability, the learning executives need to address internal customers' dissatisfaction more than fixing fine points on the organization's financial statements.

Job Competency Documentation

Creating adequate job competency documentation—a substantial task for any organization—allows learning executives to understand and manage their skills inventory, which can facilitate precise skills deployment when a learning goal is determined. High levels of job competency documentation indicate maturity of the learning function.

Integration with Business Planning

Any business function or process that is not tied to fundamental business planning has a low chance of enduring more than one business cycle, and the learning function is no exception. The learning function that maintains close ties with business planning is less vulnerable to resource reallocations, or catastrophic budget reductions, and it is consequently more aligned. High levels of integration with business planning also indicate assimilation of the learning function by senior management.

Mapping of Formal Learning and Competencies

The results of a successful formal learning program often include enhancement of an organization's skills inventory. Learning functions that make the effort to increase this important, yet often intangible organizational asset, and can demonstrate success in doing so, will often be more highly aligned with the larger organization.

Mapping of Work-Based Learning and Competencies

The results of a successful work-based learning program often include enhancement of an organization's skills inventory. It encourages senior management to consult the learning function when attempting to improve some aspect of the workplace. Learning functions that make the effort to produce important contributions to the workplace environment, and can demonstrate success in doing so at a lower cost than other potential workplace enhancements, will often be more highly aligned with the larger organization.

Mapping of Formal Learning and Individual Learning Plans

The evaluation stages of successful formal learning programs often reveal information about individual learner characteristics and how those characteristics could be developed to the maximal benefit of the organization. Learning functions that make the effort to feed such knowledge back into individual learning plans often increase their alignment with the larger organization. A high degree of mapping of formal learning and individual learning plans may also indicate a learning function less likely to be called upon in a reactionary manner, or to address an organizational deficit that could be addressed more effectively outside the learning function.

Mapping of Work-Based Learning and Individual Learning Plans

As with formal learning programs, the evaluation stages of successful work-based learning programs often reveal information about individual learner characteristics and how those characteristics could be developed to the maximal benefit of the organization. Learning functions that make the effort to feed such knowledge back into individual learning plans will often be more highly aligned with the larger organization. A high degree of mapping of work-based learning and individual learning plans may also indicate a learning function less likely to be called upon to address a deficit in organizational workplace structure inappropriately.

C-Level Satisfaction

A high standard of C-level satisfaction is critical in ensuring alignment at the outset of any learning program. Yet as learning strategy becomes crafted and executed, it is critical for workplace learning professionals to understand senior management requirements and criteria for judging the effect of learning programs on organizational objectives to maintain their satisfaction.

Summary

The WLP Scorecard is a powerful tool that will transform the learning function into a value-producing, results-driven business function. This chapter equips workplace learning professionals with the same business management techniques available to their non-learning counterparts and describes techniques for tying the learning function to the overall organization profit plan, as well as creating a WLP Value Plan.

Perhaps the most important tidbit for WLP Scorecard users starting this journey is to always use the WLP Scorecard as a way of turning the black box of learning into the glass box of workplace learning and performance. One set of measures will not satisfy the needs of every learning executive in every organization. As a guide, select the appropriate number of measures for any step in the WLP Value Plan by choosing one or two fewer metrics than what can be effectively monitored (without requiring excessive attention) and will not cause confusion.

The purpose of measurement is to collect data to enhance management and drive organizational outcomes. The WLP Scorecard helps the WLP profession to break free from oppressive measurement systems, so the profession can discover the core measures that drive organizational results.

Chapter 13

Conclusion:
Focusing on Value

In This Chapter

- Focusing on the scarcest resource
- Addressing intangible assets and future wealth
- Developing learning function strategies for success

This book has probably seemed more like something that belongs in an MBA program than a workplace learning environment. Indeed, in many places, this book tries to equip users with analytical tools most commonly used in business management. In that spirit, let's conclude like any good MBA class by reviewing some key takeaway points.

If you get only one thing out of this book, understand that there is an unbroken thread that begins with human performance. The thread leads to organizational performance, and it ends with financial performance. If the thread is broken, it is because the WLP profession lacks the methods for linking these kinds of performance.

In these terms, performance refers to both financial and human behavior. Financial behavior proceeds from human behavior, and the two can be aligned and managed using the same set of tools. The profit plan and the WLP Value Plan clarify and communicate performance expectations, and they provide the means to evaluate managerial performance rationally and organically.

Figure 13-1: The Unbroken Thread

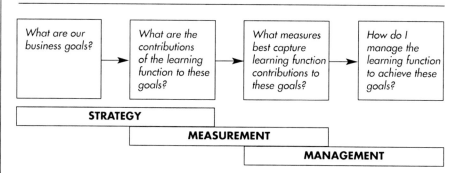

The Scarcest Resource

Workplace learning professionals have probably heard this before, but this conclusion would be remiss if it neglected this reminder: attention is the scarcest resource in any organization and with any manager. Think of all the techniques used to get the most out of time spent at work to create more time for personal and professional life. Diligently applying those techniques, workplace learning professionals are sometimes able to squeeze more time out of the day.

Can the same be done with attention? Can you squeeze more attention out of a day? Treat the WLP Scorecard as a means of devoting attention to the areas where it is most deserved, not where it is urgently needed at the moment. Many professions, such as accounting, have used some of the concepts presented in this book in the past but not all worked. So what can be learned from their mistakes? Use the WLP Scorecard to help determine where to devote your scarcest resource. The purpose of the WLP Scorecard is to free workplace learning professionals from burdensome details and to disentangle the fundamentals that require constant monitoring from those measures that need only occasional attention.

Intangible Assets and Future Wealth

Intangible assets, meaning unique capabilities and competencies, will likely represent the difference between the success or failure of organizational initiatives. Learning is the means by which organizations increase and accumulate intangible assets, and it affects the growth and value of nearly every intangible asset under an organization's control. Learning even defines whole categories of intangible assets. Yet most intangibles never make it to financial statements unless some transaction has occurred.

Intangibles created and increased by learning are fluid and ever-changing. Some intangible assets become obsolete while others will develop and emerge as fundamental value drivers. A well-managed organization adapts its competencies to market changes and strategic directives. Management of intangible assets therefore requires special measurement to feed back timely information into processes to achieve desired performance. Traditional hard financial measurements are just too blunt and coarse to do that. The WLP Scorecard will provide a refreshed insight into the new profession of wealth creation. It will equip workplace learning professionals with a new set of measures to manage any organization's greater accumulations of wealth.

Summary of Learning Function Strategies for Success

Workplace learning professionals need to develop a deep understanding that the value they contribute can and should be quantified. Well-managed learning functions return tremendous value to any organization.

Using a balanced scorecard approach provides a logical framework for aligning initiatives with an organization's strategic goals and sets up measures and targets as the basis for measurement, evaluation, and gauging performance. Once that foundation is laid, workplace learning professionals need to focus on communicating the value of learning as a strategic driver that contributes to achieving organizational outcomes.

To accomplish this end, focus on these key points:

- Workplace learning professionals need to set clear goals, measure outcomes, and be driven by performance and not "hitting the numbers."
- They need to be open to new ways of doing things and explore metrics that are meaningful and essential to senior management.
- The balanced scorecard forces workplace learning professionals to communicate strategically and to focus on measurement, targets, benchmarks, and accountability for achievement of goals.
- Scorecards enable workplace learning professionals to focus their measurement on more than just a financial dimension and to communicate as a strategic partner in more non-traditional measurement areas.
- Partner with various business unit leaders in the organization to identify the measures that matter most in driving their businesses and determine how learning can help them accomplish department goals.
- For organizations that are not currently using a balanced-scorecard-type system and it isn't likely to happen any time soon, leverage the key concepts presented in this book by asking questions about measurement and targets early in the planning process.
- Adapt these core ideas by facilitating and forcing discussions about metrics and benchmarking.

Appendix A:
WLP Scorecard Reports Input Indicators Map

Use the information in this appendix to quickly identify the required and optional input indicator fields in each report. This tool can help you to plan your "staged approach" to implementing more progressive levels of the WLP Scorecard reports with your organization.

Legend:

R = Required Input Indicator

X = Optional Field

▨ = Field Not Available

Tab	Sub-category	Input Field	(Level 1) Key Free Indicators Report	(Level 2) Scorecard Reports	(Level 3) Index Reports
Workplace	Workforce	Workforce Size	R	R	R
		Workforce Compensation		X	X
		Hourly Employees			X
		Employees Outside Home Country			X
		Workforce Dispersion		X	X
		Workforce Education Level		X	X
	Compensation	Payroll	R	R	R
		Total Compensation		X	X
	Talent Management	Turnover		X	X
		Tenure		X	X
		Promotions			X
		New Hires			X
		Job Competency Documentation		X	X
		Individual Competency Profiles		X	X
		Succession Planning			X

(continued on next page)

Tab	Sub-category	Input Field	(Level 1) Key Free Indicators Report	(Level 2) Scorecard Reports	(Level 3) Index Reports
Workplace	Performance Management	Individual and Organization Goal Linkage		X	X
		Individual Performance Goals		X	X
		Individual Learning Plans			X
		Alignment of Individual Performance Goals and Learning Plans		X	X
	Employee Engagement	Employee Alignment with Culture/Values		X	X
		Employee Satisfaction		X	X
		Employee Satisfaction with Learning Opportunities		X	X
		Absenteeism			X
	Innovation	Investment in R&D			X
		New Products and Services		X	X
		Employee Time on New Products and Services			X
		Employee Time on Process Improvement/Innovation			X
		Employee Idea Solicitation			X
		Employee Idea Conversion			X
		Number of Patents Applied For			X
		Number of Patents Received			X
		Total Patents			X
		Industry/University Partnerships			X
Learning	Investment	Total Direct Learning Investment	R	R	R
		Total Indirect Learning Investment	R	R	R
		Percentage of Direct Cost for Learning by Type of Solution	R	R	R
		Integration with Business Planning		X	X
		Unplanned Learning Expenditure		X	X
		Budget Centralization		X	X
		External Services Expenditure	R	R	R
		Tuition Reimbursement Expenditure	R	R	R
		Learning Staff Costs (Including Benefits and Taxes)		X	X
		Learning Staff Costs (Excluding Benefits and Taxes)		X	X
		Expenditure on Technology Infrastructure		X	X
		Expenditure by Employee Group		X	X

Tab	Sub-category	Input Field	(Level 1) Key Free Indicators Report	(Level 2) Scorecard Reports	(Level 3) Index Reports
Learning	Learning Function Staff/Talent	Learning Staff Size	R	R	R
		Learning Staff Allocation by Activity		X	X
		Learning Staff Reporting		X	X
		Learning Staff Turnover		X	X
		Learning Staff Tenure			X
		Learning Staff Education level		X	X
	Learning Function Processes	Learning Staff Time Allocation by Activity		X	X
		Learning Staff Time Allocation by Type of Solution		X	X
		Standardization		X	X
		Documentation		X	X
		Automation		X	X
		Shortest Cycle		X	X
		Longest Cycle		X	X
	Output (Formal Learning)	Total Formal Hours Available	R	R	R
		New Formal Hours		X	X
		Updated Formal Hours		X	X
		Formal Hours Retired		X	X
		Formal Hours by Content Area	R	R	R
		New Formal Hours by Content Area		X	X
		Formal Hours by Delivery Method	R	R	R
		Customization of Formal Content		X	X
	Output (Work-Based Learning)	Knowledge Repositories		X	X
		New Hours of Expert Knowledge Entered into Repositories		X	X
		Knowledge Sharing		X	X
	Infrastructure	Maturity of Management of Formal Learning		X	X
		Maturity of Work-Based Learning Infrastructure		X	X
		Infrastructure Standardization		X	X
		Measurement Maturity		X	X

(continued on next page)

Tab	Sub-category	Input Field	(Level 1) Key Free Indicators Report	(Level 2) Scorecard Reports	(Level 3) Index Reports
Learning	Outsourcing	Number of Providers		X	X
		Longevity of Relationships		X	X
		Management of External Providers			X
		Learning Activities Outsourced		X	X
	Integration	Formal and Work-Based Learning		X	X
		Work-Based Learning and Work		X	X
		Enterprise Data		X	X
		Formal Learning and Competencies		X	X
		Formal Learning and Individual Learning Plans		X	X
		Work-Based Learning and Individual Learning Plans		X	X
	Usage (Formal Learning)	Formal Hours Used		R	R
		Formal Hours Used by Employee Group		X	X
		Formal Hours Used by Delivery Method		R	R
	Usage (Work-Based Learning)	Knowledge Repository Access			X
		Knowledge Repository Time		X	X
		Knowledge Repository Time by Employee Group		X	X
		Knowledge Sharing Time as a Novice		X	X
		Knowledge Sharing Time as an Expert		X	X
		Time on Challenging Work Assignments		X	X
		Time on Other Discretionary Learning		X	X
Performance	Capability	Competence Gap			X
		Human Capital Readiness		X	X
		Reduction in Time to Competence/Performance		X	X
	Productivity	Individual Productivity Improvement		X	X
		Business Unit Productivity Improvement		X	X
	Business Outcomes	Customer Satisfaction		X	X
		Revenue	R	R	R
		Income/Profit	R	R	R
		Revenue from New Products and Services		X	X
		Organizational Readiness		X	X

214

Tab	Sub-category	Input Field	(Level 1) Key Free Indicators Report	(Level 2) Scorecard Reports	(Level 3) Index Reports
Performance	Perceptions	C-Level Satisfaction		X	X
		Business Unit Leader Satisfaction		X	X
		Learner Satisfaction (Formal)		X	X
		Learner Satisfaction (Work-Based)		X	X

Appendix B:
WLP Scorecard Planning Worksheets

This appendix includes three worksheets for each of the respective WLP Scorecard input categories—Workplace, Learning, and Performance. Each worksheet contains a complete list of the input indicators by sub-category.

To get started, copy and review the worksheets. Begin collecting data using the worksheets before accessing the WLP Scorecard website. In large or highly decentralized learning functions, it might be useful to distribute sections of the worksheets to persons most familiar with specific learning function elements.

Tip! The required fields needing data to generate a Scorecard report are denoted by the "Required" text and gray shading.

Workplace Tab Inputs	
WORKFORCE	
Workforce Size (Required)	FTE
Workforce Composition	
Executives and Senior Managers	FTE
Middle Managers	FTE
First Line Supervisors	FTE
Production/Technical	FTE
Administrative	FTE
Customer Service	FTE
Sales	FTE
IT	FTE
Other	FTE
Hourly Employees	FTE
Employees Outside Home Country	%
Workforce Dispersion	num
Workforce Education Level	years
COMPENSATION	
Payroll (Required)	$
Total Compensation	$
TALENT MANAGEMENT	
Turnover	%
Tenure	years
Promotions	num
New Hires	num
Job Competency Documentation	%
Individual Competency Profiles	%
Succession Planning	%

(continued on next page)

PERFORMANCE MANAGEMENT	
Individual and Organization Goal Linkage	(0–10)
Individual Performance Goals	%
Individual Learning Plans	%
Alignment of Individual Performance Goals and Learning Plans	(0–10)

EMPLOYEE ENGAGEMENT	
Employee Alignment with Culture/Values	(0–10)
Employee Satisfaction	(0–10)
Employee Satisfaction with Learning Opportunities	(0–10)
Absenteeism	days

INNOVATION	
Investment in R&D	$
New Products and Services	%
Employee Time on New Products and Services	%
Employee Time on Process Improvement/Innovation	%
Employee Idea Solicitation	Yes/No
Employee Idea Conversion	%
Number of Patents Applied For	num
Number of Patents Received	num
Total Patents	num
Industry/University Partnerships	num

Learning Tab Inputs

INVESTMENT	
Total Direct Learning Investment (Required)	**$**
Total Indirect Learning Investment (Required)	**$**
Percentage of Direct Cost for Learning by Type of Solution	
Formal Learning (Required)	%
Work-Based Learning (Required)	%
Non-Learning Solutions (Required)	%
Integration with Business Planning	(0–10)
Unplanned Learning Expenditure	$
Budget Centralization	%
External Services Expenditure (Required)	%
Tuition Reimbursement Expenditure (Required)	%
Learning Staff Costs (including benefits and taxes)	%
Learning Staff Costs (excluding benefits and taxes)	%
Expenditure on Technology Infrastructure	%
Expenditure by Employee Groups	
Executives and Senior Managers	%
Middle Managers	%
First Line Supervisors	%
Production/Technical	%
Administrative	%

INVESTMENT (continued)	
Customer Service	%
Sales	%
IT	%
Other	%

LEARNING FUNCTION STAFF/TALENT	
Learning Staff Size (Required)	**FTE**
Learning Staff Allocation by Activity	
Administration	FTE
Needs Analysis/Planning/Requirements/	
Performance Analysis/Competency Modeling	FTE
Task Analysis/Content Analysis	FTE
Design	FTE
Development	FTE
Content Maintenance	FTE
Delivery	FTE
Measurement and Evaluation	FTE
Learning Staff Reporting	%
Learning Staff Turnover	%
Learning Staff Tenure	years
Learning Staff Education Level	years

LEARNING FUNCTION PROCESSES	
Learning Staff Time Allocation by Activity	
Administration	%
Needs Analysis/Planning/Requirements/	
Performance Analysis/Competency Modeling	%
Task Analysis/Content Analysis	%
Design	%
Development	%
Content Maintenance	%
Delivery	%
Measurement and Evaluation	%
Learning Staff Time Allocation by Type of Solution	
Formal Learning	%
Work-Based Learning	%
Non-Learning Solutions	%
Standardization	(0–10)
Documentation	(0–10)
Automation	(0–10)
Shortest Cycle	days
Longest Cycle	days

(continued on next page)

OUTPUT (FORMAL LEARNING)	
Total Formal Hours Available (Required)	**hours**
New Formal Hours	hours
Updated Formal Hours	hours
Formal Hours Retired	hours
Formal Hours by Content Area (all are required)	
Executive Development	%
Managerial and Supervisory	%
Sales (not including Product Knowledge)	%
Customer Service	%
Mandatory and Compliance	%
Processes, Procedures, Business Practices, and Quality	%
Information Technology and Systems	%
Interpersonal Skills	%
New Employee Orientation	%
Basic Skills	%
Profession-Specific or Industry-Specific	%
Product Knowledge	%
Other (Required)	%
New Formal Hours by Content Area	
Executive Development	%
Managerial and Supervisory	%
Sales (not including Product Knowledge)	%
Customer Service	%
Mandatory and Compliance	%
Processes, Procedures, Business Practices, and Quality	%
Information Technology and Systems	%
Interpersonal Skills	%
New Employee Orientation	%
Basic Skills	%
Profession-Specific or Industry-Specific	%
Product Knowledge	%
Other	%
Formal Hours by Delivery Method (all are required)	
Live instructor-led real classroom,	%
Live instructor-led virtual (online) classroom	%
Live instructor-led remote, but not online	%
Self-paced online	%
Self-paced stand-alone	%
Mobile technology	%
Technology other than computer	%
Self-paced non-technology delivered	%
Other	%
Customization of Formal Content	%

OUTPUT (WORK-BASED LEARNING)	
Knowledge Repository Hours	hours
New Hours of Expert Knowledge Entered into Repositories	hours
Knowledge Sharing	hours

INFRASTRUCTURE	
Maturity of Management of Formal Learning	(0–10)
Maturity of Work-based Learning Infrastructure	(0–10)
Infrastructure Standardization	(0–10)
Measurement Maturity	(0–10)

OUTSOURCING	
Number of Providers	num
Longevity of Relationships	years
Management of External Providers	%
Learning Activities Outsourced	
Planning, analysis, competency modeling	%
Content design, development, acquisition, maintenance, and delivery	%
Learning management/administration	%
Measurement and evaluation	%
Infrastructure	%
Other	%

INTEGRATION	
Formal and Work-Based Learning	(0–10)
Work-Based Learning and Work	(0–10)
Enterprise Data	(0–10)
Formal Learning and Competencies	(0–10)
Work-Based Learning and Competencies	(0–10)
Formal Learning and Individual Learning Plans	(0–10)
Work-Based Learning and Individual Learning Plans	(0–10)

USAGE (FORMAL LEARNING)	
Formal Hours Used (Required)	**hours**
Formal Hours Used by Employee Group	
Executives and Senior Managers	hours
Middle Managers	hours
First Line Supervisors	hours
Production/Technical	hours
Administrative	hours
Customer Service	hours
Sales	hours
IT	hours
Other	hours

(continued on next page)

Formal Hours Used by Delivery Method (all are required)	
Live instructor-led real classroom	%
Live instructor-led virtual (online) classroom	%
Live instructor-led remote, but not online	%
Self-paced online	%
Self-paced stand-alone	%
Mobile technology	%
Technology other than computer	%
Self-paced non-technology delivered	%
Other	%

USAGE (WORK-BASED LEARNING)

Knowledge Repository Access	num
Knowledge Repository Time	hours
Knowledge Repository Time by Employee Group	
Executives and Senior Managers	hours
Middle Managers	hours
First Line Supervisors	hours
Production/Technical	hours
Administrative	hours
Customer Service	hours
Sales	hours
IT	hours
Other	hours
Knowledge Sharing Time as a Novice	hours
Knowledge Sharing Time as an Expert	hours
Time on Challenging Work Assignments	%
Time on Other Discretionary Learning	hours

Performance Tab Inputs

CAPABILITY

Competence Gap	(0–10)
Human Capital Readiness	(0–10)
Reduction in Time to Competence/Performance	%

PRODUCTIVITY

Individual Productivity Improvement	(0–10)
Business Unit Productivity Improvement	(0–10)

BUSINESS OUTCOMES

Customer Satisfaction	(0–10)
Revenue (Required)	$
Income/Profit (Required)	$
Revenue from New Products and Services	$
Organizational Readiness	(0–10)

PERCEPTIONS OF LEARNING FUNCTION PERFORMANCE	
C-Level Satisfaction	(0–10)
Business Unit Leader Satisfaction	(0–10)
Learner Satisfaction (Formal)	(0–10)
Learner Satisfaction (Work-Based)	(0–10)

Appendix C:
Further Reading

Anthony, R. N. 1988. *The Management Control Function*. Boston: Harvard Business School Press.

Beatty, R.W., et al. 2003. Scoring on the Business Scorecard. *Organizational Dynamics*, 107–21.

Bucknall, H., and Z. Wei. 2005. *Magic Numbers for Human Resource Management: Basic Measures to Achieve Better Results*. New York: Wiley.

Cyert, R. M., and J. G. March, 1963. *A Behavioral Theory of the Firm*. Englewood Cliffs, NJ: Prentice-Hall.

Eccles, R.G. 1991. The Performance Measurement Manifesto. *Harvard Business Review*, 131–7.

Fitz-enz, J. 2000. *The ROI of Human Capital: Measuring the Economic Value of Employee Performance*. New York: American Management Association.

Gharajedaghi, J. 1999. *Systems Thinking: Managing Chaos and Complexity: A Platform for Designing Business Architecture*. Boston: Butterworth-Heinemann.

Govindarajan, V., and A. K. Gupta. 1985. Linking Control Systems to Business Unit Strategy: Impact on Performance. *Accounting, Organizations and Society*, 51–66.

Holton, E. F., and S. S. Naquin. 2004. New Metrics for Employee Development. *Performance Improvement Quarterly 17*(1): 56–80.

Hope, J. 2006. *Reinventing the CFO: How Financial Managers Can Transform Their Roles and Add Greater Value*. Boston: Harvard Business School Press.

Huselid, M. A., et al. 2005. *The Workforce Scorecard: Managing Human Capital to Execute Strategy*. Boston: Harvard Business School Press.

Kaplan, R. S., and D. P. Norton. 2006. *Alignment: Using the Balanced Scorecard to Create Corporate Synergies*. Boston: Harvard Business School Press.

———. 2004. Measuring the Strategic Readiness of Intangible Assets. *Harvard Business Review*, 82(2): 52–63.

———. 1996. *The Balanced Scorecard: Translating Strategy into Action*. Boston: Harvard Business School Press.

Lazear, E. P. 1998. *Personnel Economics for Managers*. New York: Wiley.

Lev, B. 2004. Sharpening the Intangibles Edge. *Harvard Business Review*, 109–16.

———. 2001. *Intangibles: Management, Measurement, and Reporting*. Washington, DC: Brookings Institute.

McPherson, P., and S. Pike. 2001. Accounting, Empirical Measurement and Intellectual Capital. *Journal of Intellectual Capital 2*(3): 246–60.

March, J. G. 1994. *A Primer on Decision Making: How Decisions Happen.* New York: Free Press.

Romer, P. 1999. The Woft Revolution: Achieving Growth by Managing Intangibles. *Journal of Applied Corporate Finance 11*(2): 8–14.

Raybould, B. 1995. Performance Support Engineering: An Emerging Development Methodology for Enabling Organizational Learning. *Performance Improvement Quarterly 8*(1): 7–22.

Shapiro C., and H. Varian. 1999. *Information Rules: A Strategic Guide to the New Economy.* Boston: Harvard Business School Press.

Simons, R. 1994. *Levers of Control: How Managers Use Innovative Control Systems to Drive Strategic Renewal.* Boston: Harvard Business School Press.

———. 1987. Accounting Control Systems and Business Strategy: An Empirical Analysis. *Accounting, Organizations and Society 12*(4): 127–43.

Standfield, K. 2002. *Intangible Management: Tools for Solving the Accounting and Management Crisis.* San Diego: Academic Press.

Sugrue, B. et al. 2005. What in the World Is WLP? *T+D 59*(1): 51–2.

Swanson, R. A. 2001. *Assessing the Financial Benefits of Human Resource Development.* Cambridge, MA: Perseus.

Teece, D. J. 2000. *Managing Intellectual Capital: Organizational, Strategic, and Policy Dimensions.* Oxford: Oxford University Press.

Ulrich, D., and N. Smallwood. 2004. Capitalizing on Capabilities. *Harvard Business Review 82*(6): 119–27.

References

Accenture. 2004. *The Rise of the High-Performance Learning Organization: Results from the Accenture Learning 2004 Survey of Learning Executives.* Available at http://www.accenture.com.

———. 2006. *The High-Performance Workforce Study 2006.* Available at http://www.accenture.com.

Bingham, T., and P. Galagan. 2006. You Won. *T+D 60*(3): 34–40.

Bingham, T., and T. Jeary. 2007. *Presenting Learning.* Alexandria, VA: ASTD Press.

Bernthal, P. R., et al. 2004. *2004 ASTD Competency Study: Mapping the Future.* Alexandria, VA: ASTD Press.

Collins, J. 2001. *Good to Great: Why Some Companies Make the Leap...and Others Don't.* New York: HarperCollins.

IBM. 2004. *Global CEO Study.* Available at http://www1.ibm.com.

Kaplan, R. S., and D. P. Norton. 1992. The Balanced Scorecard—Measures That Drive Performance. *Harvard Business Review* (January–February): 71–80.

Nesheim, J. L. 2005. *The Power of Unfair Advantage: How to Create It, Build It, and Use It to Maximum Effect.* New York: Free Press.

O'Driscoll, T., B. Sugrue, and M. K. Vona. 2005. The C-Level and the Value of Learning. *T+D*, 70–8.

Rivera, R. J., and A. Paradise. 2006. *2006 State of the Industry Report.* Alexandria, VA: ASTD Press.

Sugrue, B., and D. Lynch. 2006. Profiling a New Breed of Learning Executive. *T+D*, 51–6.

Sugrue, B., and R. J. Rivera. 2005. *2005 State of the Industry Report.* Alexandria, VA: ASTD Press.

Vanthournout, D., et al. 2006. *Return on Learning: Training for High Performance at Accenture.* Chicago: Agate Bolden.

About the Author

Ray J. Rivera is the director of the WLP Scorecard within ASTD's Research Department and coauthor of ASTD's 2005 and 2006 *State of the Industry* reports. In his three years at ASTD, he has served in several roles, including consulting with organizations about ASTD research study results and communicating both the practical and strategic implications of research findings to the WLP profession.

Rivera is a doctoral candidate at Stanford University. His dissertation work focuses on using intangible asset valuation methods in evaluating the effects of training and learning interventions on human performance within firms and their use in capitalizing knowledge assets. He holds a master's degree in instructional design and technology from the University of Iowa and received his undergraduate education from St John's College in Annapolis, Maryland.

Rivera has published numerous articles, reports, and book chapters in the areas of business impact measurement, financial performance of organizations with high-impact learning programs, global integration of the learning function, and changing workforce demographics due to a maturing workforce.

Index

Printed in the United States
135804LV00002B/7/A